Israel's Lost Empires

By

Steven M. Collins

"History is the unfinished drama of which our lives are a part. We cannot understand ourselves except we have some knowledge of history." -H.G. Wells

Dedication

This book is dedicated to the Glory of the Creator God and the Restoration of His Truth and Knowledge.

About The Cover

The cover features an original painting of the port city of ancient Carthage by talented artist Ruth Amelia Lincoln. Carthage was one of the wealthiest cities of the ancient world, and its large fleets of merchant vessels sailed the world's oceans as they united a global commercial empire. For centuries, its warships controlled Gibraltar and barred the ships of Greece and Rome from the Atlantic Ocean and the New World. Until it was destroyed after the Third Punic War, Carthage was the great rival of Rome, and its famous general, Hannibal, almost conquered Rome before it could become an empire. The cover conveys well Miss Lincoln's artistic effort to portray the power, energy and essence of ancient Carthage.

Israel's Lost Empires

Book Two of the Series:

"The Lost Tribes Of Israel"

By
Steven M. Collins

Published by:

Bible Blessings
www.bibleblessings.net
Box 1778
Royal Oak, MI 48068-1778
USA

ISRAEL'S LOST EMPIRES

Written by Steven M. Collins
Editor-In-Chief, Pastor Jory Steven Brooks
Original Cover artwork by Ruth Amelia Lincoln
U.S. Library of Congress Control Number 2002115948
I.S.B.N. 0-9725849-1-9
Copyright Number TX-5-853-948

This book includes material published previously under
Library of Congress Copyright Number TX-4-266-787
Copyright 1996, Steven M. Collins

Additional Studies may be read online:
Website: www.israelite.info

First Edition

ORDERING INFORMATION:
For information on ordering copies of this book, other volumes in this series, and other books distributed by *Bible Blessings Book and Tract Ministries,* see our website or the order notice at the back of this book.

About The Author

Steven Collins' first book was *The "Lost" Ten Tribes of Israel...Found!* During its second printing, that book attracted sufficient attention that its subject matter was substantially expanded into this four-book series tracing the history and modern locations of the biblical Israelites.

Mr. Collins is a former *National Merit Scholar,* and a graduate of the *University of Minnesota* with a B.S. in Public and Personnel Management.

While employed in the office of the Mayor of St. Paul Minnesota (1973-1974), Mr. Collins researched the fields of air transportation and radiation safety as well as applicable government regulations while drafting the nation's first airport ordinance (at *Minneapolis-St Paul International airport*) monitoring the air transportation of radioactive materials. This ordinance was examined by CBS Television on a national telecast entitled *"Magazine"* in 1974.

The author was employed by the *Minneapolis-St. Paul Metropolitan Airports Commission* in a number of capacities from 1974 to 1983, the most recent position being that of Personnel Manager. In addition to personnel management duties, the author performed many research and writing projects, and also prepared formal exhibits for air route hearings of the former *Civil Aeronautics Board* (CAB). These projects involved research and analysis of a wide variety of economic, demographic and air transportation data, and in an International Route Case, the author also served as an oral witness as part of the CAB proceedings.

After a career-ending injury, the author directed his research skills to a comparison of secular historical records with the historical accounts of the Bible. This led to the publication of his first book, *The "Lost" Ten Tribes of Israel...Found!* The author is a former Board Member of the *Association for Christian Development* (ACD), based in the Seattle area, and a member of the *National Epigraphic Society.* However, this book represents the analysis and judgments of the author, and does not claim to represent the views of any organization.

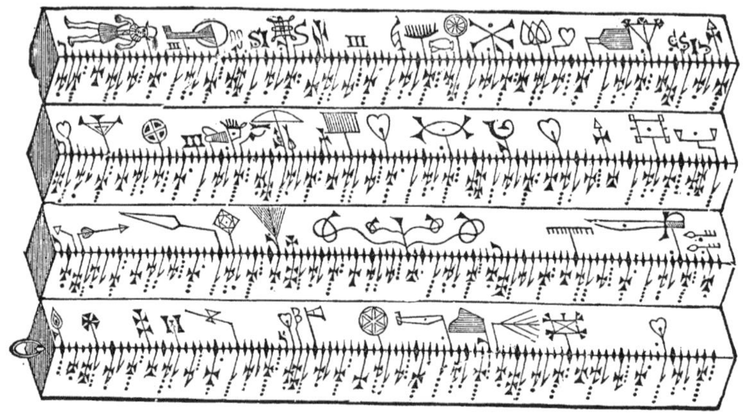

Ancient Clog Almanac

Acknowledgements

This series of books on the history of the Israelite tribes is the result of years of research, writing and ongoing review. The process of writing four books involves considerable effort and time, but it has been a "labor of love" for me. During this time, I have been aided by the assistance and encouragement of others, to whom gratitude must be expressed.

I would first like to recognize the profound pioneering work of the late Dr. Barry Fell, Harvard University Professor Emeritus who was the Founder and President of the National Epigraphic Society. Dr. Fell deciphered many ancient inscriptions which confirmed that several Old World civilizations were present in the ancient Americas. The books and writings of Dr. Fell and other contributors to the publications of The Epigraphic Society have been most helpful in providing source material for historical facts and observations cited in this book. Indeed, it was the striking information in Dr. Fell's books, *America B.C.* and *Saga America* which inspired my own writing efforts. Whenever I personally contacted Dr. Fell to seek his assistance in directing me to past publications of the National Epigraphic Society dealing with specific research topics, he was always most helpful and cordial. He was that rarest of individuals: a person who possessed great talent while displaying personal humility.

I am also indebted to the late Dr. Charles V. Dorothy (a graduate of Claremont Graduate School, Claremont, CA, and formerly the Director of Biblical Research for the Association for Christian Development, Auburn, WA), for checking many of my transliterations from ancient languages into English. Dr. Dorothy studied Hebrew, Greek, Aramaic, Syriac, Akkadian and Ugaritic at the Fuller Theological Seminary in Pasadena, CA., and was an Assistant Professor of Biblical Studies at Faith Lutheran Seminary in Tacoma, Washington before his untimely demise. Like Dr. Barry Fell, Dr. Charles Dorothy combined scholarly and academic ability with personal humility. I have been privileged to know two such individuals.

There are a number of individuals whose assistance and support has made this current series of books on Israelite history a reality. I want to thank Pastor Herb Teitgen for performing the data conversions necessary to upgrade my data disks to a "modern" software format suitable for publication. I am one of those people who is most comfortable writing at a keyboard with word processing software that is now archaic. While doing so enables me to write more effectively, the downside is that no modern computer or publisher can utilize my old software's data. Herb was able to perform the data upgrades accurately and effectively.

Special credit must be given to Pastor Jory Steven Brooks, Editor-In-Chief, for his able assistance in providing additional research, source documentation, and illustrations. This series of books has greatly benefited from the inclusion of material from his own research at various libraries and historic sites. He has also assisted in editing my books, and in preparing them in desktop publishing software for publication. His support in the preparation of these books has been crucial to the success of this effort.

Finally, I also wish to thank the many people who have contributed in various ways to the inspiration for, and writing of, these books. Their collective contributions have provided valuable assistance and encouragement to me during my writing efforts.

Steven M. Collins

The Fall Of Carthage:
Roman Soldiers Enter the City

Illustrations

The Fall of Carthage:
Roman soldiers storming the Bursa Citadel

Table of Contents

Introduction

The previous volume in this series on Israelite history, *The Origins and Empire of Ancient Israel,* concluded with the tribes of Israel united and leading the ancient Phoenician Alliance. King David of Israel allied Israel to the Phoenicians of Tyre and Sidon, and his conquests of Assyria and other nations catapaulted Israel onto the world stage as a great power. The Israelite role in the greatness of the Phoenician Empire from 1000-700 B.C. is confirmed by the ancient Greeks who gave the "Phoenicians" their name and included Israel in Phoenicia's territory.

Under King Solomon of Israel, Phoenicia's sailors, miners and traders explored both the Old and New Worlds. Israel, Tyre and Sidon merged their nations, their navies and their destinies. Phoenicia's naval might allowed it to exploit the mineral wealth of Europe and the ancient Americas even as it also barred the Greeks from the world's oceans. Because the modern world's concepts of the ancient world are based on Greek sources, today's educational system is based on the ignorance of the ancient Greeks about the world's oceans and continents rather than on the Israelite/Phoenician awareness of world geography.

King Solomon's reign of global power and greatness began to fade and decay during his waning years. Solomon abandoned biblical laws, and served pagan gods. Because Israel's greatness was built on the favor of God's direct actions, Solomon's idolatries began to remove God's favor from the tribes of Israel.

This second book in the series on Israelite history contains many historical surprises. It documents, via biblical and secular evidence, what happened to the tribes of Israel after Solomon's death. The tribes of Israel divided into two separate nations of "Israel" and "Judah," and their great civil war devastated the power of the Phoenician alliance led by Israel. Freed from Israelite dominance, Assyria recovered and began a long series of wars against Israel. Both Israel and Judah experienced periods of renewed power, but they entered irreversible slides toward national destruction as their sins worsened. The ten tribes of Israel remained in the Phoenician alliance, but the Jews of Judah were no longer a part of that alliance. The ten tribes of Israel and Jews of Judah became rival nations that charted separate courses.

This book will answer one of the great mysteries of ancient history: What happened to the "lost ten tribes of Israel?" While the history of the Jews, who take their name from the old kingdom of Judah, is well-documented, efforts to locate the ten tribes have generally failed to trace their migrations and whereabouts. This book solves that mystery, and the Biblical evidence is entirely consistent with the records of ancient secular historians.

One clue for locating the "lost" ten tribes of Israel is the realization that Israel's tribes had access to Phoenicia's fleets and overseas colonies. Many Israelites evaded captivity by simply sailing to new homelands in the Phoenician colonial system. This book reveals where they went! However, Israel's population was far too large to relocate the entire nation via the Phoenician fleets. Many Israelites did go into captivity and were forcibly resettled eastward into the Assyrian Empire. Forgotten and overlooked historical accounts record that a large body of escaping Israelites voluntarily fled Palestine and migrated overland to a new area.

There are two major reasons why efforts to locate the mysterious ten tribes of Israel have failed. The first reason is that such efforts look for small bands of people with Jewish customs. This approach is doomed to failure. Because the ten tribes of Israel were not "Jewish" to begin with, their descendants will not be found by looking for overtly-Jewish bands in ancient history. However, the Israelites were "Hebrews" and they took their Semitic language and culture with them when they migrated elsewhere. The second reason for failure to locate the ten tribes of Israel is the pathetically "minimalist" approach of these efforts.

The history and destinies of the ten tribes of Israel were determined by the conditions and blessings of the Covenant made between Abraham and the God of the Bible. These blessings included large population growth, national wealth and greatness, and possession of strategic geopolitical "gates." While the Mosaic Covenant made at Mt. Sinai was conditional on Israel's obedience, the blessings of the Abrahamic Covenant were unconditional. God had bound Himself to implement the blessings of that Covenant with Abraham's descendants. This book will confirm that God kept those promises!

When one searches for the Israelites via the "maximalist" approach of determining which nations inherited the blessings of the Abrahamic Covenant, the descendants of the ten tribes can easily be found in the many new locations to which they migrated after the ancient kingdom of Israel fell. In fact, the search is so easy that you may wonder why modern history texts take such pains to ignore the nations and empires with obvious Israelite roots.

While many mysteries will be revealed in this book, two historical clues about the Israelites will be offered here. Some readers have heard of ancient Carthage, the great enemy of early Rome. Carthage was its Greco-Roman name. The great city of Carthage, one of the wealthiest and most powerful in ancient history, continued the Phoenician tradition of naval power and its war-fleets prevented the Greeks and Romans from leaving the Mediterranean region for many centuries. This fact has had a profound impact on our mistaken views of the ancient world, as this book will reveal. Much evidence will be offered that the Phoenician/Carthaginian fleets of the ancient Israelites explored and settled parts of the New World. Their artifacts, inscriptions and ruins in the New World still exist today. You will not learn about them in the establishment history books that omit these facts. However, you will find the evidence in this book.

Carthage actually called itself by a Hebrew name, and its heritage and language had obvious Hebrew origins. Historians of Carthage acknowledge these facts, but your history texts didn't tell you this important truth! Carthage inherited the wealth and power of the Abrahamic blessings, and it controlled Gibraltar, one of the most strategic "gates" on the globe. This book will give you the real history of Carthage, the maritime empire which almost destroyed Rome.

This book will also give you considerable historical evidence about the Israelite origins of the Scythians of the ancient Russian steppes. The evidence of their Israelite origins is voluminous, and they destroyed the Assyrian Empire and twice crushed the mighty Persian Empire in warfare. Yet your history books and encyclopedias offer many pages about Assyria and Persia while ignoring the history of the more powerful Scythian Empire which defeated both Assyria and Persia! The Greeks preserved much of Scythia's history, but this information has been almost totally censored out of the history books. Why has this happened? Many Scythian tribes were named after the Israelite patriarch, Isaac. When you see the extensive evidence of the Israelite origins of the "Sacae" Scythians, it will become obvious that the ten tribes were never "lost" at all. Secular histories, which bow down at the altar of the theory of evolution, have ignored the history of Scythia because it offers evidence that the Bible's prophecies about the ten tribes of Israel came to pass.

Those of you who read this book (and the following two volumes in this series on Israelite history) will learn the truth: some of the greatest empires in world history have been ignored or de-emphasized in historical accounts of the ancient world. Interestingly, it is the ancient nations and empires with Israelite origins that have been de-emphasized.

This book challenges the politically-correct version of ancient history now being taught. It also challenges and exposes the shameless Greco-Roman ethnocentricity of our current versions of ancient history. While Greece and Rome truly were great empires, other empires were more powerful and scientifically advanced than either

Greece or Rome. This book has no political or ethnic agendas and it is non-denominational in content and approach. It simply "tells the truth" about the ancient world. Readers of this book will enjoy a feast of new information about the true history of the ancient world.

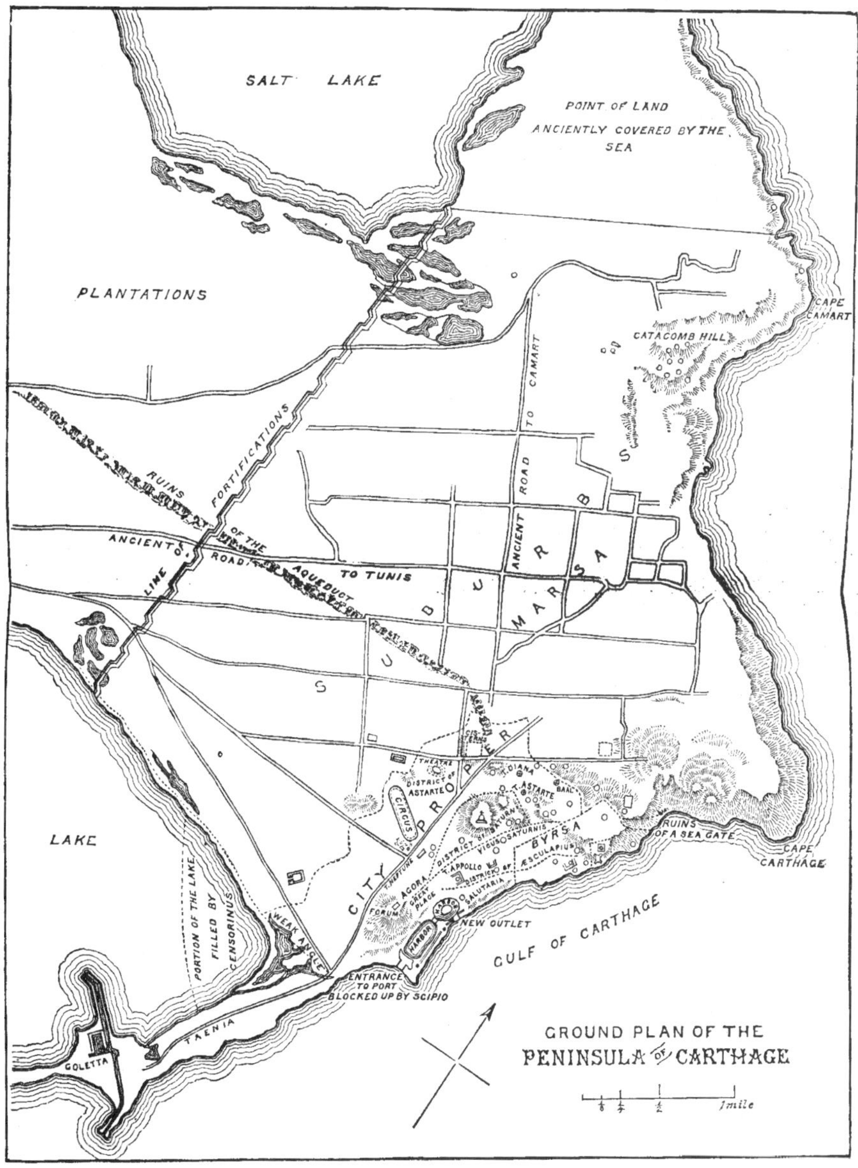

GROUND PLAN OF THE
PENINSULA OF CARTHAGE

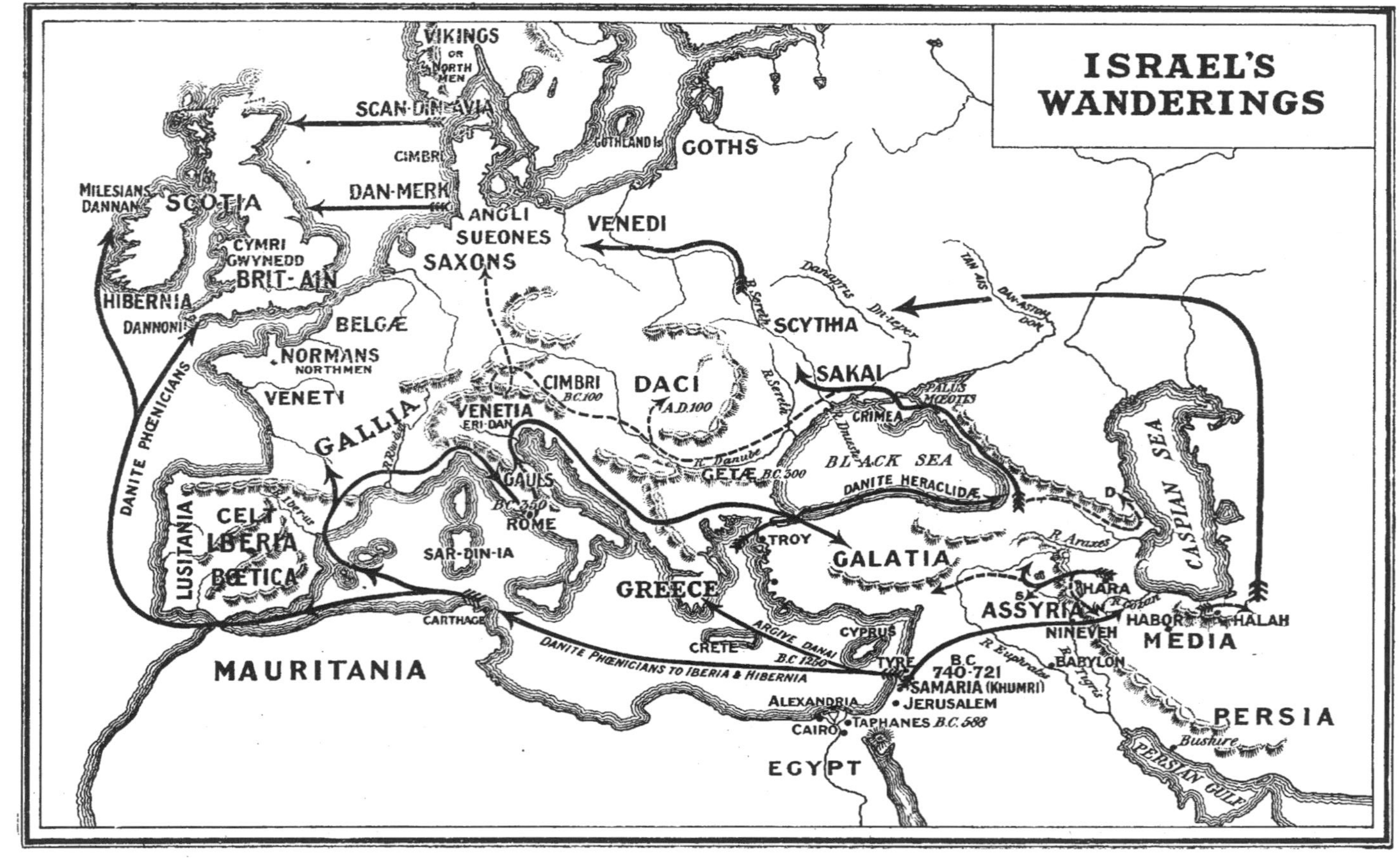
ISRAEL'S WANDERINGS
VIKINGS OR NORTH MEN
SCAN-DIN-AVIA
CIMBRI
DAN-MERK
GOTHLAND Is
GOTHS
MILESIANS DANNAN
SCOTIA
CYMRI GWYNEDD
BRIT-AIN
HIBERNIA
DANNONII
ANGLI
SUEONES
SAXONS
VENEDI
BELGÆ
NORMANS NORTHMEN
VENETI
GALLIA
DANITE PHŒNICIANS
SCYTHIA
Danapris
Dn-ieper
TAN AIS
DAN-ASTON DON
R. Sereth
SAKAI
PALUS MÆOTIS
CIMBRI B.C.100
DACI
A.D.100
VENETIA
ERI-DAN
CRIMEA
R. Dniester
R. Danube
BLACK SEA
GETÆ B.C.300
DANITE HERACLIDÆ
GAULS
B.C.350
ROME
LUSITANIA
CELT
IBERIA
BŒTICA
Iberus
SAR-DIN-IA
TROY
GALATIA
R. Araxes
CASPIAN SEA
GREECE
CARTHAGE
HARA
ASSYRIA
HABOR
HALAH
NINEVEH
MEDIA
CYPRUS
CRETE
ARGIVE DANAI B.C.1280
DANITE PHŒNICIANS TO IBERIA & HIBERNIA
TYRE
B.C. 740-721
SAMARIA (KHUMRI)
JERUSALEM
R. Euphrates
R. Tigris
BABYLON
MAURITANIA
ALEXANDRIA
CAIRO
TAPHANES B.C.588
EGYPT
PERSIA
Bushire
PERSIAN GULF

Chapter 1
The Golden Age of the Israelite-Phoenician Empire

Most readers are aware of the Greco-Macedonian Empire of Alexander the Great, the Roman Empire of the Caesars, and other ancient empires discussed in history lessons. However, few realize that centuries before the empires of Greece and Rome, there existed an empire whose domain, colonies and influence included both the Old and the New World. Its great antiquity is one reason for our ignorance of it. There are ancient historical references to it, but only recently have archaeological and epigraphic discoveries made it possible to determine the scope of this empire. The forgotten world empire was that of Israel, which began under Kings David and Solomon and continued for almost three centuries.

The reader of the first book in this series on Israelite history, *The Origins and Empire of Ancient Israel,* already has some knowledge of this empire and why its history was so obscured. In the previous book, we saw evidence from secular historians that the "Phoenicians" established an international empire in the time frame of 1000-700 B.C. We also learned that the Greeks gave the name "Phoenicia" to the region on the Eastern Shore of the Mediterranean Sea. In doing so, they applied the name "Phoenicia" to groups of Semitic people living in Israel, Tyre and Sidon. Maitland Edey comments concerning the Phoenicians:

"...there never was a country or empire called 'Phoenicia'...they spoke of themselves as Tyrians, Sidonians...and so on. The very word 'Phoenician' was unknown to them; the label...was pasted on them by the Greeks and preserved by the accident that the Greek language and its literature, and not the Phoenician, have been passed down to us."[1]

The "Phoenicians" called themselves "Sidonians," "Tyrians," or as we shall see in this chapter, various Israelite names. The Israelite alliance with Tyre and Sidon was called "Phoenicia" by the Greeks, and that name initially designated a whole region which included Biblical Israel, not merely a few city states on the shores of ancient Lebanon. The previous book also documented that under King Solomon of Israel and King Hiram of Tyre, their allied people became virtually one society with mingled work forces laboring together on huge building projects and with their navies crewed jointly by sailors from both nations.

The city-states of Tyre, Sidon, etc., were junior partners to the Israelites during Phoenicia's Golden Age. Since the Israelites and the inhabitants of the city-states shared a common language, common customs and a common race, the differences between them were mere nuances when viewed from a perspective almost three thousand years after their existence. The Israelite dominance in that empire was forgotten because the Israelites left the region when their kingdom fell. Since the inhabitants of the non-Israelite city-states remained in that region, the name "Phoenicia" remained on the non-Israelite city-states after 700 B.C. However, when historians refer to the Phoenician Empire and its international power and influence around 1000-700 B.C., they are actually identifying the empire of Israel to which Tyre and Sidon were allied.

Historians acknowledge that the "Phoenicians" planted many colonies throughout the Mediterranean world, which were tied to the "mother country" on the eastern Mediterranean. It is likely that some of these colonies started as trading posts founded by the city-states of Tyre and Sidon before their alliance with Israel. It has long been acknowledged that the Phoenicians traded, mined and settled throughout the shores of the Mediterranean, the west coasts of Africa and Europe, the British Isles and into the Baltic Sea. When Tyre and Sidon allied themselves to the emerging power of Israel during the reigns of David and Solomon, the Israelites — with a much larger population base — expanded many of these trading stations into larger colonies. In this chapter, we shall see the evidence of many Hebrew and Israelite names in colonies that have traditionally been called "Phoenician."

The Scope of the Israelite-Phoenician Empire

Before examining Israel's colonial empire, let us first review their area of direct rule in the Mideast. The Bible tells us that King David subdued the Philistines, the Moabites, the Ammonites, the Edomites, the Amalekites and sufficient Syrian territory to reach the Euphrates River. *(I Chronicles 18:1-17)* This area would roughly correspond to the modern nations of Israel and Lebanon together with much of Jordan, a sizable portion of Syria and a part of western Iraq. Israel's army, when fully mobilized, numbered 1,500,000 men! *(I Chronicles 21:5-6)* As documented in the first book of this series, I Chronicles 19:1-19 shows that the Mesopotamian powers, led by Assyria, engaged Israel in combat by the subterfuge of having their national armies "hired" as mercenaries by the small nation of Ammon, which wanted to rebel against David's rule. Many Syrians were also allied to the Mesopotamians fighting against Israel.

David speaks of this war in Psalm 83:1-8 when he names the nations which aided the Ammonites' (the "children of Lot") rebellion. David specifically names the Assyrians *(verse 8)* as being part of the enemy alliance fighting against him. This war resulted in the defeat of all the nations warring against Israel, and greatly expanded David's rule and the empire of Israel. As documented in the first book in this series, this Israelite victory over Assyria accounts for the sudden eclipse of Assyrian power at the beginning of the second millennium B.C.[2]

During the rule of Kings David and Solomon, Assyria and Babylon were subordinate to the kingdom of Israel. It is an oversight that historians have not linked Assyria's period of severe decline with the simultaneous ascent of King David, whose army routed the Assyrians in a major war. *(I Chronicles 19:6-15 and Psalm 83:1-8)*

Unlike most conquerors who only exalted themselves, David desired to exalt the God of Israel. *(Psalm 83:9-18)* Consequently, the writings of David in the Psalms dwell on glorifying God, and the self-praise so characteristic of other triumphant ancient monarchs is lacking. If David's ego had been paramount, his writings would have dwelt on his own accomplishments and he would have built monuments to commemorate them. II Samuel 7:9 acknowledges that King David had a name "among the great men of the earth," so his international fame is attested to in the Bible.

The Israelites even constructed great edifices. Under King Solomon, the Israelites and their subject peoples labored for decades to finish Solomon's immense building projects. Their greatest monument, the Temple in Jerusalem, was constructed to honor God and was likely one of the wonders of the ancient world while it stood. It was later destroyed in warfare, as were all the other great projects of King Solomon.

Upon concluding his war with the Assyrians and their allies, King David's Israel ruled, either directly or via its influence over vassal kings, the entire Mideastern world from Egypt and southern Asia Minor to the region of the Tigris and Euphrates Rivers. I Chronicles 19:16-19 records that David had also defeated Syrians (Aramaeans) who lived east of the Euphrates River. David claims a victory over Assyria and its allies in Psalm 82, and secular records affirm Assyria's great national decline occurred during David and Solomon's reigns.

Since David also defeated the Arabians in the Israelite-Assyrian war (Psalm 83:6 refers to Arabians as "Ishmaelites"), Israel's dominance also extended into the Arabian Peninsula. This description sets the bounds of Israel's Mideastern territory ruled by Kings David and Solomon either directly or through vassal kings. However, this was only the beginning of Israel's empire!

The city-states of Tyre and Sidon first allied themselves to Israel during David's reign, and during Solomon's reign, the Phoenicians shared the skills of long-range ocean travel with the Israelites. *(I Kings 9:26-27)* The Israelites, Tyrians and Sidonians operated a common fleet with international ports-of-call. *(I Kings 9:28, 10:22)* Artifacts and inscriptions left around the world by this alliance today are called "Phoenician," as named by the Greeks. The King James Version of the Bible records in I Kings 10:22 that King Solomon "had at sea a navy of Tharshish" (other versions simply say "Tarshish"). What was this "navy of Tharshish?" Let us examine possible explanations.

One possibility is that Solomon had a fleet of ships based in Spain because Tartessus, in ancient Spain, is often identified as "Tarshish." It was noted in the previous book that ancient American inscriptions indicated that the "ships of Tarshish" made voyages to the New World, and that these fleets of Tarshish had Semitic-Phoenician crews. It is also significant to note that I Kings 10:22 has the Bible's first mention of "ships of Tharshish." This record may be a reference to a Phoenician-Israelite colony in Spain that became the homeport of a major Phoenician-Israelite fleet during Solomon's reign. Tartessus, or Tarshish, was a logical jumping-off point for Phoenician voyages throughout the Atlantic. When the author of I Kings wrote his words, he was not writing for a readership in the twentieth century A.D. He was writing at a time when it would have been known whether "ships of Tarshish" identified an Israelite-Phoenician fleet based in ancient Spain or whether some other meaning was intended.

The fact that the prophet Jonah sailed "to Tarshish" from Joppa **away** from the direction of Nineveh *(Jonah 1:3)* supports the conclusion that Tarshish had to be located in the western Mediterranean, as noted in *Harper's Bible Dictionary.*[3]

Another explanation involves the possibility that the extra "h" in the word **Tharshish** identifies this navy with one of the clans of the Israelite tribe of Benjamin, which was named "**Tharshish.**" *(I Chronicles 7:10)* Since "Tharshish" was an Israelite clan name, the reference to "ships of Tharshish" could mean that this fleet was primarily crewed by members of this Benjaminite clan. This possibility has a biblical precedent as Judges 5:17 records that the tribe of Dan was identified with a particular fleet of ships circa 1200 B.C., during the days of the "Sea Peoples." The tribe of Dan's role in the Sea Peoples was examined in the first book of this series.

It is also possible that the term "ships of Tarshish" later came to describe a particular class of large, ocean-going vessels used by the Phoenicians. This possibility is supported by I Kings 22:48 that over a century later Judah's King Jehoshaphat built a fleet of such ships at the Red Sea port of Ezion-geber. *Young's Analytical Concordance* also

PHOENICIAN GALLEY
A Model Exhibited in the Commercial Museum, Philadelphia
Based on the Sennacherib relief excavated by Layard

states that "mighty ships fitted for long voyages" is one possible meaning of the term: "ships of Tarshish."[4]

"Tarshish" likely came to be a word which could either describe the substantial Israelite-Phoenician colony in ancient Spain (Iberia) or a class of ocean-going vessels which were common in the Israelite-Phoenician fleets. It is well known that ancient Spain contained a Phoenician colony and major ports for their fleets.

Dr. Barry Fell observed that the language of Tartessus or Tarshish in ancient Spain was "no more than a dialectal variant of Phoenician."[5] The fact that Tarshish spoke a dialect of the Phoenician language clearly shows that it was a Semitic colony in the Phoenician Empire. The language of Phoenicia's colony in Spain came to be known as "Iberian-Punic." The Israelite nature of the Tartessus/Tarshish colony is apparent in many ways. The fact that this colony apparently bore the name of a clan of the Israelite tribe of Benjamin is one of many pieces of evidence. More evidence will be cited later in this chapter.

I Kings 10:22 states "once in three years came the navy of Tharshish, bringing gold, and silver, ivory, and apes and peacocks." That it returned, laden with trade goods and exotic animals, after a voyage of three years confirms its voyage included ports-of-call in other continents. A three-year voyage is also associated with Ferdinand Magellan's circumnavigation of the globe in 1519-1522.[6] A span of three years allows sufficient time for sailing ships to travel around the globe, trading and exploring on their voyage. Magellan's voyage

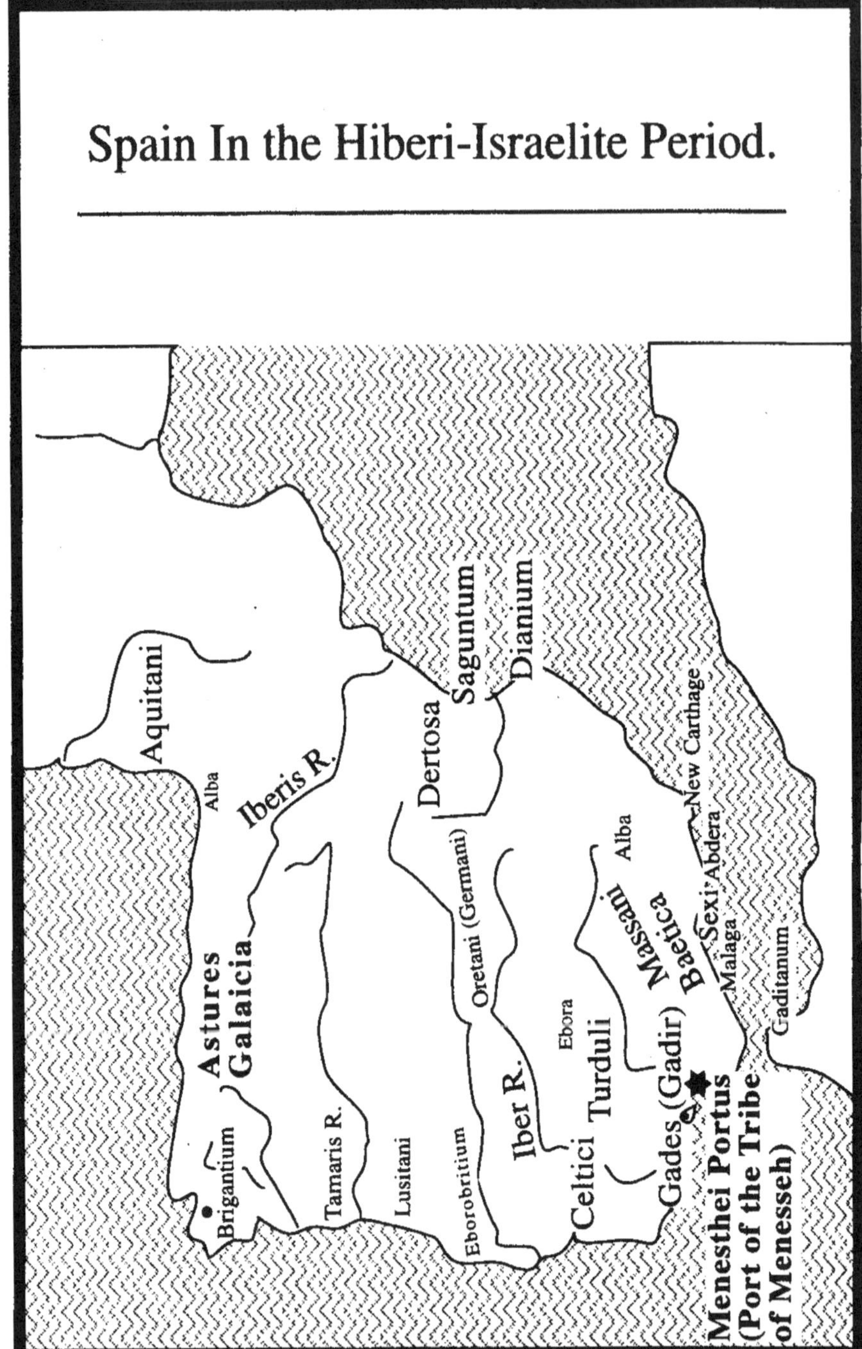
Spain In the Hiberi-Israelite Period.
Aquitani
Alba
Iberis R.
Dertosa
Saguntum
Dianium
New Carthage
Abdera
Sexi
Malaga
Gaditanum
Alba
Massani
Baetica
Oretani (Germani)
Astures
Galaicia
Brigantium
Tamaris R.
Lusitani
Eborobritium
Iber R.
Ebora
Turduli
Celtici
Gades (Gadir)
Menesthei Portus
(Port of the Tribe
of Menesseh)

involved a large loss of life, including his own, due to it being a path-finding expedition in hostile areas. However, Solomon's fleet could utilize the already established trading routes of the Phoenicians and Egyptians in the Atlantic, Pacific and Indian Oceans (as documented in the previous book), making for a tranquil voyage. The above does not "prove" that Solomon's fleet sailed around the world, but the length of its voyage does parallel the length of Magellan's voyage in a sailing ship, and its cargo of exotic animals from other continents also supports such a conclusion.

Barry Fell's book, *America B.C.* offers evidence that "ships of Tarshish" were involved in ancient explorations of North America,[7] arguing that the biblical "Tarshish" was located on an Atlantic shore such as in ancient Spain. The highly-regarded archaeologist, Dr. Cyrus Gordon, agrees, asserting that "Tarshish...must therefore lie on the shores of the Atlantic...[and adds]...Mexico, rich in silver and other metal ores, is a possible identification of Tarshish..."[8] It is particularly worth noting that an eminent archeologist like Dr. Cyrus Gordon did not find it strange to propose that biblical Tarshish may have been located in the ancient New World.

The Phoenicians planted many colonies wherever their navies sailed. Maitland Edey has observed that many Phoenician colonies were located in Mediterranean Africa, Sicily, Sardinia, Corsica, Spain and the coast of Morocco.[9] George Rawlinson adds "in the space of about three hundred years, from B.C. 1100 to B.C. 800, Phoenician colonists occupied...the mid-African sites [on North Africa's coast] from Leptus Magna...to Hippo Regina."[10] This time of Phoenician colonial expansionism directly coincided with the period of Israel's dominant role in the "Phoenician" alliance, strongly indicating that most of the "Phoenician" colonists in that time frame were Israelites.

The sailors of Tyre and Sidon founded trading stations in the Mediterranean and Western Atlantic regions prior to their formal alliance with the Israelites. Author Richard Harrison notes that: "Historical tradition credits the Phoenicians with voyages to southern Spain in the twelfth century BC and places...their base at Gadir (Cadiz) around

1100 BC, by a fleet which sailed from Tyre. A few years later was founded Utica, close to Carthage on the African coast."[11] Harrison adds that: "the pace and intensity of contact [between the Phoenician homeland and its Spanish colony] quicken after 900 BC..."[12] Even 3000 years after the events, archeological evidence confirms that Phoenicia's colony in Spain expanded during the time Israel was allied to Tyre and Sidon. This further indicates that it was Israel's much larger population base which furnished the colonists for Phoenicia's growing colonial system.

The Spanish Peninsula in ancient times was known by its Hebrew name: **Iber**ia. Spain was originally named after **Eber**, the namesake of the H**ebre**ws. Israeli writer, Yair Davidy, has noted the Hebraic nature of other ancient geographical names in Spain. Davidy notes that ancient names for Spanish rivers included the **Iber**is, the **Iber** and the **Tamar**is.[13] The former two names are obviously named after Eber, but the **Tamar**is River preserved the name of two biblical women.

Ancient Utica, sister city of Carthage

A daughter-in-law of Judah, one of Jacob's sons, was named Tamar *(Genesis 38:6)*, as was a daughter of King David. *(II Samuel 13:1)* Because ancient Iberia was in the Phoenician orbit during King David's lifetime, it is logical that one of its rivers would be named after a member of the royal household that ruled the Phoenician alliance.

Phoenician Scientific and Navigational Skills

At this juncture, some comments about the scientific knowledge of the ancient world is necessary in order for readers to appreciate the remaining material in this book. Most modern writers take a very "minimalist" view concerning ancient mankind's scientific knowledge and maritime skills. This is due to several factors. One is the corrosive influence of evolutionary theory, which can not explain why ancient mankind was far more advanced technologically than human societies only a few centuries previous to the modern era. Also, the inexplicable academic bias against pre-Columbian explorations of the Americas has blinded many to the obvious evidence of Old World colonies in ancient America. Another reason for a warped view of the ancient world is the tendency to assume uncritically that whatever Greco-Roman writers asserted about the ancient world had to be (A) factual and (B) the most advanced viewpoint then extant in the ancient world. While Greco-Roman sources do offer valuable insights into the ancient world, there is one area where the Greco-Roman writers were profoundly backward and benighted.

The backwardness of the Greco-Roman writers and historians is most evident in the field of international geography and trans-oceanic navigation. However, their backward state in these fields has been assumed by modern historians to be the highest standard of awareness in the ancient world. There is an unspoken dogma in academia that ancient Greece and Rome "had to" represent the pinnacle of ancient man's awareness in all fields of knowledge at all times. There is a nonsensical assumption that no one in the ancient world could possibly have known anything significant until a Greek or Roman first "discovered" it. This "Greco-Roman ethnocentric bias"

PHŒNICIAN FLEET ON A VOYAGE OF DISCOVERY.
Drawn by P. Philippoteaux.

has led to gigantic errors in our perceptions of the ancient world. In the previous book in this series, *The Origins and Empire of Ancient Israel,* we examined evidence that ancient Phoenicians mastered trans-oceanic navigation via the science of astronomical and mathematical calculations, assisted by their invention of the compass so they could navigate in cloudy or stormy weather. The Phoenicians sailed the world's oceans and knew the world was a sphere about a millennium before the Greeks or Romans figured this out.

The Phoenician-Carthaginian awareness of world geography was far superior to that of the Greco-Romans. One of the oldest books of the Bible, the book of Job, includes geographical and astronomical knowledge that may shock modern readers. It confirms this knowledge was extant in the Hebrew-Israelite culture long before the empires of Greece and Rome ever existed! Job 26:7 preserves this statement in a discourse about God's creation of the earth:

> "He **stretcheth out the north over the empty place**, and **hangeth the earth upon nothing**." *(KJV)*

Consider the scientific knowledge underlying this statement. Job knew that the far northern part of the earth was "over an empty place," and that God had "hung the earth upon nothing." Job's description of the far north as "an empty place" is a suitable description for the Arctic region where there is no continent and only an "empty" wasteland of ice. Job's statement that "the earth is hung upon nothing" confirms that he knew the earth was a sphere "hung" by God in the void of space, "upon nothing." Other ancient cultures had silly ideas about the earth being flat, or being supported on the back of a giant turtle, but Job in very ancient times knew the earth was suspended in the void of space, placed there by a Creator God.

Who is responsible for the false notion that the Bible is an unscientific book? The Bible contains scientific truths that were known millennia before mankind "rediscovered" these facts in recent centuries. Where did Job learn about these geographical and astronomical truths? Some modern writers take the "minimalist" view that the book of Job dates to the exilic period after the fall of Samaria. *Harper's Bible Dictionary* expresses that assumption. [14] However, the Open Bible Edition of the *King James Version* of the Bible (published in 1975) states regarding the book of Job:

> "The name of the book and its hero...appears in extra-biblical texts as early as 2000 B.C...Many conservative scholars favor a date in Solomon's time, the great age of Biblical Wisdom literature..."[15]

Phoenician ships were built for long oceanic voyages and we know their presence in the British Isles was extensive. Author Thomas Johnston asserts that ancient Phoenician commerce reached Norway.[16] It would be only a short trip for Phoenician ships to sail far enough northward from Norway to learn that the Arctic region was "an empty place." The book of Job was a part of the Israelite-Phoenician heritage. Where could such knowledge have originated?The intrepid explorers of Phoenicia's fleets would seem to be the only source for learning such knowledge.

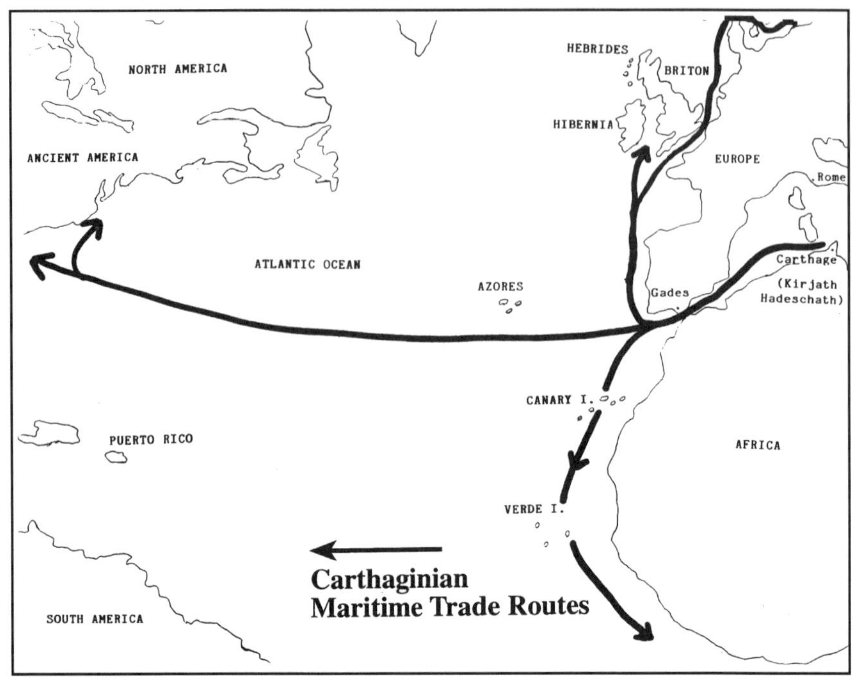

Job's comment that he knew the earth was an object "hung on nothing," a sphere "hung" in the ether of space, attests to an ancient knowledge of astronomical science that was far superior to that of ancient Greece, Rome, or even Medieval Europe. The first book in this series documented that Phoenician-Israelite ships traversed the Atlantic Ocean and, with their allies the Egyptians, explored the Indian and Pacific Oceans as well. Their voyages would have led them to the obvious conclusion that the earth was a sphere. At any rate, this remarkably accurate scientific knowledge is first manifested in ancient Israelite literature, not Greco-Roman sources.

The Greco-Romans were the rivals of the Phoenicians and Carthaginians. Greece and Rome were land powers with armies conquering territories to add to a contiguous empire. Phoenicia and Carthage were maritime empires that linked their widely scattered colonies together with large fleets. The Phoenicians and Carthaginians exploited the commerce and mines in their maritime empire to become quite wealthy. The Phoenicians and Carthaginians were capitalists who developed the ancient equivalent of a "global economy." They explored for natural resources throughout the world and traded with nations located on different continents. They developed a monopoly as the only "middlemen" who could link various customers together. Rome and Greece were autocratic empires primarily concerned with extending and preserving their power over conquered nations. Phoenicia and their Carthaginian offspring protected their empire's secrets from Greece and Rome via powerful war fleets, their possession of Gibraltar and misinformation campaigns.

Their dominance over Gibraltar , the "Pillars of Hercules," kept enemies and rivals of Phoenicia and Carthage out of the Atlantic Ocean, hiding colonies, mines, and trading stations in Atlantic regions from Greek and Roman eyes. In possessing the strategic gateway of Gibraltar, the Israelite-Phoenician Empire, and Carthage after them, enjoyed one of the specific promises of the Abrahamic Covenant that Abraham's seed would "possess the gate of his enemies." *(Genesis 22:17)* Phoenicia and Carthage kept Greek and Roman ships out of the Atlantic Ocean for centuries, ensuring that the Greco-Roman powers would stay largely ignorant of Phoenicia's and Carthage's Atlantic empires.

A Roman historian, Strabo, recorded what lengths Phoenicia and Carthage would go to preserve the secrecy of their Atlantic destinations from other nations. Aylett Sammes was a British writer from Christ's College in Cambridge; his 1676 book, *Antiquities of Ancient Britain*, cites Strabo's account:

> "The Phoenicians very studiously concealed this treasure [the location of their colonies] from them [the Greeks], as we find they did from the Romans, because they being the great trading nation of the world, they were jealous lest...they should lose the advantages...which had hitherto been a peculiar monopoly unto themselves...That this is true, Strabo... witnesseth: At the beginning the Phoenicians alone traded to Britain from Gades, and concealed from all others this navigation; but when a Roman vessel followed a certain master of a ship, that they themselves might learn this traffic of merchandise, he...ran his ship on purpose upon the sands...and out of the common treasury received the worth of the commodities and wares he had lost."[17]

The account of Strabo details an event where a Carthaginian trading vessel grounded itself rather than reveal to a Roman ship the whereabouts of Carthage's colonies and trading routes. The fact that the scuttled ship's master received replacement funds from the Carthaginian Treasury indicates that it was a state policy to conceal Carthage's oceanic routes and destinations from the Greeks and Romans. The same author, Aylett Sammes, also wrote the following caustic comment about the ancient Greeks:

> "In the days of Solomon...the Phoenicians were arrived to a great perfection in the art of navigation, they made long voyages, and imported many rich commodities...But the Grecians...made it their business to fasten all the great actions and inventions of the Ancients, upon something of their own nation, and being better able to write than perform great matters, they brought down the original of arts and sciences to their own low and pitiful epoch."[18]

Sammes wrote as long ago as 1676 that there was a tendency to ascribe to the Greeks certain inventions, arts and sciences that were actually invented by earlier cultures. Herodotus, a famous Greek geographer, wrote of a Phoenician fleet which sailed around the continent of Africa, starting in the Red Sea and eventually arriving in Egypt by way of Gibraltar on their return trip. Herodotus declares his disbelief of the Phoenicians' account that as they sailed along Africa's coasts, the sun eventually rose on their right hand instead of at their left hand.[19] Obviously, the Phoenician account was completely accurate, but Herodotus' disbelief of their account is evidence that the Greeks could not comprehend what the Phoenicians knew to be true about world geography.

The Phoenicians and Carthaginians were successful at embargoing the Greeks and Romans from Atlantic destinations for centuries. Thomas Johnston writes:

> "Until 500 B.C. no Greek ship had penetrated beyond the pillars of Hercules. **Phoenicia was at that time the only navigating power in the world**."[20] *(Emphasis added)*

Keep in mind that the Greek definition of "Phoenicia" included the kingdom of Israel from 1000-700 B.C. So for the first three centuries of the first millennium B.C., it was an Israelite navy, allied to the navies of Tyre and Sidon, which kept the Greeks out of the Atlantic Ocean.

In writing about the skills of the ancients and that of the Greco-Romans, the respected Dr. Cyrus Gordon rightly observes:

> "There were ancient mariners in a remote...past who could determine longitude, which modern science could not duplicate until the 18th century A.D. **Worldwide exploration and interconnections were more highly developed in the Bronze Age than in Europe before the Age of Columbus and Magellan**...In certain ways, such as **in navigation and geography, the Greco-Roman world was inferior to that Golden Age of old, as Strabo rightly infers**."[21] *(Emphasis added)*

It is doubtful that you were taught the above facts in any of your school history textbooks. Dr. Cyrus Gordon also acknowledges the dominant Israelite role among the "Phoenicians of old." He writes:

> "**Herodotus tells us that the Phoenicians came from the Red Sea**...**The fleets sent out by Hiram and Solomon... undertook long voyages including regularly-scheduled missions that took up to three years for the round trip**...The quest for metals, stones, special woods and other valued materials...impelled **the ancient merchant kings such as Hiram and Solomon to launch expeditions to the ends of the earth**. The skill and drive were there. **Naval architecture, along with celestial and other methods of navigation, had been refined**, and exploration and cartography had gone through a long development."[22] *(Emphasis added)*

The evidence offered by Dr. Barry Fell in his books confirms Dr. Gordon's statement that the Phoenician-Israelites launched expeditions "to the ends of the earth." Dr. Gordon mentions Herodotus' record that the Phoenicians "came from the Red Sea." Here is a fuller version of Herodotus' statement cited by Dr. Gordon:

> "**The Phoenicians lived of old**, so they say, **about the Red Sea, but they came out of there** and settled in that part of Syria that is next to the sea. **That piece of Syria**, and all as far as Egypt, **is called Palestine**."[23] *(Emphasis added)*

Although Herodotus was writing about "Phoenicians" who were Persian subjects centuries after the kingdom of Israel fell, **he says that the "Phoenicians of old" had "come out" of the Red Sea and migrated to a new homeland in Palestine.** Even in the time of Herodotus, the memory remained of real events about the biblical Israelites, whom the Greeks called "Phoenicians." Obviously, it was the Israelites who came through the Red Sea when God parted the waters in the time of Moses and who went on to settle in Palestine, making it their home. This account of Herodotus strongly confirms the dominant Israelite role in the "Phoenicians of old." Herodotus lived circa the fifth century B.C., so the time of Moses and King Solomon would have been ancient history to him.

Not only would the Phoenicians wreck their own vessels rather than betray their secrets to their rivals, the ancient Phoenicians had a deliberate disinformation campaign to scare their Greek and Roman rivals off the oceans. Sharon Turner's epic 1805 work, *The History of the Anglo-Saxons*, includes this commentary on the confusion of ancient people about the location of the ancient Cassertides, Phoenicia's tin-mining region in British Cornwall and the Scilly Islands. Turner writes:

> "**Much of the false description** with which the position of the Cassertides has been confused, **may have been designedly circulated by the Phoenicians themselves**. We know from Strabo that they were anxious to deprive the rest of the world of any acquaintance with these islands."[24] *(Emphasis added)*

Many readers have, no doubt, seen ancient maps that include drawings of monstrous sea-creatures inhabiting the oceans. We already know that the Phoenicians and Carthaginians had state policies of keeping their trans-oceanic colonies and mines secret from their rivals. What better way to retain their monopoly on trans-oceanic trade routes than to "leak" inaccurate maps to their rivals and scare them off the high seas with lurid tales of sea-monsters waiting to consume sailors and ships? These actions would obviously serve Phoenician-Carthaginian national policy by duping their rivals into believing great "dangers" lurked on the oceans. Since: (A) the ancient maps depicting

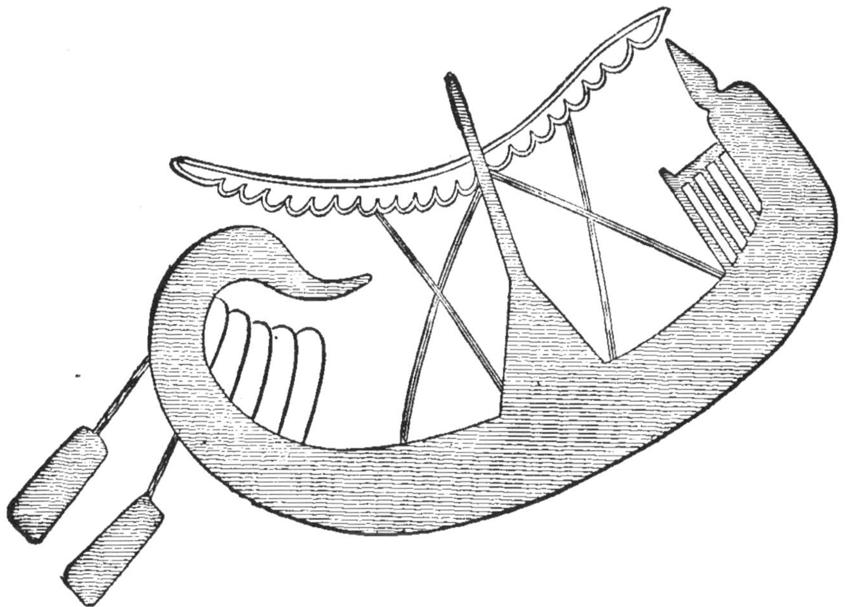

PHŒNICIAN GALLEY FROM A PAINTING.

PHŒNICIAN BIREME.

scary sea-creatures in the oceans have come to us through the Greco-Roman tradition, and (B) neither the Greeks nor Romans had much of an ocean-going reputation, it is likely that an ancient disinformation campaign of the Phoenicians and Carthaginians was successful beyond their wildest dreams!

Not only did they deceive the Greeks and Romans about what was "out there" on the oceans, but they are still deceiving modern mankind as well! Modern man has been deceived into thinking **all** ancient cultures feared the sea because modern history texts have preserved Greco-Roman superstitions about the oceans. The ancient Greco-Roman maps are knowledgeable about Mediterranean regions, but are often wildly inaccurate about regions beyond the Mediterranean. This inaccuracy is a testimony to Greco-Roman ignorance about the regions outside the Mediterranean Sea. Their maps likely were their best effort to piece together what limited knowledge of the outside world they had obtained from Phoenician and Carthaginian sources. The Phoenician and Carthaginian sea-charts and maps would have been far more accurate, but those precious maps were never shared with Greeks or Romans.

Even after Carthage fell to Rome in 146 B.C., Rome remained mostly a land power. They did build large grain ships, which crossed the Mediterranean Sea from Africa to Rome and other cities, but Rome exhibited little interest in trans-oceanic exploration. A century after Carthage's fall when Julius Caesar invaded Britain, Sharon Turner wrote about Rome's ignorance of what lay beyond Europe.

> "When Caesar invaded Britain, we know from his Commentaries, that he was unacquainted with its magnitude, its harbours, or its people...**This ignorance of other nations, and the designed misinformation given by the Phoenicians** may have occasioned...the Cassertides [to] become imperfectly known to the Romans."[25] *(Emphasis added)*

The above digression about the great difference in the nautical skills of the Phoenician-Carthaginians and the Greco-Romans was necessary to assist the reader in grasping that trans-oceanic navigation was common during the Phoenician Golden Age led by the kingdom of Israel. Modern mankind has assumed that because the Greco-Roman writers were unfamiliar with oceanic travel and world geography that all ancient civilizations shared that ignorance. This is not true. If Phoenicia and Carthage had emerged the ultimate winners instead of Greece and Rome, modern schools would all teach the truth that international maritime travel and commerce was commonplace in the time of King Solomon, and they would marvel at the backwardness of the Greco-Romans in matters of maritime navigation and related sciences. However, the victors always write the history books, so Greco-Roman ignorance has been exalted as the standard of knowledge in ancient times and the far more advanced Phoenicians and Carthaginians have been called "barbarians." Now you know the truth.

Israel's Role in the Phoenician Empire

We know that the Phoenician-Israelite alliance established many colonies and trading posts throughout the Mediterranean Sea. Their dominance of the region's maritime commerce during the time of the kingdom of Israel meant the Mediterranean Sea was an "Israelite Sea" much as it was a "Roman Sea" during the time of the Caesars. Israel had a large population that extended inland for a considerable distance while the city-states of Tyre, Sidon, etc. occupied small coastal areas around their respective city-states. Therefore, the population base to support the founding of Phoenicia's many colonies had to come from the population of Israel, not that of Tyre or Sidon.

God promised Abraham that his progeny (especially the "birthright" descendants: the Israelites) would give birth to populations too large to number. *(Genesis 13:16, 22:17)* When the Israelites occupied the Promised Land, it was described as a "land of milk and honey" which could easily support a growing population. That the Israelites numbered in the millions is obvious from the fact that David's army could muster 1,500,000 men when all reserves were mobilized, and that total would exclude all females, children, the tribe of Levi, the elderly and maimed males. Commenting on the population of Israel, based on the above number of mobilized males, the *McClintock and Strong Cyclopedia* states:

> "According to the general laws observable in such cases, these numbers may be said to represent an aggregate population of from **five and a half to six millions**, of which about one third, or two millions, may be fairly assigned to the kingdom of Judah at the time of separation."[26] *(Emphasis not added)*

That estimate is likely on the conservative side. If we double the number of military-age adults to allow for adult females, we reach a total of three million. However, the Bible confirms that many ancient families had large numbers of children, and the *McClintock and Strong* estimate allows for barely two children per adult pair. Some adults were too old to fight in military service so that number needs to be added to the nation's population. Based on the above facts, Israel's population may have been significantly higher than six million people.

However, the physical territory of the twelve tribes in Palestine remained relatively static. The obvious question is "where did their expanding population go?" We now know the answer: their expanding population furnished the settlers for Phoenicia's colonies. Let us examine those colonies for evidence of specific Israelite involvement.

The Phoenician settlements in Spain originally bore several Hebrew names. We have already seen that Spain itself was named Iberia, after Eber, the forefather of the Hebrews. Iberian rivers were also named after Eber and Tamar, a daughter of King David. One principal settlement was named Gades, Gadir or Gadeira (now called Cadiz). Located on the Atlantic Ocean, it served as a major port for Phoenician expeditions to Britain and North America. The prominent historian, George Rawlinson, cites the Phoenician word for "enclosure" or "fortified place" as the source for the name of this ancient port city.[27] He could just as easily have given it an Israelite origin as the Hebrew word "gadar" means the same thing.[28] Since the Hebrew word "gadar" would have been written without consonants at that ancient time, its consonants G-D-R serve precisely as the root word for the names Gadir or Gadeira.

Another writer, L.A. Waddell, suggests Gades could be rendered as House "of the Gads."[29] **Gad** was the name of one of the twelve tribes of Israel, and may have given its name to the colony at

Gades. The tribe of Gad was prophesied in Deuteronomy 33:20 to "be enlarged" (i.e., experience growth in population and territory). As its population expanded, Gad would have been one of the tribes most needing to export some of its population to Israel's colonies. Ephraim and Manasseh were the "birthright" tribes that needed to expand their growing numbers to the Phoenician colonial system as well. Yair Davidy, an Israeli author, asserts that a site near ancient Gades was called "Menesthei Portus," which he dubs: "Port of the tribe of Menesseh [Manasseh]."[30]

Historian Philip Hitti, writes that Gades was founded as a colony of the Phoenicians around 1000 B.C.,[31] while the *Encyclopedia Britannica* states that it was founded "as early as 1100 B.C."[32] This time frame for Gades' founding is at the beginning of Israel's rise to empire status under Kings David and Solomon, when we would expect to see Israelite dominance in Phoenicia's Empire.

George Rawlinson cited the Hebrew word "malakh" as the root word for the Phoenician settlement now called Malaga in Spain.[33] The *Encyclopedia Americana* states: "Malaga, the Malakka of the Phoenicians, was founded in the eleventh century B.C."[34] Both Gades (or Gadir) and Malakka were founded around 1000 B.C., or a little prior to that date. In the previous book of this series, we learned that King David imported vast amounts of copper ores for eventual use in the Temple to be built by Solomon, and that the ancient copper mines of Lake Superior's shores were worked to exhaustion by 1000 B.C. We also learned that the Israelites constructed a large copper-smelting facility in Ezion-geber around this same time. For King David to import copper ores from ancient Lake Superior for use in the Temple, the Israelites and their allies from Tyre and Sidon would have needed several ports of call between North America and Israel to maintain their fleets and rest their sailors. All such shipments would have to pass through the Strait of Gibraltar, and Cadiz and Malaga (to use their modern names) gave them twin ports on both the Atlantic and Mediterranean sides of Gibraltar. It is likely that these ports were built in the eleventh century B.C., and expanded in the tenth century B.C., to serve David and Solomon's need for metal imports to construct the Temple of God and Solomon's expansive building projects.

The ancient Iberian ports with Hebrew names were likely sited by skilled mariners from Tyre or Sidon. Locating a port on either side of the Strait of Gibraltar would ensure the choice of a windward or leeward port for all ships transiting the strait, whether they were heading toward the Atlantic Ocean or the Mediterranean Sea. Supporting the view that Solomon's Israelites were heavily involved in Phoenicia's Spanish ports are Hebrew sepulchral inscriptions found in Spain and discussed in 1846 as follows by Moses Margoliouth:

> "...a sepulchral monument, bearing a Hebrew epitaph, is mentioned as being of far greater antiquity than the Roman monuments; for the characters were more ancient than the square alphabet now in use...the following is a literal English translation:
>
> '**This is the grave of Adoniram, the servant of King Solomon, who came to collect the tribute, and died on the day**...'"[35] *(Emphasis added)*

Moses Margoliouth opines that the Adoniram buried in Spain was the same Adoniram mentioned in I Kings 4:6 and 5:14 who literally was King Solomon's official "over the tribute" and the conscripted labor force. In other words, Adoniram was King Solomon's chief tax collector and impressment official. This would have made him a very unpopular person. If he was buried in ancient Iberia (modern Spain), it is debatable whether he died a natural death or whether he was slain by locals who resented Solomon's high taxes. I Kings 12:1-15 relates that the ten tribes of Israel revolted from Solomon's son, Rehoboam, soon after Solomon died. The reason? They were angry and fed up with Solomon's high taxes. The eventual split between Israel and Judah was caused by an ancient "tax revolt!" The Bible's confirmation that there was widespread anger and resentment about Solomon's high taxes indicates that Adoniram may have been given a very proper funeral after dying from an unfortunate "accident" when he tried to collect the onerous taxes from the Israelite-Phoenician colony in ancient Iberia. Adoniram had to be a very high-ranking Israelite official to warrant such a prominent burial monument.

Biblical accounts that a national "tax revolt" among the Israelites occurred soon after Solomon died indicate Adoniram, the tax collector, may have died in the waning years of King Solomon when

Working in Metal.

the Israelites lost their respect for King Solomon. It would have been logical for Solomon's tax collector to be present in ancient Spain, which was famous for its rich silver mines. The Bible confirms an immense amount of silver flowed into Israel during Solomon's time. *(I Kings 10:21)* The presence of King Solomon's tax collector in ancient Spain indicates much of that silver came from ancient Iberia's silver mines.

The Phoenicians also mined tin and other ores in Britain, and exported them to other nations in the Mideast. George Rawlinson states:

> "Phoenician ships from Gadeira...crossed the mouth of the English Channel...to the Scilly Isles and conveyed thither a body of colonists...The attraction which drew them was the mineral wealth of the islands and of the neighboring Cornish coast...It is reasonable to suppose that the Phoenicians both worked the mines and smelted the ores."[36]

The Bible records that Kings David and Solomon amassed metal ores and products for the Temple of God in Jerusalem. The previous book in this series offered evidence that copper ores were imported to Israel from the New World. Therefore, it can easily be understood that metal ores also came from Phoenician mines in ancient Spain and Britain. A British historian of the nineteenth century, Sir Edmund Creasy, wrote that ancient British mines contributed to the glorious adornment of Solomon's Temple."[37]

We have seen that the name "Iberia," based on the Hebrew namesake, Eber, was placed on the Phoenician settlement in ancient Spain. Dr. Barry Fell wrote that an ancient name of Ireland was **Ibheriu** or **Iberiu**, and that ancient Gaelic histories record that Ireland's Gaelic ancestors **came from Iberia** ("Phoenician" Spain).[38] It is known that

IRELAND & SOUTH BRITAIN ACCORDING TO PTOLEMY

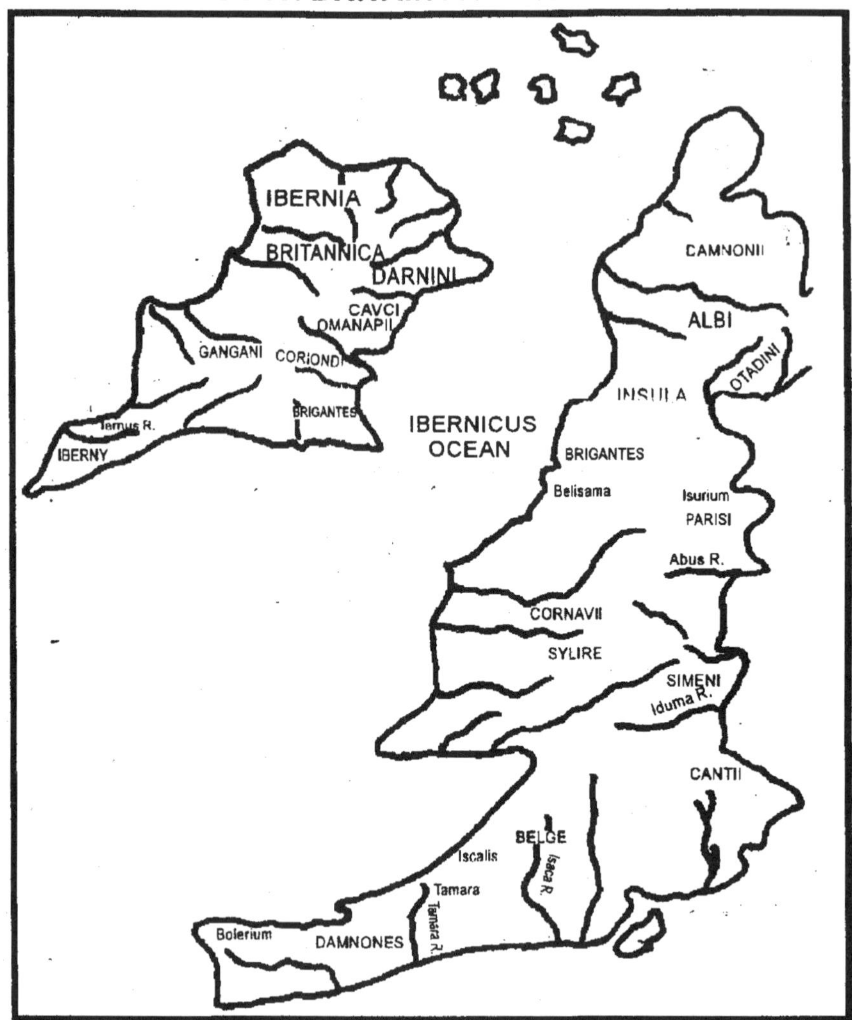

ancient Ireland was also called **Hibernia**, a name that also preserved the Hebrew root word "Eber." L.A. Waddell noted that **Hibernia** and **Hebrides** also derive from the words **Eber** or **Iber**ia (ancient Spain)..."[39] The placement of the name of a Hebrew patriarch on ancient Ireland, Spain and Britain's isles further confirms that their early settlers were Israelites, colonizing these areas during the centuries of the "Phoenician Golden Age."

One other possibility exists for these early names in the British Isles. One clan of the Israelite tribe of Asher was named the **Heberites** (Numbers 26:44-45), a precise root word for such names as **Hibernia** and the **Hebrides**. This possibility argues that the tribe of Asher was active in early Phoenician-Israelite Britain.

Yair Davidy's book, *Lost Israelite Identity*, reproduces an ancient Ptolemaic map (at left) of the British Isles replete with Israelite names. The names **Iber**nia and **Iber**ny are found on ancient Ireland and the names **Simen**ii and the **Tamar**a River are found in ancient Britain.[40] The name of the Israelite tribe of **Simeon** is evident in the name **Simen**ii, and the **Tamar**a River reprises the same name which was found in ancient Iberia/Spain: the name of King David's daughter.

Ancient place-names confirm a substantial Israelite role in the early Phoenician period of the British Isles. The abundance of Israelite names in ancient Spain, Ireland and Britain argue that these "Phoenician" colonies were mostly settled by Israelites. Tyre and Sidon were small city-states, which could not provide settlers for numerous Phoenician colonies on several continents. However, Israel had an expanding population that readily supplied the manpower for these efforts.

The first book in this series documented that Israelite-Phoenician explorers and colonists were present in ancient North America. It was documented that the Ten Commandments, written in ancient Hebrew, was found on artifacts in Ohio and New Mexico.[41]However, most Israelite-Phoenicians in North America were followers of Baal and the "mother-goddess," the same pagan gods that Israel served from the death of Solomon to the fall of Samaria. The reader is referred to the first book in this series for additional evidence confirming a widespread Israelite-Phoenician presence in ancient North America.

HEAD AND WHOLE FIGURE OF PHŒNICIAN BAAL.
From Coins in the British Museum.

The Phoenician "Mound Builders" of Ancient America

How large and viable was the early Hebrew-Phoenician civilization in the New World? Evidence now exists that it was expansive and long-lived. The following passage is taken from *The Adena Tablets*, written by Robert Lenhart, and published in *The Epigraphic Society Occasional Publications*, Volume 13, 1985.

> "When the first settlers moved westward from the American colonies...they discovered the great burial mounds and earthworks of the Ohio Valley. The mounds were obviously the work of man, but...not within the capacity or tribal memories of the tribes who inhabited the valley at that time. Presidents Thomas Jefferson and William Henry Harrison, scientists, many eminent clergymen and others speculated that the mounds and earthworks were built either by Egyptians, Norsemen or **the lost tribes of Israel**."[42] *(Emphasis added)*

Concerning this early Adena civilization, Lenhart also states that:

> "**they reached a very high cultural level** over 1500 years and then disappeared about 500 A.D."..."**the Adena People dominated the Ohio Valley from about 1000 B.C.**"[43] *(Emphasis added)*

Charles Sullivan, Del. *Baker & Co., Engr.*

SKETCH.—ANCIENT WORKS AT MARIETTA, OHIO.

The Adena People and their offshoot, the Hopewell Culture *(their Chillicothe, Ohio mounds are at left)*, were the first of the North American "Mound Builders" who constructed impressive burial mounds that have survived to the present. The *Encyclopedia Americana* also traces the earliest Mound Builders in ancient America to **1000 B.C.**[44] The mound builders had an impressive civilization. The *Americana* comments as follows:

> "Whites who settled west of the Appalachians were so impressed by the number and size of these earthworks that they imagined a super-race of 'Mound Builders' **antedating the Indians**."[45] *(Emphasis added)*

It also describes the Adena earthwork mounds as follows:

> "The Adena people buried their dead in large conical mounds of earth, together with rich grave goods of copper, mica and stone. They left many ornaments and pieces of jewelry, **as well as stone tablets covered with curvilinear designs**."[46] *(Emphasis added)*

The term "curvilinear designs" *(the Serpent Mound in Ohio, at left, is in curvilinear coils itself)* is actually a euphemistic phrase describing Old World inscriptions! Alphabetic writing involves "curved lines" written in a "linear" (straight-line) manner. Therefore, "curvilinear designs" should more accurately have been written "ancient inscriptions." Dr. Barry Fell, in his book *Saga America*, discussed these "curvilinear designs:"

> "The so-called Curvilinear is in fact writing — ancient Punic, Greek, and Libyan Arabic of North Africa — using alphabets that are proper to those tongues. Similar texts, including also Celtic, Iberian and Hebrew, were inscribed in other parts of America..."[47]

The Adena People flourished in the American Midwest as noted above, beginning around 1000 B.C. An example of their megalithic work is the Newark Mounds below. Their arrival in ancient America was part of the expansionary phase of ancient Israel under Kings David and Solomon **around 1000 B.C.** as the "Phoenician" empire grew very powerful. Let us examine what languages have been found on artifacts in ancient American burial mounds.

Newark Mounds, Newark, Ohio

In 1838 a tablet, skeleton and copper arm rings were excavated in Grave Creek, West Virginia, from an Adena burial mound site.[48] Concerning this tablet, Dr. Barry Fell wrote:

> "It was at once recognized by Professor Rafn of Copenhagen as being Iberian...**the language of the tablet is Punic (Phoenician), written in the form of alphabet used in Spain during the first millennium B.C.** It may be translated...reading from right to left: 'The mound raised-on-high for **Tasach** this tile (His) queen caused-to-be-made.' The alphabet of the tablet was deciphered by Spanish scholars, and published by the English epigrapher D. Diringer in 1968. **The language is basic Semitic, and all words occur in standard literary Semitic dictionaries**."[49] *(Emphasis added)*

Another excavated tablet, found in a different burial mound in West Virginia, was:

> "**inscribed in Iberian script and employing the Punic language**, shares some of its vocabulary and all of its basic style characters with the historic tablet of Tasach excavated in 1838 [in] West Virginia...**Its vocabulary is found in standard Semitic dictionaries**, and yields the following translation: "The memorial of Teth this tile (His) brother caused-to-be-made."[50] *(Emphasis added)*

Grave Creek Mound West Virginia.

The presence of Iberian Punic inscriptions on these tablets indicates their makers had their origins in the Phoenician colony in ancient Iberia (Spain). That the Adena people buried their dead with Semitic inscriptions of the Hebrew-Phoenician language group confirms that the Adena People were a large colony of Semitic settlers from the Old World. Given the proximity of these finds to the "Decalogue Tablet" found in Ohio, inscribed with the Ten Commandments in ancient Hebrew, it seems evident that ancient America was inhabited for many centuries by Israelite settlers. Though Israel ceased to be a nation in the eighth century B.C., its American colony outlived its parent nation for many centuries, linked to its sister Phoenician colonies in Carthage, Iberia and Britain.

It is significant that the Adena Civilization began around 1000 B.C. The first book in this series documented that the Lake Superior copper mines were apparently worked to exhaustion around 1000 B.C. when King David was importing massive amounts of copper ores into Israel. It seems evident that the Israelites, together with their Tyrian and Sidonian allies, founded the Adena colonies to exploit the natural resources of ancient North America. A Michigan author, Betty Sodders, wrote the following about the widespread utilization of ancient America's natural resources by these people:

> "... Michigan was 'THE' copper mining center of the New World, still other prehistoric diggings for various minerals became clearly evident across our entire nation...mica was mined in North Carolina, serpentine in Pennsylvania and lead mines were found in Kentucky, just to name a few...the most baffling endeavor was located along the Mississippi Valley where prehistoric oil wells were actually discovered. Additional oil operations can be noted in Ohio, Pennsylvania and Canada.[51]

Did your history texts teach you that a sophisticated ancient civilization, with Semitic inscriptions in their graves, built elaborate mounds and mined the mineral wealth of ancient America? Probably not. Unfortunately, the truth about ancient America's links with Old World civilizations has not been taught in America's schools. The truth would be fascinating! However, if the truth were widely told, the Bible's historical accounts would be given dramatic new credibility and the theory of evolution would be given a mortal blow. Therein lies the most likely explanation for the truth being withheld from the American people.

The Grave Creek mound tablets date to approximately 300-200 B.C.,[52] a time when North American Semites were linked to Punic cultures in Spain and Carthage. Since it is apparent that the late Adena civilization was a Semitic culture, like those in Iberia and North Africa, sharing a common culture and language, it is evident that these groups shared a common origin. That common origin was the Phoenician alliance of Israel, Tyre, and Sidon.

It is significant that an ancient Adena personage interred in an American burial mound was named "Tasach." In Genesis 21:12, God promised Abraham that "through Isaac shall your descendants be named." *(RSV)* God promised that Isaac's name would be an identifying "marker" for locating the birthright descendants of Abraham. The name "Ta-**sach**," found in ancient America, is derived from the name "**Isaac**." Tasach must have been a prominent Israelite in the ancient Semitic colony in North America to warrant such a burial mound. Also, the "Decalogue tablet" found in an Ohio burial mound indicates that it was the final resting-place of an ancient Levite or Priest because the Levites and Priests were the custodians and teachers of the laws of God.

The Phoenicians in Ancient South America

The Phoenicians also explored South America. This is not surprising because South America's shores are closer than North America to Phoenician colonies in Iberia and Carthage. In 1872, a stone with a Phoenician inscription was found in Brazil that describes an expedition of Sidonians who practiced human sacrifice and appealed to Baal and other "gods and goddesses." It states its Sidonian makers were part of a ten-ship expedition sent in the nineteenth year of King Hiram's reign from the port of Ezion-geber in the Red Sea, and that they arrived in the "Island of Iron" after a two year voyage around Africa. These facts are based on a translation by Dr. Cyrus Gordon in his book,

Before Columbus.[53] Others have doubted the authenticity of the inscription, but Dr. Gordon outlined reasons why the inscription is authentic. One is that these ancient sailors referred to themselves as "Sidonians," not "Phoenicians." This is consistent with the factual reality that they would not have referred to themselves as "Phoenicians," the name the Greeks used for them.

At first glance, the reader may be tempted to think this inscription dates to the "King Hiram" who was contemporaneous with Kings David and Solomon. However, there are strong reasons to think otherwise. One is a reference to the practice of human sacrifice by this group of Sidonians. Kings David and Solomon would never have tolerated such a practice in their navies. A second reason is the lack of any dedication to Yahweh, the God of Israel. This inscription was made at a time when Baal worship permeated Phoenician society and when the Red Sea port of Ezion-geber was functioning. This argues for a date well after the time of King Solomon. Ezion-geber was in the territory of Judah, and Judah was not an ally of the Sidonians, so this fact argues that Sidonians could only launch fleets from Ezion-geber after the fall of Judah circa 586 B.C.

A. PHŒNICIAN AND CYPRIOTE INSCRIPTION

The South American inscription makes no mention of any Israelites. During the Israelite portion of the Phoenician Golden Age, Israel, Tyre and Sidon mingled their naval crews together *(I Kings 9:26-27)*, so this inscription apparently was made after the Israelites had departed the region and were no longer in the Phoenician alliance.

Dr. Cyrus Gordon's dating agrees with the above historical context. He asserts this inscription was made in 534 B.C. during the reign of King Hiram III, a vassal of the Achaemenid Persian Kings. Why did these Sidonians take a circuitous route around Africa to Brazil when a direct route through Gibraltar was the quickest way? Dr. Gordon answers:

> "...Gibraltar was controlled by the Carthaginian rivals of Cyrus the Great. The historical setting explains why the [Sidonian] fleet sailed from Ezion-geber, taking the long (but open) way to the Atlantic."[54]

The Phoenicians' large colony, Carthage, had grown powerful and could bar Persian fleets from the Atlantic Ocean. Sidon was under Persian rule and, therefore, had to do the bidding of the Persian King. The Sidonians were likely looking for raw materials in the Atlantic regions, relying on their old records that such raw materials were exported from the New World in King Solomon's time. Indeed, the Phoenician inscription calls the land of ancient Brazil the "Island of Iron."

Dr. Gordon makes a good case that the ancient Phoenicians even called Brazil by its modern name. He writes that the Hebrew word for iron is "BRZL," and that iron ore is one of Brazil's main resources:

> "...no country in the world merits the name BRZL "Iron" more than Brazil, whose chief resource is still iron. Indeed it is reported that 25 percent of the world's known iron reserves are in the Brazilian province of Minas Gerais. Other parts of Brazil are also rich in iron..."[55]

The Sidonian fleet serving Persia may have been looking for a way to exploit New World iron ore without the knowledge of the Carthaginians, who guarded access to the Atlantic Ocean by controlling Gibraltar. The above argues that the modern nation of BRAZIL still bears a Hebrew/Semitic name (BRZL) given to it by the ancient Phoenicians. This raises the likelihood that even as the Lake Superior copper mines were exploited around 1000 B.C. by King David's Israelites, the mariners of Kings David and Solomon found a source for iron ore in ancient Brazil. That is why Sidonian mariners arriving in South America still called the region by the name of "BRZL" ("iron") when they landed there in 531 B.C. Dr. Gordon dismisses the idea that these Sidonians arrived in the New World by accident. He writes:

> "The crossing was probably not an accident...the winds and currents are all in favor of east-to-west crossings at that latitude where the Atlantic happens to be much narrower than it is in the Northern Hemisphere...There is every reason to believe that the ship that reached Brazil in 531 B.C. sailed intentionally to a land (already known...by its name "Island of Iron") to get raw materials..."[56]

"Phoenicia's" most prominent ruler, King Solomon, wrote about the very trade winds that Dr. Gordon mentions. In Ecclesiastes 1:6, Solomon wrote:

> "The wind blows to the south, and goes round to the north; round and round goes the wind, and on its circuits the wind returns." *(RSV)*

This is exactly what the circular trade winds do over the oceans, and Solomon's awareness of this fact affirms that the Phoenicians knew about the oceanic trade winds five centuries before Sidonian sailors landed in Brazil in 531 B.C. The Phoenicians, capitalists who knew the truth of the adage "time is money," no doubt used the trade winds to their commercial advantage by routing their ships to take advantage of the trade winds in their voyages across the Atlantic Ocean in either direction.

There is further evidence of the presence of ancient Phoenicians (and Israelites) in South America. Dr. Gordon notes the widespread presence of the word "Para-" on South American Rivers from Venezuela to Argentina (Paragua, Para, Paranaiba, Paraiba, Paraguacu, etc.) Two nations of South America still bear this same root word (Paraguay and Peru).[57] He wrote that this word root indicates that these rivers were named by people whose linguistic roots were from Mesopotamia where Semitic languages were spoken, and he specifically cites the "Hebrew Pra-t (with f. sg. suffix -t)."[58] This presents an intriguing possibility: If the Hebrew word **Pra-t** is the origin of the common South American word "**para-**," we have a form of the Hebrew word for "covenant" (B-R-T). Dr. Gordon notes the language of the Aztecs (Nahuatl) did not distinguish between the letters "p" and "b."[59] As long ago as 1676 A.D., Aylett Sammes wrote that the letters "p" and "b" were "easily convertible" in ancient Phoenician place-names.[60] This would make Dr. Gordon's suggested root word of "Prat" another form of the word "B-R-T." The fact that the national name "Brazil" preserves the Hebrew word for "iron" argues for a Hebrew-Semitic origin for the "para-" words naming many rivers along Brazil's Atlantic coast.

This leads to another possible explanation for an ancient mystery. Dr. Gordon discusses the ancient "Piri Reis" map found in Turkey in 1929. This map (shown on next page) includes a strikingly accurate depiction of Brazil's South American coastline, noting many of its rivers. Dr. Gordon describes this amazing ancient map in these words:

> "The principal map was painted...in 1513 by the Turkish Admiral Piri...Piri Reis tells us in his writings that the map embodies ancient sources, some of which came via the great library at Alexandria, which was destroyed by fire...in the seventh century A.D. There are features of the map that must antedate Columbus' discovery of America in 1492: notably, **the essentially correct east coastline of South America in its right longitudinal relationship with the Atlantic coast of the Old World**."[61] *(Emphasis added)*

The computation of longitude at sea was not "rediscovered" in the modern world until the 18th century.[62] Yet, the Piri Reis map confirms an ancient culture knew how to make "longitudinally correct" maps of continents and seacoasts. It is this book's conclusion that the original map (from which the Piri Reis map was copied) was made by the ancient world's navigational experts: the Phoenicians! When Israel, Tyre and Sidon fell or lost their independence, Carthage carried on their seafaring skills for centuries. The Piri Reis map is likely a

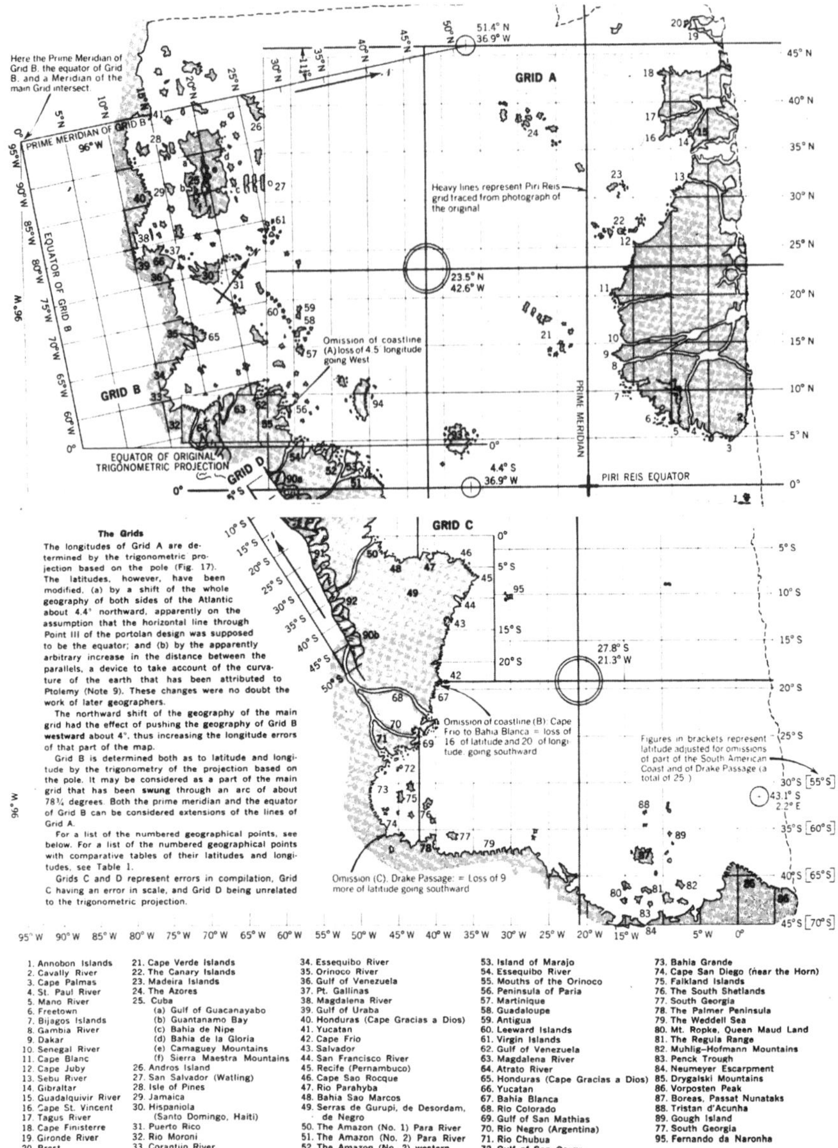

1. Annobon Islands
2. Cavally River
3. Cape Palmas
4. St. Paul River
5. Mano River
6. Freetown
7. Bijagos Islands
8. Gambia River
9. Dakar
10. Senegal River
11. Cape Blanc
12. Cape Juby
13. Sebu River
14. Gibraltar
15. Guadalquivir River
16. Cape St. Vincent
17. Tagus River
18. Cape Finisterre
19. Gironde River
20. Brest
21. Cape Verde Islands
22. The Canary Islands
23. Madeira Islands
24. The Azores
25. Cuba
    (a) Gulf of Guacanayabo
    (b) Guantanamo Bay
    (c) Bahia de Nipe
    (d) Bahia de la Gloria
    (e) Camaguey Mountains
    (f) Sierra Maestra Mountains
26. Andros Island
27. San Salvador (Watling)
28. Isle of Pines
29. Jamaica
30. Hispaniola (Santo Domingo, Haiti)
31. Puerto Rico
32. Rio Moroni
33. Corantijn River
34. Essequibo River
35. Orinoco River
36. Gulf of Venezuela
37. Pt. Gallinas
38. Magdalena River
39. Gulf of Uraba
40. Honduras (Cape Gracias a Dios)
41. Yucatan
42. Cape Frio
43. Salvador
44. San Francisco River
45. Recife (Pernambuco)
46. Cape Sao Rocque
47. Rio Parahyba
48. Bahia Sao Marcos
49. Serras de Gurupi, de Desordam, de Negro
50. The Amazon (No. 1) Para River
51. The Amazon (No. 2) Para River
52. The Amazon (No. 2) western mouth
53. Island of Marajo
54. Essequibo River
55. Mouths of the Orinoco
56. Peninsula of Paria
57. Martinique
58. Guadaloupe
59. Antigua
60. Leeward Islands
61. Virgin Islands
62. Gulf of Venezuela
63. Magdalena River
64. Atrato River
65. Honduras (Cape Gracias a Dios)
66. Yucatan
67. Bahia Blanca
68. Rio Colorado
69. Gulf of San Mathias
70. Rio Negro (Argentina)
71. Rio Chubua
72. Gulf of San Gorge
73. Bahia Grande
74. Cape San Diego (near the Horn)
75. Falkland Islands
76. The South Shetlands
77. South Georgia
78. The Palmer Peninsula
79. The Weddell Sea
80. Mt. Ropke, Queen Maud Land
81. The Regula Range
82. Muhlig–Hofmann Mountains
83. Penck Trough
84. Neumeyer Escarpment
85. Drygalski Mountains
86. Vorposten Peak
87. Boreas, Passat Nunataks
88. Tristan d'Acunha
89. Gough Island
77. South Georgia
95. Fernando da Naronha

The famous Piri Reis Map, drawn in very early times, clearly shows the South American coastline near present-day Brazil as discovered by ancient explorers. *(Copyright: Hapgood, Maps Of The Ancient Sea Kings, pages 36-37. Used by permission.)*

copy of an ancient Carthaginian-Phoenician map that was preserved in the great library at Alexandria. This is supported by the fact that (A) the South American seacoast so accurately depicted on the map still bears a Hebrew name ("Brazil"), and (B) its rivers are known by an Old World root word from the Mesopotamian/Semitic tradition (according to Dr. Gordon).

The Israelites even founded colonies in the Black Sea region of Asia during their Golden Age. Herbert Hannay, a British historian, wrote about:

> "that **other Hebrew colony in the Caucasus**, called **Iberia**, which...was **founded in the Hebro-Phoenician Era**."[63] *(Emphasis added)*

We will examine more information about the Israelite kingdom called Iberia in the Caucasus region in the third book of this series on Israelite history. The Israelites in their Phoenician glory days founded colonies named "Iberia," honoring their forefather "Eber," in both ancient Spain and in the Caucasus region of Asia east of the Black Sea. In Genesis 28:4, Abraham was promised that his birthright seed would "spread abroad to the west, and to the east, and to the north and to the south." This prophecy was being fulfilled as the Israelites expanded all over the globe during Israel's "Golden Age" of the Phoenician Empire.

The Phoenician alliance of Israel, Tyre and Sidon founded numerous colonies in the Mediterranean region, Spain, the British Isles, and in ancient North and South America during the reigns of Kings David and Solomon "around 1000 B.C." Under these kings, the Israelite (Phoenician) Empire began to plant colonies and to export Hebrew-Phoenician culture around the world. The evidence that the ancient Israelites founded a large empire has been in the Bible for thousands of years, but there now is archeological evidence which confirms that the biblical accounts were correct all along. At its zenith, the "Phoenician" empire of Israel ruled portions of five continents: Asia, Africa, Europe, North America and South America!

The "Covenant" Empire

While we have seen that the Greeks used the term "Phoenicia" to describe the alliance of Israel, Tyre and Sidon, it is time to address the question: **What did the ancient Israelite empire call itself?**

The answer to this question is not difficult to ascertain. The Israelites were descended from Abraham, with whom God made a solemn **covenant** *(Genesis 12:1-3, 15:18, 17:1-21, and 22:15-18)* to make "many nations" and "kings" out of his descendants. In the above scriptures the word "**covenant**" appears many times. This **covenant**, with its many blessings, was passed on to Isaac *(Genesis 26:24-25)* and to Jacob. *(Genesis 35:9-12)* Jacob's name was changed to "Israel" *(Genesis 35:10)*, and God's **covenant** promises were conveyed to Israel's twelve sons, the progenitors of the "twelve tribes of Israel." However, the name "Israel" was most specifically placed on the Israelite tribes of Ephraim and Manasseh. *(Genesis 48:8-16)* Note Israel's statement in verses 14-16:

> "**Israel** stretched out his right hand, and laid it upon Ephraim's head...and his left hand upon Manasseh's... ...And he blessed...the lads...**let my name ["Israel"] be named on them**...and let them grow into a multitude in the midst of the earth." *(KJV)*

Consequently, from that point on, any entity called "Israel" in the Bible usually identifies the tribes of Ephraim and Manasseh because they were the primary inheritors of the Abrahamic "covenant."

Ephraim and Manasseh received the "birthright" blessings of the Abrahamic covenant, which divinely promised them a large population, many nations, possession of the "gates of their enemies," abundant natural resources, and many more physical and Spiritual blessings. *(Genesis 49:22-26; Deut. 33:13-17)* The other tribes shared in these covenant promises, but the "lion's share" of the covenant blessings was inherited by the tribes of Ephraim and Manasseh.

While the tribe of Judah did not receive the birthright blessings of the Abrahamic Covenant, they did inherit one prominent blessing that no other tribe received. Abraham was told in Genesis 17:6 that his

ISRAELITES

THE "COVENANT" PEOPLE

The Bible records that the tribes of Israel, under Moses, made a "covenant" with God. The Israelites retained the unique awareness that they were the "covenant" people as an enduring part of their culture. The Hebrew word for "covenant" ("B-R-TH") was placed on people, places and Phoenician/Carthaginian coins. The presence of the Hebrew word for "covenant" on ancient peoples or places is a strong identifier for locating where the ten tribes of Israel migrated after leaving Palestine. Listed below are important examples.

HEBREW WORD FOR "COVENANT"

Without Vowels:	**B-R-T, B-R-TH**
With Vowels:	**BERITH, BARAT, BRYTH, BRIT, B'RITH, etc.**

TRIBAL AND PLACE NAMES ASSOCIATED WITH MIGRATING ISRAELITES:

BRITON, BRETON, BRITTANY, BRYTHONIC CELTS, etc.

Place Name		Greek Name
BRITANNIC ISLANDS	=	PRETANIC ISLANDS
BRITHIA or B'RITHIA	=	PARTHIA

descendants would include kings. Before he died, Israel (Jacob) prophesied in Genesis 49:10 that:

> "**The sceptre [kings and dynasties] shall not depart from Judah**, nor a lawgiver from between his feet, until Shiloh come..." *(KJV)*

The word "Shiloh" is defined by *Young's Analytical Concordance* as "a description of Messiah..." The Messiah will ultimately rule all nations (Zechariah 14:9-16), and Genesis 49:10 prophesied that the Messiah must come from the tribe of Judah. Christians note that one of Jesus Christ's credentials as Messiah is that he was a Jew from the tribe of Judah.

After the kingdom of Israel divided into northern and southern kingdoms, Ephraim and Manasseh became the chief tribes of the Northern Kingdom of Israel, and Judah became the chief tribe of the southern kingdom named Judah. This fact will become critically important in the remaining books of this series as we trace their descendants through history up to (and including) the modern era. The Bible consistently refers to the Jews and their related tribes by the name "Judah" (both in history and prophecy), while Ephraim and Manasseh and their related tribes are referred to as "Israel" (in both history and prophecy). **It is critically important to realize that, after the division of the tribes that occurred soon after the death of King Solomon, the terms "Israel" and "Judah" are not synonymous and in a national sense designate different groups of people.**

The above discussion illustrates the importance of the word **"covenant"** in the history of Israel. Israel's tribes were well aware that they were the "covenant people," indeed, it was the central theme of their heritage. The Hebrew word for covenant is **"Berith."**[65] With vowels absent in ancient Hebrew, this word would be represented by the consonants **B-R-T** or **B-R-TH**. A modern form of this Hebrew word is contained in the name of a well-known Jewish organization: B'nai **B'rith**.

Before continuing, the reader should know that the final symbol of **B-R-T** or **B-R-TH**, although written as "T" or "TH," is based on the same Hebrew consonant (its pronunciation could vary). I wish to acknowledge the assistance of the late Dr. Charles V. Dorothy, a graduate of Claremont Graduate School, Claremont, CA, who wrote the following on the different forms of this Hebrew consonant: "It is no stretch at all of linguistic patterns for a spirant (especially hard to pronounce in the case of 'th') to elide into a stop: 't'."

I also thank Dr. Dorothy for noting that "B-R-T/B-R-TH" can sometimes designate a Hebrew word for "soap or alkali." Since some individuals, determined to minimize the role of the Israelites and the God of Israel in world history, may grasp at this straw to oppose the truth, we will examine this possibility in order to give it the swift dismissal it deserves. According to *Young's Analytical Concordance to the Bible*, the Old Testament translates the word "B-R-T/B-R-TH" as "covenant" (or related words) about 280 times.[66] However, those consonants are translated only twice in the Bible (Hebrew word "borith") as "soap."[67]

Anyone familiar with history knows that the Israelites were known as the "Covenant People," not the "Soap People." In terms of its national importance to the Israelites, the word "covenant" merits unique and special importance to them. Dr. Dorothy agreed, writing to this author: "...in your favor, and you may want to mention [it] whenever possible, is the much greater importance of 'covenant' or 'bond' [in Israel's history] against...'soap.'" It is beyond the scope of this book to analyze the nuances of the Hebrew language, but the reader may rest assured that either **B-R-T** or **B-R-TH**, when applied in a national sense to the Israelites, represents the Hebrew word for "covenant."

L. A. Waddell's book, *Phoenician Origin of Britons, Scots and Anglo-Saxons*, documents the prominent usage of the word "B-R-T," which Waddell generally renders "Barat," in the nation and colonies of the early Phoenicians, but a cautionary comment must be made about his book. While it contains strong evidence about the prominence of the word "B-R-T" in Phoenicia's sphere of influence, Waddell's book (first published in 1924) contains Aryan racial supremacy theories. In contrast, the book that you are now reading completely rejects and disavows any racial supremacy theories and all forms of anti-Semitism. Waddell seemed not to realize that in documenting the prominence of the Hebrew word for covenant (B-R-T) in the Phoenician Empire, he was actually offering strong evidence for Israel's dominant role in Phoenicia's empire.

Waddell's book made a key error in not grasping that there were two separate Hebrew kingdoms in the ancient Mideast: Judah in the south and Israel in the north. He mistakenly refers to the Israelites to the north of Judah as the "Hitto-Phoenicians." Waddell's lack of awareness that the terms "Jew" and "Israelite" designated different nations is evident in his notation on a chart that the "Israelites [were] carried into captivity by Nebuchadnezzar, 587 B.C."[68] It was actually the "Jews" (of the kingdom of Judah) who were taken into captivity by Nebuchadnezzar in 587 B.C. The "Israelites" of the kingdom of Israel left Palestine when Samaria fell in 721 B.C. Due to this mistake, Waddell failed to recognize the Israelite character of the "Phoenician" Empire. Tyre and Sidon lacked any identification with the word "covenant," **but the ten tribes of Israel, especially the tribes of Ephraim and Manasseh, were the covenant people**, and their use of the word "B-R-T" proclaimed their

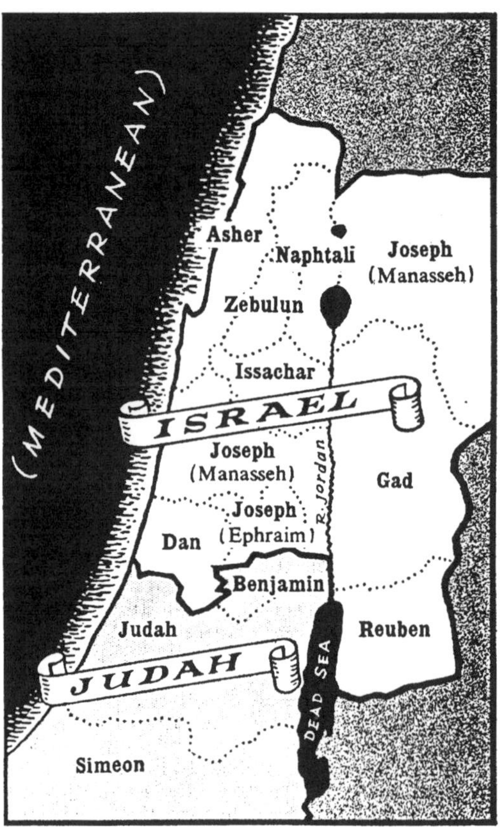

identity to the world! Besides calling themselves "Israel," "Judah," or their individual tribal names, the Israelites called themselves the "covenant" people.

Early British chroniclers record that a Trojan ruler named Brutus came from the Eastern Mediterranean with hundreds of ships to colonize ancient Britain, and that he gave it the name "Briton" or "Brittania." An approximate date for this event is 1103 B.C. Although Brutus is attributed a Trojan ancestry in the ancient accounts, he bore the Hebrew word **B-R-T** in his name (Brutus), and applied the same Hebrew word (**B-R-T**) to the British Isles. That a Trojan leader bore an important Hebrew root word in his name provides evidence that Israelites were present among the inhabitants of ancient Troy. We have seen that the tribe of Dan was involved with the Greeks and the Sea Peoples long before Troy fell and that the Israelites founded a colony named Iberia on the eastern shores of the Black Sea, so Israelites were certainly present in the area of Troas in Anatolia where Troy was located.

William Camden, in his 1610 book, *Britannia*, acknowledges the belief that the Trojan Brutus founded the British nation,[69] but not all British historians accept the Brutus story. Commonly accepted is the Phoenician involvement in ancient Britain. Aylett Sammes' 1676 book, *Antiquities of Ancient Britain (or Britannia)*, wrote:

> "when I considered...the British or Welsh language... that the main body of it consisteth of Hebrew and Greek words...I concluded this could proceed from no other root but the commerce of the Phoenicians with this nation, who using the same language with the children of Israel in Canaan, even in those primitive times were great traders and skillful mariners, and sent out their colonies through the world..."[70]

Sammes's book devotes many pages to the substantial involvement of the Phoenicians in ancient Britain, and he credits the names: Britain, Barat-anac (Britannic), etc. to a Phoenician origin. Writing in the seventeenth century, Sammes acknowledged that the Phoenicians shared a language with the Israelites, but he seems not to realize that he had stumbled on the Hebrew word for "covenant" in the ancient placenames of the British Isles.

Israel, the covenant nation, had been present in the Eastern Mediterranean for centuries before King David ruled, so the arrival in Britain of Brutus and a fleet of Israelite "Covenant People" from the Eastern Mediterranean in 1103 B.C., was certainly possible. Judges 5:17, and secular accounts of the Sea Peoples, confirm the Danites had adopted a maritime lifestyle at least a century before Brutus arrived in Britain. Who else but the Israelites, who really did have a "covenant" relationship with God, would so prominently affix the Hebrew word for "covenant" to themselves and their territories? Unique among the lands inhabited by the Israelite-Phoenicians, the island of Britain has retained its original Israelite name continuously into the modern era.

The Phoenician colony of Carthage later printed the Hebrew word B-R-T on its coins,[71] confirming the Israelite role in ancient Carthage. The Israelites knew that they were "the Covenant People," and the Hebrew word for "covenant" was a key part of their nomenclature. Would Tyre and Sidon's pagan colonists have used Hebraisms such as the Hebrew word for "covenant," Israelite tribal names, and the name of King David's daughter? Of course not! **The abundance of Israelite names during the Golden Age of the Phoenician Empire confirms that the "Phoenician" Empire was the Israelite Empire spoken of in the Bible**.

There is additional evidence about the global power of the Phoenicians during the biblical era. Remember that vowels were frequently omitted in ancient languages? The consonants of the word "Phoenicia" are **P(h)-N-C**. The Romans preserved these consonants when they called the Carthaginians the "Punic" empire. In doing so, the Romans copied the Greek designation for the Phoenicians, the founders of Carthage.

The Romans were not the only ancient nation that retained the "**P-N-C**" name for the ancient Israelite Empire. Ancient Vedic records in India also record the existence of an international empire with those consonants in their name. The ancient writings of India include the following statement:

> "The able **Panch**...brought the whole World under their sway."[72]

Also, a Rig Veda Hymn includes this statement:

> "The **Br**iha**t** singers belaud Indra...Indra hath raised the Sun on high [and] leads us with single sway — The **Panc**h leaders of the Earth."[73] *(Emphasis added)*

The consonants for the global "Panch" empire of the Vedic records are **P-N-C(h)**. These are the same consonants found in the words: Phoenician and Punic. This could conceivably be written off by skeptics as a coincidence except for the fact that this "Panch" empire is also linked with the **B-R-T** Hebrew root word for "Covenant." The first quote about the "Panch" is from the "Maha-Barata Indian Epic of the Great Barats." *(underlining added)*

The references to Indra and sun worship are not surprising. The Bible records that Israelites became devotees of the Sun-god, Baal, after Solomon's death. Sun-worship began permeating Israel even before the death of Solomon as he himself worshipped "Ashtoreth (or "Astarte)," a Phoenician name for the "mother-goddess" who was worshipped in other cultures by other names. Israel's devotion to foreign gods lasted from Solomon's death until the fall of Israel in about 721 B.C., so the fact that the B-R-T (Covenant) People of "Panch" (Phoenician) fame were associated with sun-worship is consistent with both biblical and secular accounts.

Clearly, the ancient Indian histories referred to the Israelite Empire by the **same** root words by which they were known in the Mediterranean world! The Greeks knew the Israelites by the term Phoenicia, and the Israelites named themselves the "B-R-T" ("Covenant") People. Ancient India preserved both root words in the terms Panch, and the Barats (or Brihats). Further linking these root words together is a phrase in an ancient Indian epic (the Vishnu Purana) which states:

> "The principal nations of the **B**a**r**a**t**s are the Kurus and the able **Panc**h."[74] *(Emphasis added)*

The Israelite-Phoenician Empire made a lasting impression in Asia as well as in the Mediterranean and Atlantic worlds, confirming Israel's influence was truly international in scope. The record in

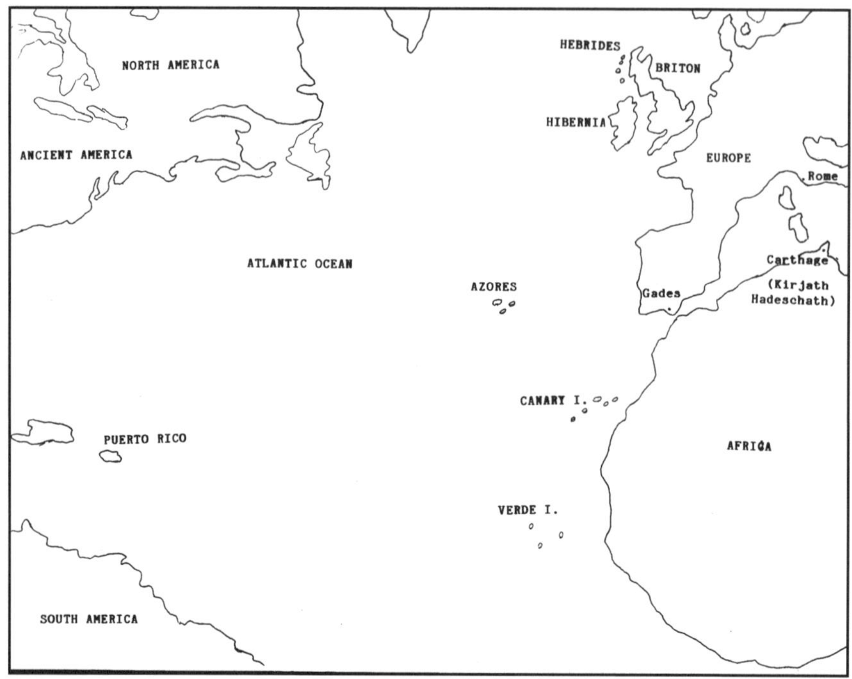

The Old World and the New

ancient Indian annals that the Barat/Panch (B-R-T/Phoenicians) "brought the whole World under their sway" gives added weight to the statement of the Bible that "all the kings of the earth sought the presence of Solomon..." *(II Chronicles 9:23-24)*

God gave King David the following promise through the prophet Nathan:

> "I have been with you wherever you went, and have cut off all your enemies from before you; and I will make for you a great name, like unto the name of the great ones of the earth." *(II Samuel 7:9, KJV)*

This passage is important for two reasons: It not only claims that God would make King David's name famous, but it also claims a divine role in David's and Israel's ascendancy. God blessed David and Israel because King David served and glorified God. A nation and its leaders are exalted when they glorify and obey God. King Solomon began his reign with great humility and great blessings linked together.

As his character deteriorated at the end of his reign, troubles and problems beset him. The next chapter will document that Israel's kingdom was progressively weakened as they forgot God and ignored God's laws in their society and culture.

To conclude this chapter, it can be seen that the Israelite empire under Kings David and Solomon at the beginning of the first millennium B.C. was an international maritime empire which spanned the globe and dominated parts of five continents. Besides its Mideast homeland, it founded colonies throughout the Mediterranean region of Europe and Africa, the British Isles, the Asian shores of the Black Sea region and in both North and South America. For decades, it exercised dominance over the nations that had been conquered by King David and ruled by King Solomon. After King David routed the Assyrian army and its allies, the fame of Israel spread far and wide. Solomon's wealth, wisdom and power further expanded the world's awareness of Israel's greatness.

King Solomon's links with Sidon, Tyre and Egypt would have made this alliance one of the most powerful empires in the ancient world. Secular histories have called this powerful empire the "Phoenician Empire," but that name obscures the fact that the Greeks included the Israelites in that empire. The prominence of Israelite proper names in the Phoenician Empire confirms Israel's dominant role in Phoenicia's Empire. Secular histories have also greatly underestimated the power and intercontinental influence of the Israelite-Phoenician Empire because they assumed this empire shared the ignorance of world geography manifested by the ancient Greeks and Romans. That assumption was wrong. While the Greeks and Romans conquered large land empires, the Phoenicians had conquered the world's oceans. The Phoenicians knew the earth was round about a millennium before the Greeks understood this fact, and the Phoenicians and Carthaginians explored, mined and colonized other continents for centuries while barring Greece and Rome from the world's oceans during most of the first millennium, B.C. Biblical assertions that the Israelite Empire under King Solomon had worldwide influence are not exaggerated. Archeological, epigraphic and historical evidence confirms that the Bible's historical accounts are, and always have been, accurate!

Secular historians have been unaware of the real scope of Israel's ancient empire. One reason for this omission is the great antiquity of Israel's empire. We must realize that the Israelite Empire's Golden Age was already "ancient history" at the time of Alexander the Great, and occurred a millennium prior to the time of the Roman Caesars. Because it existed long before the empires commonly discussed in history texts, and because its Golden Age of world power was mostly limited to the reigns of just two kings, David and Solomon, the story of the Israelite Empire has not been fully appreciated previously.

Another reason why historians may have overlooked the greatness of the Israelite Empire is the lack of ancient monuments, steles, etc. in the Mideast. We have already discussed one reason for the lack of monuments to Israel's glory: God forbade idolatry and "graven images." God tried to keep Israel's monarchs humble for the good of the nation, and self-glorifying monuments and steles would not have been made by Israel's humble kings. Kings David and Solomon, who were faithful to God at the time of Israel's greatest glory, did not build memorials and monuments to "their" conquests and accomplishments. Since they did not build boastful monuments, modern archeologists have nothing to find.

But what about later monarchs, when they ceased fearing God, some might ask? It is likely that later Israelite monarchs did, indeed, build monuments about their accomplishments, but there are several reasons why these artifacts could not have been preserved. The territory of Israel was the location for many destructive wars after the reigns of Kings David and Solomon. As Israel's enemies conquered Palestine, destroying whole cities in the process, vast numbers of monuments and records were destroyed as well. Indeed, as Assyria and Babylon conquered the Israelite homelands, Solomon's Temple, the royal palaces of David and Solomon, etc. were all razed. It is likely that Assyria and Babylon destroyed every vestige of Israelite civilization that they could find when they burnt the cities of Israel and Judah. Also, subsequent populations placed in Palestine had no use for anything "Israelite," and scavenged whatever physical materials were left for their own building materials. Palestine is a nexus where three continents (Africa, Asia and Europe) converge. For this reason, the small territory of Palestine has been fought over and its cities have been destroyed and rebuilt many times. Each of the many wars in Palestine further destroyed the physical evidence of the very ancient Israelite Empire.

There is another reason why little or nothing would have remained of the Israelite empire based in Palestine: the weathering forces of the elements. Maitland Edey writes about the role of the damp, ocean climate of the eastern Mediterranean in erasing the remnants of the Phoenician Empire.

> "Why for so long has so little been known about the Phoenicians? One reason is the climate...Anything written on papyrus quickly disappears; wood rots; clay tablets, unless safely buried in the ground, crumble. Even stone monuments or inscriptions, if exposed long enough to the weathering of wind, rain and frost, become blurred and eventually indecipherable...while the Phoenicians over a period of about a thousand years...were very busy making things, saving things and writing things down, the elements were equally busy destroying them."[75]

While the ancient tablets and monuments of Assyria, Babylon and Persia were preserved in dry desert conditions or buried under the sands of time, remaining undisturbed for centuries, Israel's monuments and records were pulverized by human action and deteriorated by natural forces. However, the abundant evidence of their global exploration and colonization provides firm evidence of their international power and worldwide influence.

The Israelite empire was at its zenith during the reigns of kings David and Solomon, but after their deaths, it was rent by a great civil war which permanently divided the tribes of Israel into the separate, and often hostile, kingdoms of Israel and Judah. Their former glory and power was never fully recaptured. The story of Israel's fall from grace, its decline and their many waves of migrations out of Palestine will be examined in the next chapter.

ENDNOTES: CHAPTER ONE

1.Edey, The Sea Traders, p. 9-10

2.Collier's Encyclopedia, Vol. 2, Heading entitled "Babylonia and Assyria," p. 637, and Halley, Halley's Bible Handbook, p. 134

3.Harper's Bible Dictionary, see word "Tarshish," p. 1018

4.Young's Analytical Concordance to the Bible, see "Tarshish-Tharshish, subhead "2," p. 961

5.Fell, America B.C., p. 93

6.Encyclopedia Americana, Vol. 18, Heading entitled "Magellan, Ferdinand," pp. 80-81

7.Fell, America BC, pp. 93-101

8.Gordon, Cyrus, Before Columbus, p. 137

9.Edey, p. 14

10.Rawlinson, Phoenicia, p. 63

11.Harrison, Richard, Spain at the Dawn of History, p. 41

12.Ibid, p. 41

13.Davidy, Yair, Lost Israelite Identity, see map, p. 170

14.Harper's Bible Dictionary, see "Job," p. 492

15.King James Version of the Bible (Open Bible Edition), Thomas Nelson Publishers (1975), see Introduction to the book of Job, p. 492

16.Johnston, Did the Phoenicians Discover America?, Introductory, p. xvii

17.Sammes, Aylett, Antiquities of Ancient Britain, p. 74

18.Ibid, p. 9

19.Herodotus, The History, 4.42

20.Johnston, Thomas, Did the Phoenicians Discover America?, p. 69

21.Gordon, Cyrus, Before Columbus, pp. 87-88

22.Gordon, Before Columbus, p. 113

23.Herodotus, The History, 7.89

24.Turner, Sharon, The History of the Anglo-Saxons, Vol. 1, p. 12

25.Ibid, pp. 13-14

26.McClintock, John and Strong, James, Cyclopedia of Biblical, Theological and Ecclesiastical Literature, Vol. X, see "Israel," p. 695

27.Rawlinson, Phoenicia, p. 68

28.Young's Analytical Concordance to the Bible, Old Testament Hebrew Lexicon, see word "Gadar," p. 16

29.Waddell, Phoenician Origin of the Britons, Scots and Anglo-Saxons," p. 74

30.Davidy, Yair, Lost Israelite Identity, see map, p. 170

31.Hitti, Philip, A Short History Of the Near East, p. 48

32.Encyclopaedia Britannica, Vol. 513, Heading entitled "Cadiz," p. 513

33.Rawlinson, Phoenicia, p. 68

34.Encyclopedia Americana, Vol. 18, Heading entitled "Malaga," p. 152

35.Margoliouth, Moses, The Jews in Great Britain, pp. 22-23

36.Rawlinson, Phoenicia, pp. 69-70

37.Capt, Raymond, The Traditions of Glastonbury, p. 28 (citing Sir Edward Creasy's History of England)

38.Fell, America BC, p. 43

39.Waddell, L.A., The Phoenician Origin of Britons, Scots and Anglo-Saxons, p. 137

40.Davidy, see map, p. 345

41.Fell, Saga America, p. 167; Bloom and Polansky, "Translation of the 'Decalogue Tablet' from Ohio," Epigraphic Society Occasional Publications, Vol. 8, Part One, 1980, pp. 15-20; and a series of articles on the "Los Lunas Inscriptions," Epigraphic Society Occasional Publications, Vol. 13, 1985, pp. 32-50

42.Lenhart, Robert, "The Adena Tablets," Epigraphic Society Occasional Publications, Vol. 13, 1985, p. 206

43.Ibid, p. 206

44.Encyclopedia Americana, Vol. 19, Heading entitled "Mound Builders," p. 565

45.Ibid, p. 565

46.Ibid, Vol. 19, Heading entitled "Mound," p. 565

47.Fell, Saga America, p. 248

48.Fell, America B.C., p. 21

49.Ibid, p. 21

50.Ibid, p. 158

51.Sodders, Betty, Michigan Prehistory Mysteries, p. 28

52.Lenhart, p. 208

53.Gordon, Cyrus, Before Columbus, pp. 124-125

54.Ibid, p. 125

55.Ibid, p. 119

56.Ibid, p. 126

57.Ibid, pp. 129-131 (and map on p. 130)

58.Ibid, p. 129

59.Ibid, p. 135

60.Sammes, p. 49

61.Gordon, Before Columbus, p. 70 (and map on p. 71)

62.Encyclopedia American, Vol. 17, see "Latitude and Longitude," p. 51

63. Hannay, Herbert, European and Other Race Origins, p. 56

64. Young's Analytical Concordance to the Bible, see First Heading entitled "Shiloh," p. 879

65. Ibid, see Heading "Covenant," subhead one, p. 207

66. Ibid, Hebrew-Lexicon Section, See word "berith," p. 8

67. Ibid, Hebrew-Lexicon Section, See word "borith," p. 9

68. Waddell, The Phoenician Origin of Britons, Scots and Anglo-Saxons, Appendix 1, p. 387

69. Camden, William, Britannia, p. 8

70. Sammes, Aylett, Antiquities of Ancient Britain (or Britannia), see Preface

71. Waddell, p.9

72. Ibid, p.1

73. Ibid, p.1

74. Ibid, p. 188

75. Edey, The Sea Traders, p. 17

Chapter 2
Israel's Decline And Their Migration From Palestine

The Israelite Empire, which once dominated the nations of the earth, was gradually weakened by foreign and civil wars, internal decay, and even by weather calamities. The Bible reveals that their decline was a result of their refusal to abide by the laws of the Creator God who had made Israel great. Israel's decline resulted in successive waves of migration exiting the Israelite homeland in Palestine as the land became increasingly untenable.

While many are familiar with the fall of Samaria, Israel's capital, in approximately 721 B.C., many readers may not realize that by the time of Samaria's fall, the vast majority of Israelites had already migrated out of the land, most of them voluntarily. Additionally, many Jews were removed from the kingdom of Judah by 700 B.C. as Assyrian captives. We read in II Kings 18:13,

> "Now in the fourteenth year of king Hezekiah did Sennacherib king of Assyria come up against all the fenced cities of Judah, and took them."

Only Jerusalem and a remnant of Judah survived until approximately 586 B.C., when the Babylonians carried the remaining Jews into an Asian captivity.

This chapter will not provide a comprehensive history of the two Hebrew kingdoms of Israel and Judah, but will examine some of the lesser-known aspects of their history as well as the many

.—Astarte. From a Phœnician terra-cotta in the Louvre.

.—Bes. From a Phœnician terra-cotta in the Louvre. Height 8 inches.

migrations of their people from Palestine. A thorough history of the two separate Hebrew kingdoms can be obtained by reading the biblical books of I and II Kings and I and II Chronicles. Also, because the history of the Jews is well known and the focus of this book is on the forgotten history of the ten tribes of Israel, this chapter will focus more on the history of the ten tribes and less on that of the Jews.

Israel and Judah Become Rival Kingdoms

After the death of Solomon, the Hebrew kingdom was soon divided into two nations: **Judah**, ruled by Solomon's son Rehoboam, and **Israel**, ruled by Jeroboam, Solomon's former governor over the tribes of Ephraim and Manasseh. *(I Kings 11:28)* Rehoboam and Jeroboam are famous for making some of the worst decisions in the entire history of the Israelite kingdoms.

The Israelites had come to greatly resent the labors and taxes that Solomon had forced on them because of his massive building projects, and they wanted relief! Rehoboam, Solomon's son, made a very foolish decision at the beginning of his reign. With Jeroboam as their spokesman, all of Israel's tribes were prepared to accept Rehoboam as king if he would only grant them tax relief. *(I Kings 12:1-5)* Rehoboam alienated most of the nation when he rashly stated that he would be even "tougher" on them than Solomon had been. *(I Kings 12:1-15)* Having had their offer of conditional submission spurned by Rehoboam, all the tribes of Israel except Benjamin and Judah — Rehoboam's own tribe — spurned Rehoboam, and made

Jeroboam their king. The division of Israel's tribes into two separate kingdoms began with a simple "tax revolt."

This event left both factions feeling "rejected" by the other side, yet I Kings 12:15 relates that God arranged this division of the tribes of Israel into two kingdoms. Rehoboam made preparations for war, but God sent a prophet to order Rehoboam to accept the division of the tribes as divinely ordained. Rehoboam obeyed God, and war was averted.

After Rehoboam's initial foolish decision, Jeroboam made one of the worst decisions any man in history has ever made! Jeroboam had been hand-picked by God to be the new ruler over the ten tribes of Israel, and God offered Jeroboam the same favor given to King David if only he would be obedient. God even offered to make Jeroboam's dynasty a permanent one if he would be obedient to God. *(I Kings 11:28-38)* What a deal! All Jeroboam had to do was say "yes," and he would have been a great king over the Phoenician alliance, and his dynasty would have been made permanent.

Phœnician Priest
(From a statuette in the Metropolitan Museum, New York)

Jeroboam spurned God's offer. He decided to worship idols in the image of cattle and forced this idolatrous practice on Israel. He rejected God's divinely ordained Holy Days in favor of new pagan celebrations he devised for them. *(I Kings 12:25-33)* He rejected the Levitical Priesthood and selected a priesthood that he could politically control. His adoption of calf worship, perhaps the apis bulls of Egypt, surely resulted from his being sheltered in Egypt for a period of time when Pharaoh gave him political asylum from Solomon's wrath.

Pharaoh's defiance of Solomon, who sheltered Solomon's adversary in Egypt, makes one wonder what was becoming of the Israelite-Phoenician-Egyptian alliance that began under Solomon? It was still intact, but internal stresses were building. When God hand-picked Jeroboam to succeed Solomon over the northern ten tribes of Israel, Solomon learned of it and sought to execute Jeroboam. Egypt's Pharaoh gave Jeroboam political asylum from Solomon's wrath, indicating that enmities were growing between King Solomon and Pharaoh even before Solomon's death.

When Pharaoh sheltered Jeroboam, they must have forged a personal friendship and alliance that made them immediate allies when Jeroboam became king over the largest portion of Solomon's old kingdom. Therefore, while Egypt drifted away from Solomon, and Solomon's dynasty, it remained allied to Jeroboam, who succeeded Solomon over most of Israel. Jeroboam's sojourn in Egypt led him to become familiar with Egypt's religion. Therefore, his adoption of Egyptian idols was a move to cement political ties with Egypt as soon as he became king over Israel's northern ten tribes.

After Jeroboam disenfranchised God's Levitical priesthood, the whole tribe of Levi migrated into Judah. *(II Chronicles 11:13-16)* Since the worship of God was being "kicked out" of Israel, the northern Israelites who wished to serve God followed the Levitical priests into Judah, since only the Levites could perform God's services. This resulted in infusions of contingents from all the other tribes into Judah's kingdom. *(verse 16)* Jeroboam's plan totally backfired. He had instituted a phony religious system to keep his people from going to Jerusalem and Judah. *(I Kings 12:26-28)* However, because he kicked out the Levites and disobeyed God, many of his subjects decided to emigrate to Judah.

The division of Israel's tribes was fully accomplished: most of the northern ten tribes followed Jeroboam of Israel, and the three tribes of Judah, Benjamin and Levi — along with contingents from the other tribes — followed Rehoboam of Judah. This initial division of the tribes resulted in a two-to-one numerical superiority of Israel over Judah. *(II Chronicles 13:3)*

Rehoboam obeyed God for three years *(II Chronicles 11:17)*, and then he made another foolish decision by also abandoning the laws of God. *(II Chronicles 12:1-2)* He did not have to wait long for God's punishment.

Just five years after Solomon died, and two years after Rehoboam forsook God, Egypt attacked Judah. Since there was no love lost between Israel and Judah, the Egyptians attacked Judah knowing their friend, King Jeroboam of Israel, would render no aid to Judah. *(II Chronicles 12:2-12)* When Egypt defeated Judah, it looted Jerusalem of its gold treasures that Solomon had amassed, leaving Judah a much poorer kingdom. However, Rehoboam and Judah repented and humbled themselves, so God did not allow Egypt to inflict further damage upon Judah.

While Israel was glad to see Egypt "teach Judah a lesson," Judah felt "stabbed in the back" by Israel's refusal to aid it against Egypt's attack. Though they were brother nations, the Hebrew kingdoms of Israel and Judah became bitter enemies.

The Bible records that there was constant fighting between Israel and Judah during the reigns of Jeroboam and Rehoboam. *(I Kings 14:30)* This internal fighting among the tribes of Israel weakened the Israelite/Phoenician Empire that had developed under Kings David and Solomon. It was now composed of Israel's ten tribes, the cities of Tyre and Sidon and Egypt. Jerusalem, which had been the resplendent capital of the Phoenician Empire, was no longer even in the Phoenician alliance. Jerusalem and Judah were expelled from the Phoenician alliance.

Rehoboam died after ruling seventeen years, and Abijah succeeded him on the throne of Judah. The hatred between the Hebrew kingdoms of Israel and Judah continued as II Chronicles 13:2 states, "there was war between Abijah and Jeroboam." Israel and Judah, less than two decades after they were united in ruling over a world empire, were now so alienated that they routinely warred against each other. Judah had been stripped of its gold, and had no empire. Israel's power was about to be sapped as well.

The Great Civil War Between the Israelites and the Jews

The Israelites of the Northern Kingdom of Israel fought a massive war against the Jews of Judah that engaged 1.2 million combatants. *(II Chronicles 13:3)* Note the consistency of the Bible's account regarding the armed forces available to Israel's tribes. Under King David, Israel could muster 1,510,000 soldiers. *(I Chronicles 21:2-6)* Several decades and internecine wars later, 1,200,000 soldiers were mustered for a war pitting Israel against Judah. Due to the need of both warring nations to maintain garrisons in various cities and conquered lands, their combined total military reserves would have been close to the number of reserves cited under King David.

Israel, trusting in their golden calves, fought against Judah. However, King Abijah of Judah proclaimed that his forces would trust in God. Although the Israelites outnumbered the Jews, God gave the Jews a huge victory over Israel. Israel alone suffered 500,000 battle deaths *(II Chronicles 13:17)*, and we are not told the amount of Jewish casualties. The hatred between the Israelites and the Jews must have been immense to cause such unimaginable bloodletting among brother tribes! Considering that such ancient battles were hand-to-hand contests, this means that heads, limbs and chunks of flesh and

Terra-cotta chariot. Louvre. Height 8 inches.

viscera must have been flying in all directions as thousands of swords were flailed like scythes. Readers can view the movies "Braveheart" or "Gladiator" to get an insight to what ancient combat was like. Those who want to "live in Bible days" may change their minds after considering the ancient realities. Visualize what it must have been like to identify and bury over a half-million dead bodies after the battle between the Israelites and the Jews!

This costly civil war between Israel and the Jews had vast international repercussions. II Chronicles 13:20 tersely states concerning the aftermath of this horrendous loss of life: "neither did Jeroboam recover strength again..." Israel's military was greatly depleted after this battle, and it could no longer control or defend its large empire. Israel's area of direct rule had to shrink to a smaller territory that the weakened army could defend. Many nations in Syria and Mesopotamia which had been dominated by Israel now became independent by default as Israel's garrisons were called home.

This devastating defeat of Israel at the hands of Judah is dated 913 B.C. in Bibles offering dates with chapter headings. That date is likely quite accurate. The previous book's chapter about King David noted that the *Encyclopedia Americana* stated the following about Assyrian history:

> "...Assyria was reduced to dire staits [from 1012-935 B.C.], and the poverty of its people is vividly described in the inscriptions of Asshur-**dan** II (934-912), under whom the Assyrian Empire began its long climb back to its former power...Asshur-**dan** II and his son Adad-nirarii II (911-891) were chiefly concerned with the restoration of Assyrian strength by procuring cavalry horses..."[1]

Notice the profound inverse symmetry between Biblical events in Israel and secular accounts of Assyria's fortunes. Prior to the costly war between Israel and Judah in 913 B.C., Assyria was in "poverty," but it began reasserting itself right after the Israelite-Jewish war. Interestingly, Assyria's ruler during the period of Israelite domination even had an Israelite tribal name ("**Dan**") in his title (!), perhaps implying Israelite domination of Assyria during its period of national weakness.

Ancient Assyrian Bowmen and Slingers.

Assyria's sudden freedom to rearm and reassert itself attests to the power vacuum created when Israel lost a half-million soldiers in a single war! Assyrian resurgence, made possible by Israel's crushing defeat at the hands of Judah, would eventually lead to the end of Israel's nationhood two centuries later. Assyria resented being subjugated by Israel, and would seek revenge in many wars to come.

Soon after Judah crushed Israel's army, it was attacked from the south. Judah mobilized all reserves and mustered 580,000 soldiers to face an Ethiopian army of 1,000,000 men. Judah's king Asa humbly asked for God's help in the battle, and God responded. Judah crushed the Ethiopian army, and gained a considerable amount of war booty. *(II Chronicles 14:1-15)* Even though Judah had been expelled from the Phoenician alliance, it was still obedient to God and was routing one huge army after another.

With terrible wars raging between factions that once had formed a great worldwide alliance, there was great hardship for all the people in the entire region. II Chronicles 15:5-6 says:

> "In those times there was no peace...great vexations were upon all the inhabitants of the countries. And nation was destroyed of nation, and city of city..." *(KJV)*

This chaos was created when the old established order in the region, the Phoenician Empire led by the united tribes of Israel, came apart. It is a stark commentary on what happens when God's laws are ignored. When God and his laws were preeminent in the glory days of

King Solomon, there was peace, international harmony, and time for scientific and artistic pursuits. Soon after God's laws were forgotten throughout Israel, chaos, death and destruction followed on a scale we can scarcely imagine. Following the victory of Judah over Ethiopia, God sent a prophet to King Asa of Judah promising God's continuing favor if they remained obedient to God's laws. *(II Chronicles 15:1-7)* This time a king made a wise decision.

King Asa of Judah obeyed God, and removed foreign idols out of all lands under his jurisdiction. II Chronicles 15:9 records that:

> "...he gathered all Judah and Benjamin, and those from Ephraim, Manasseh, and Simeon who were sojourning with them, for great numbers had deserted to him from Israel when they saw that the Lord...was with him." *(RSV)*

The above account records that many people from the northern ten tribes of Israel moved to Judah in order to follow King Asa who was willing to obey God. After King Asa's death, his son, Jehoshaphat became king over Judah. He also served God enthusiastically, and assigned the Levites to teach all his subjects the laws of God. *(II Chronicles 17:1-9)* God gave him favor, power and tranquillity reminiscent of the glory years of King Solomon. Judah received tribute payments from Philistines and Arabians, and King Jehoshaphat and his nation became very wealthy. *(II Chronicles 17:5,11-13)* As in the days of King Solomon, King Jehoshaphat launched a construction program, building "fortresses and store-cities" throughout the nation.

King Jehoshaphat was so respected by the surrounding nations that none of them dared fight him. Indeed, his army numbered 1,160,000 men. *(II Chronicles 17:14-18)* In comparison, the combined forces of the tribes of Judah and Benjamin had not previously exceeded 580,000 men. *(II Chronicles 14:8)* Clearly, Jehoshaphat's army was being swelled by many hundreds of thousands of men from the northern ten tribes of Israel who had migrated to Judah from Israel. Why did so many people move from Israel to Judah at that time? To answer that question, we need to examine what had been occurring in the northern Hebrew kingdom of Israel.

Evil King Ahab and the Devastating Drought of the Prophet Elijah

During much of King Jehoshaphat's reign, the king of Israel was named Ahab, a man described in I Kings 16:30 as one whom:

> "did evil in the sight of the Lord **above all** that were before him." *(KJV)*

Ahab was the son of King Omri of Israel, who built and fortified Israel's capital city of Samaria. Omri was a general when he became Israel's king, and although little is said of King Omri in the Bible — except for the fact he followed the sins of Jeroboam — significant events must have occurred in his reign. As Werner Keller wrote in his book, *The Bible as History:*

> "**King Omri made an impression on the Assyrians**. A century after his dynasty had crashed, Israel was still officially called 'the House of Omri' in cuneiform texts."[2] *(Emphasis added)*

Keller further notes that during King Omri's reign, Assyria's King Ashurnasirpal II had conquered his way through Syria, north of Israel, and proclaimed: "I washed my weapons in the Great Sea."[3] The "Great Sea" was the Mediterranean Sea, and Assyria's army reached it during King Omri's reign. The fact that Assyria bragged about its march to the "Great Sea," but is silent about Israel during that campaign implies that King Omri decisively defeated the Assyrians in battle. Assyria respected power and since "King Omri made an impression on the Assyrians" which lasted well over a century after Omri died, this book concludes King Omri gave the Assyrians a beating they never forgot! There is no way King Omri would have made a great and lasting impression upon the Assyrians if Omri had simply hidden in the mountains and declined battle.

Assyrian King and Cupbearer.

King Omri's experience with the Assyrians likely motivated him to build Israel's capital, Samaria, in an impregnable area that could withstand a military siege. Omri foresaw the future would bring more Israelite-Assyrian wars. As Werner Keller opines about Omri's building a fortress capital at Samaria: "He (Omri) was certain that Israel would need it, and need it badly."[4]

Harper's Bible Dictionary also comments on Assyria's lasting respect of King Omri:

> "The name 'Omri' became an established term in Assyrian documents to indicate the Israelite kings even after the death of Omri and his descendants...Assyrian annalists continue to refer to Israel as the 'land of (the house of) Omri' for a hundred years after the end of his dynasty."[5]

Assyria's names for Israel's people will become significant later in this account. Herbert Hannay wrote:

> "The great mass of the...Hebrew race consisted of the Israelites, or House of Isaac, who are also...called the **House of Omri (Beth Omri), the Assyrian equivalent for which was Bit-Khumri**..."[6] *(Emphasis added)*

Remember the Assyrian name for the Israelites: "Khumri." We will see Israelites bearing that name after they migrate from Palestine. Although Assyrian writers were long impressed by Israel's King Omri, he ruled only twelve years before his evil son, Ahab, replaced him. With the exception of Omri's short rule, there had been much instability in Israel that included royal assassinations and internal warfare. *(I Kings 15:25-16:30)* With wicked rulers and civil instability prevailing in Israel, is it any wonder that many thousands of citizens of the northern ten tribes migrated toward the peace, stability and prosperity of Judah?

Ahab's wife was a Phoenician princess named Jezebel, daughter of the king of Sidon. *(I Kings 16:31)* This marriage confirmed that Israel's role in the Phoenician alliance was still very strong. King Ahab and his wicked wife defied the God of Israel as they led the nation in embracing the Phoenician god, Baal. Verse 32 states that Ahab built an "altar for Baal in the house of Baal, which he had built in Samaria."

He built a "grove," apparently a place for state-sponsored prostitution. One translation for the word "grove" is a "pagan shrine for pleasure."[7] *Harper's Bible Dictionary* describes "groves" as "places of worship of the pagan gods Baal and Astarte."[8] The Hebrew word translated as "grove" is "asherah,"[9] a place dedicated to the worship of Baal, Tanit, and Astarte, or Ashteroth. The worship of these gods was evil and degenerate, with orgiastic sex rites and human sacrifices, mostly of children.[10]

THE AMMONITE FIRE-GOD MOLOCH.

The "religion" of Baal featured the murder of little children as part of the "worship" services.[11] Another malignant religion, the worship of the Canaanite deity, Moloch, was present during King Ahab's reign. God warned the Israelites not to practice the human sacrifice rites of Moloch. *(Leviticus 18:21, 20:2-5)* Some may think that God was harsh in ordering the Israelites to kill or drive out all the Canaanites and to avoid their religion when they entered the land under Joshua. *(Numbers 33:51-53)* When one realizes that the Canaanites murdered their own children as part of their "religion," one can see why God ordered the Israelites to destroy both the adherents and the symbols of this degenerate religion. However, Moloch was worshipped in Israel during the latter years of Solomon *(I Kings 11:7)*, and the evil gods, Baal and Moloch, were both worshipped during King Ahab's reign.

Today, there is a myth that "all religions are equal," but reality shows that some religions are terribly destructive to their adherents, others reduce the "faithful" to poverty, and some do inspire their followers to a higher standard of conduct and morals, benefiting societies that embrace such religions. The worship of the God of Israel was one which greatly benefited its adherents — witness the peace, wealth and prosperity of Solomon's reign in his faithful years — while Baalism was one of the most malignant religions ever devised.

God warned the Israelites that if they did not destroy this religion and its practitioners when they came into Canaan, they would be corrupted by its practices, and then God would punish the Israelites as he had the Canaanites. *(Numbers 33:53-56)* This began to come to pass in the reign of Ahab. Just as God was determined to drive the Canaanites out of the land for their gross sins, he began, literally, to drive out the Israelites also.

Whereas Judah's army under Jehoshaphat numbered over a million men, King Ahab of Israel could barely muster 7,000 soldiers *(I Kings 20:15)* as a garrison to defend his capital city. It was noted above that many Israelites from the northern ten tribes had moved to Judah, and served in Jehoshaphat's army of Judah instead of staying in Israel. Given the wickedness in Israel's ruling house, decent people left Israel to serve Judah's king instead. Anyone who wanted to avoid raising their children in an environment where they and their playmates could be murdered by the state religion moved! The fact that so many moved to Judah is a testimony that many in the ten tribes of Israel were still decent people even though Israel's leaders were hopelessly corrupt.

Ahab and his wicked Phoenician wife, Jezebel, became worse and worse. One episode indicates that Ahab was a weak-willed man dominated by a strong-willed, ruthless wife. Ahab wanted a particular property that belonged to a private citizen, but the private citizen didn't want to sell. Ahab sulked about the situation, but was willing to respect the rights of the citizen not to sell his land to the king. However, when Jezebel heard of it, she cavalierly had the citizen murdered and gave the land to Ahab. *(I Kings 21)* This episode confirms that Jezebel was far more evil than King Ahab. It also indicates that, even under the rule of a wicked king, respect for private property rights was very strong in ancient Israel. Even wicked King Ahab was still respectful of a citizen's property rights.

A STELE TO TANIT.

The situation cried out for God's intervention, and he acted. God sent a powerful prophet named Elijah who became the nemesis of Ahab and Jezebel. Elijah declared that Israel would be punished for its sins by a national drought, and I Kings 18:1 and James 5:17 record that this drought lasted for three and one-half years!

Before examining the major geopolitical effects of this drought, let us consider the evidence that Ahab's Israel, though weakened, still was the head of a considerable empire. We saw in the previous chapter that Israel's empire, built with the cooperation of Egypt, Tyre and Sidon, had explored and colonized parts of Europe, Africa, Asia and North and South America. Israel's devotion to the pagan gods of Phoenicia and Egypt deepened Israel's alliance with them. King Ahab still ruled over Israel's many foreign colonies.

Since Israel adopted both the Baal worship of Tyre and Sidon and the calf-worship of the Egyptians, the religious and political bonds would have kept these nations united. The presence in ancient Iowa, in North America, of a trilingual ancient stele depicting a pagan religious ceremony from approximately 800-700 B.C. supports this contention.[12] Dr. Barry Fell, in his book *America B.C.*, commented that the languages on this ancient American stele are Egyptian, Libyan (the sailors of the Egyptians) and "Iberian-Punic." Iberian-Punic is a Hebrew-Phoenician language, and its presence in the New World indicates that Israelites, Tyrians and Sidonians were still closely allied to the Egyptians during the time of the divided kingdoms of Israel and Judah. Dr. Fell noted the Hebrew-Phoenician origin of this Iberian-Punic language, as he states that the stele had "some signs resembling Hebrew and others resembling Phoenician."[13] On the same subject, *Collier's Encyclopedia* states:

"The Iberian language is extant in about one hundred inscriptions in a national alphabet generally believed to be of Phoenician origin."[14]

There would have been no need for such tri-lingual inscriptions so far from the homelands of Israel, Egypt, Tyre and Sidon unless their colonists and sailors were still allied together throughout the world! Since their sailors ventured deep into the American Midwest during the period of the divided Hebrew kingdoms (circa 800-700 B.C.), it indicates the worldwide power of the Phoenician alliance was still very great. Although Israel was a weakened land power, the allied navies of Israel, Tyre, Sidon and Egypt still ruled the oceans.

Dr. Fell noted that this ancient Iowan stele depicts a pagan religious ceremony honoring the Egyptian deities Osiris and Ra, which involved human sacrifices (a trait of the Baal worship mentioned in the Bible.) Interestingly, Dr. Fell wrote that this ancient stele was mistakenly branded a "forgery" by a scientific establishment that at the time of its discovery could neither comprehend nor translate the ancient languages contained on the stele.[15] The stele from ancient Iowa confirms the Phoenician alliance was still actively exploring and exploiting the New World even after the time of King Ahab.

A critical fact needs to be stressed at this point to understand why the ten-tribed kingdom of Israel is generally unrecognized in accounts about ancient Phoenicia. **It cannot be overemphasized that from the time that Israel and Judah became separate, Hebrew kingdoms, they became estranged from one another.** Although they experienced brief interludes of cordial relations, they generally were enemies. The first Israelite king after they separated was Jeroboam. He sought to sever cultural and religious ties between the Israelite and Jewish kingdoms by replacing God's Holy Days with pagan

VOTIVE STELE TO TANIT.

GODDESS ASHTORETH, ISHTAR.

festivals to keep the Israelites of the northern kingdom from traveling to the Jewish capital at Jerusalem. As time went by, Israel became progressively more linked to Tyre and Sidon, adopting their worship of Baal, Ashtoreth, and Tanit. The Israelite and Phoenician royal houses intermarried, and their economies and military forces had been merged since the days of King Solomon. During this same time, Judah had several good kings who worshipped God, causing Judah to have progressively less in common with Israel.

Therefore, the kingdoms of Israel and Judah not only separated politically from one another, but they also drifted apart religiously, economically, and culturally. **Since the economic, religious and cultural life of Israel was, for centuries, linked much closer to Tyre and Sidon than to Judah, the northern ten tribes of Israel would have also become linguistically merged with the Phoenicians as well!** Therefore, the language of the ten tribes of Israel would have become almost indistinguishable from that of their close Phoenician allies. Their language would have been increasingly **less** like the Hebrew language of Judah, with whom they had generally hostile relations. **By the time the kingdom of Israel fell, Judah's language would still be "Hebrew," but the language of the ten tribes of Israel was like that of Tyre and Sidon!** For this reason, after their migrations from Palestine, the descendants of the ten tribes of Israel would be found in those places where the language was labeled "Phoenician," "Punic," or "Iberian-Punic." The ancient stele found in Iowa with an inscription in "Iberian-Punic... [with] some signs resembling Hebrew and others resembling Phoenician" confirms that the Israelites had so intermingled with the people of Sidon and Tyre that their language was merging into the "Phoenician" tongue.

BAAL AND ASHTAROTH.

The orgiastic rites of Baal and Ashtoreth also permeated the Phoenician-Israelite colonies in ancient America. Phallic symbols and inscriptions of the "mother-goddess" religion, the religion of King Ahab and Queen Jezebel of Israel, have been found, photographed and detailed in the former Phoenician colony in the New England region of ancient America. Barry Fell's book, *America B.C.* describes and depicts many of the artifacts confirming that the worship of Baal and the "mother-goddess" had spread to ancient America.[16] The fact that one of ancient America's representations of the mother-goddess is Tanith, the Carthaginian goddess who was worshipped as the spouse of Baal,[17] will become significant in the next chapter. Carthage was a colony of the Israelite-Phoenician alliance, founded during the century when King Ahab ruled Israel.

Dr. Fell describes one of the Phoenician sites in ancient America as "an open-air fertility precinct."[18] In other words, it was what the Bible called a "grove," an outdoor "pagan shrine for pleasure."

Dr. Fell also observed that:

> "The Celtic festival of Beltane, held on May Day, originally in pagan times included revels danced around an erect phallus. In Europe, after Christianity was introduced, the phallus was replaced by a maypole."[19]

The Celtic god, "**Bel**tane," preserves the root word of the ancient Phoenician/Israelite sun god: **Ba**a**l**. We see in these ancient American archeological records that Baal worship, so deeply rooted in Israel-Phoenicia, also permeated their ancient American colonies. The above evidence confirms the idolatrous degeneracy of the Israelites as recorded in the Bible. [Modern readers may be disquieted by the realization that the "maypoles" of May Day festivities actually represent erect phalli.]

We now resume the narrative of Israel's decline in the middle of the ninth century B.C., during the reign of King Ahab of Israel. God intervened by sending Elijah to Israel when the corruption of Israel's leaders reached intolerable levels. It was by Elijah's word that a three and one-half year drought occurred in Israel. *(I Kings 17:1, James 5:17)* During this period of time rivers dried up, there was scarcely any vegetation left, and starvation gripped both Israel and the Phoenician city-states. *(I Kings 17:7-12, 18:5)*

Since Israel was usually a food exporter *(Ezekiel 27:17)*, this drought caused unprecedented hardship in a nation accustomed to an abundance of food. Tyre and Sidon had smaller populations,[20] and, therefore, had fewer people to feed than the much larger kingdom of Israel. Nevertheless, I Kings 17:8-12 shows that even Tyre and Sidon were in desperate straits as starvation was occurring in Zarephath, a suburb of Sidon. The situation would have been absolutely catastrophic for Israel with its much larger population. Much of Israel's population faced a brutally simple choice: either stay in Israel and die, or migrate elsewhere and live. People's desire for self-preservation being what it is, much of the population left the land of Israel to live somewhere else. We have already seen that those who "feared God" and

ISRAEL and JUDAH

wanted no part of Baal worship migrated to Judah where King Jehoshaphat ruled according to God's laws. **The fact that Judah could support a population that included an army of over one million men while its northern neighbor, Israel, was starving provides striking evidence that the drought did not affect Judah!** This was a stark contrast between the two Hebrew nations, and offered daily proof of God's role in the drought. He gave rain to Judah, which obeyed God, while He denied rain to Israel, which served Baal, even though Israel and Judah directly bordered each other.

As seen in previous chapters, international commerce in the ancient world was far more developed than modern man has realized. We now know that transoceanic travel between the Old World and the New World was well established by the time of Elijah and Ahab. Indeed, during this time of drought, King Ahab made an intense search to locate the prophet Elijah who had gone into hiding. I Kings 18:10 states that when Elijah came out of hiding, an aide to King Ahab told Elijah that:

> "As the Lord your God lives, there is no nation or kingdom whither my lord has not sent to seek you; and when they say, 'he is not here,' he would take an oath of the kingdom or nation, that they had not found you." *(RSV)*

Some critics of the Bible regard this statement as sheer hyperbole by the writer of I Kings. However, now that we know the truth about the ancient world's advanced state of nautical commerce, this statement can be taken literally! The Phoenician alliance of Tyre, Sidon and Israel had long had the world's most powerful navy, and the kingdoms of the earth became known to them when Solomon's "Phoenician" navy sailed the oceans and the "kings of the earth" gave gifts to King Solomon. Solomon amassed flora and fauna from all over the globe as his Phoenician Empire explored and/or colonized at least five continents. Consider also this fact: The drought in Israel, Tyre and Sidon made it necessary to greatly enlarge the Phoenician fleets so: (A) their people could be relocated to Phoenicia's colonies elsewhere and (B) available foodstuffs could be transported back to Israel. Because of this dire need to export much of its population, the navies of Israel, Tyre and Sidon may have been at their largest and most powerful status during the reign of King Ahab.

That King Ahab would send messengers to "all nations" to look for Elijah is reasonable when we realize that the missing prophet could have easily booked passage to distant lands via Phoenicia's maritime routes. Jonah 1:3 relates that the prophet Jonah fled Israel by simply booking passage on a Phoenician ship heading to Tarshish. Since it would be logical to assume that Elijah had journeyed far from Israel to hide from King Ahab, the above biblical statement includes the possibility that Ahab sent messengers to the Israelite-Phoenician colonies in Europe, Asia, Africa and North and South America to look for Elijah. In fact, the elusive Elijah had hidden in a place that Ahab and Jezebel would least expect to find him: in a suburb of Jezebel's home town of Sidon, the very heart of the pagan religion that had brought such suffering upon Israel.

The fact that King Ahab of Israel was able to exact an oath from the nations of the earth indicates that the king of Israel still had much "clout" among the nations. If he had been an impotent leader of a small, starving kingdom, he would have been ignored. Because he was one of the leaders of the world's most powerful maritime alliance, he was treated with deference. Any nation declining to cooperate with King Ahab would have been quickly frozen out of world commerce, and Phoenician warships would have sunk their ships.

While Israel's homeland could only support a "skeleton crew" during the drought, the rest of its population sought refuge elsewhere. While those Israelites who served God sought refuge in the Jewish kingdom of Judah, those Israelites "who served Baal" sought refuge from the drought in Israel's far-flung "Phoenician" colonies where Baal was worshipped.

Undoubtedly, some of Israel's refugees found new homes in Israel's colonies in Spain, North Africa, the British Isles and even North America. Since those migrating Israelites had abandoned their Hebrew religious customs, they would have become indistinguishable from the "Phoenicians" of Tyre and Sidon. Embracing the culture, religion and the dialect of Tyre and Sidon, migrating Israelites would not exhibit an "Israelite" identity to modern archaeologists, but would be known to us today simply as "Phoenicians," "Iberians," "Celts," or "Celtiberians."

However, the colonial system could only accommodate so many new arrivals, and the majority of refugees — such as the elderly and those with small children — surely did not wish to travel any further than was necessary. Many would have sought refuge in Phoenicia's North African colonies which were founded during the time of Israelite power "from B.C. 1100 to B.C. 800."[21] However, so many Israelites, Tyrians, and Sidonians needed to emigrate from their parched homelands that a large new colony was needed.

During the same century as the great drought of Elijah, a large exodus of Israelites, Tyrians and Sidonians founded a new colony in North Africa called **Kirjath-Hadeschath,** which the Romans later called **Carthage**. Carthage's origin as a colony of Israelite refugees from the catastrophic drought in Israel has not been appreciated. Why did "Phoenicia" establish a large, new colony in the ninth century B.C. when it already had colonies and trading posts in the Mediterranean region? Clearly, they had a sudden, compelling need to relocate more people out of their homelands than their existing colonies could accommodate. The devastating drought of Elijah in that century explains the need for such a massive resettlement of their people.

Cape Carthage and ruins of the ancient sea-gate

While it is known that the original Hebrew name of Carthage was Kirjath-Hadeschath,[22] it eventually came to be known to the Greeks as "Karchedon," and to the Romans as "Carthago."[23] Since ancient history is taught in today's western world from an ethnocentric Greco-Roman viewpoint, we today know Israel's colony by its Roman name instead of its original Hebrew name. Therefore, few realize that Carthage began as a Hebrew-Phoenician colony.

The Hebrews who founded Carthage were Israelites from the Northern Kingdom of Israel; they were not Jews from the southern kingdom of Judah. As noted above, Judah's population and its Israelite immigrants had no need to migrate anywhere, as Judah's King Jehoshaphat was loyal to God. Therefore, the searing drought did not affect Judah. Its land could support a million soldiers!

The drought finally ended after Elijah's famous confrontation with the priests of Baal. I Kings 18:20-46 records the episode in which Elijah challenged the priests of Baal to see whether God or Baal was more powerful. In this test, Baal and God were both asked to send fire to consume a sacrifice of oxen. The priests of Baal made frenzied appeals to Baal, and even cut themselves till they were bloody. Self-flagellation was common among the worshippers of Baal and Astarte.[24] After they failed to accomplish anything, Elijah called on God to consume the offering with heavenly fire, and he did so. When God consumed the offering with fire, the crowd was shocked into an acknowledgment that the God of Israel was greater than Baal, and their devotion to Baal was shaken. In an atmosphere where the people were likely afraid that God might also consume them for their Baal-worship-

EASTERN END OF MOUNT CARMEL (PROBABLE OF ELIJAH'S SACRIFICE).

ping past, they cooperated with Elijah in executing 450 priests of Baal. This execution of 450 priests was poetic justice, because the priests of Baal had murdered thousands of innocent children in their rituals of human sacrifice.

In I Kings 18:33-35, Elijah directed that the animal sacrifice be drenched with barrels of water. Modern readers tend to gloss over the significance of this event. The rivers had dried up, and it had not rained in three and one-half years! Water would have been very scarce. Yet twelve barrels of water were poured on an altar of twelve stones, one each for the tribes of Israel, before Elijah called on God to send fire from heaven to consume the sacrifice. At a time when water was more priceless than gold, the water poured on the altar was an exceptionally sacrificial offering!

I Kings 18:40 records that Elijah had the people apprehend all 450 priests of Baal and hold them captive while Elijah personally killed each one. Can you picture yourself personally thrusting a sword into the guts of human beings and disemboweling them as they died in front of you? Not a pretty picture, is it? Few of us could do this to even a single evil person deserving of death. Elijah did it to 450 human beings, one right after the other in assembly-line fashion! He no doubt heard each one pleading and begging for mercy, and Elijah just went on cutting them to pieces. In sending Elijah as his prophet to Ahab and Israel, God had sent a very, very tough individual!

In spite of Elijah's total victory over the prophets of Baal, the experience seems to have drained the energy from him. Ahab's Sidonian wife, Jezebel, vowed to execute Elijah to avenge the death of the priests of Baal. *(I Kings 19:1-2)* In spite of the fact he had just called divine fire down from heaven, Elijah fled from Jezebel, and forty days later he found refuge in a cave at Mt. Horeb, the same place where Moses received the Ten Commandments. *(I Kings 19:3-8)* The first book in this series offered evidence that the real Mt. Horeb is Jabal al Lawz in Northwest Saudi Arabia. Further affirming its identity as the real "Mountain of Moses" is the fact that there is a prominent cave near its summit. Author Larry Williams calls it "the cave of Elijah" in his book, *The Mount Sinai Myth,* which includes a photograph of this very cave.[25]

One aspect of Elijah's life has a future implication, and we will make a brief observation for the benefit of those readers who have an interest in biblical prophecy. Many readers will understand that the Bible contains many prophecies about events between now and the return of Jesus Christ at the climax of this age. It is often overlooked that Elijah and Elisha (Elijah's protégé) formed a duo of powerful prophets sent by God to ancient Israel. *(II Kings 2)* Malachi 4:1-6 contains a prophecy that God will send an "Elijah" work to the world just prior to the "day of the Lord" at the climax of this age. Revelation chapter 11 prophesies that a duo of two powerful prophets will plague the nations, withhold the rain, call fire down from heaven, and kill those who try to harm them for a period of three and one-half years. Elijah did all these things *(I Kings 17-18, II Kings 1)*, and his drought upon Israel lasted three and one-half years. The parallel is clear. Of all the prophets in the Bible, the final two prophets of God — called the Two Witnesses in Rev. 11 — are likened to be most like the Prophet Elijah. *(Malachi 4)* As John the Baptist went before Jesus Christ's first coming, the Two Witnesses will precede Jesus Christ's Second Coming. John the Baptist came in the "spirit" but not the "power" of Elijah, but the two Witnesses will come in both the "spirit **and power**" of Elijah. *(Luke 1:17)* Those who oppose these two powerful prophets of God will likely end up as dead as the 450 priests of Baal. Much will be written about biblical prophecies in a later book, but now we will return to our narrative about ancient Israel.

It is doubtful that the kingdom of Israel ever recovered from the extreme drought in Elijah's time. The exodus of so many Israelites from their native land greatly reduced the population and military potential of Israel's homeland. While many Israelites surely returned to Israel when the drought was over, many others would have remained in Israel's colonies to pursue new lives. Israel's growing weakness was obvious to Israel's enemies. The Bible details many wars between Israel and the Syrians. I Kings 20 relates that an outnumbered Israelite army of 7,232 men crushed an alliance of thirty-two Aramaean kings and killed 100,000 enemy soldiers in a surprise attack during Ahab's reign. These were Israelite soldiers who were besieged with King Ahab in-

Samaria — The Street of Columns. (*From a Photograph.*)

side the city of Samaria. King Omri had built Samaria well, as the Aramaeans could not take the city. Interestingly, verse 13-14 shows that God actually intervened to help King Ahab and the Israelites win this battle in spite of Ahab's personal sins. This is an important sidebar to the story of Israel's history as it confirms that sometimes God will be merciful and helpful to his people even when they don't deserve his help or even ask for it.

During this time, Judah was sometimes allied with Israel in wars against the Syrians. *(I Kings 22:1-4)* Why did righteous King Jehoshaphat of Judah ally himself to wicked King Ahab of Israel? The answer was likely a political one. There were hundreds of thousands of Israelites from the northern kingdom serving in Jehoshaphat's army of Judah, and Jehoshaphat may have feared a revolt if he asked them to fight against their native Israel. Also, although Judah was then dominant on land, Israel's "Phoenician" alliance was dominant on the oceans. Judah needed favor with King Ahab to ensure its access to the world's maritime commercial routes. King Jehoshaphat tried to assert maritime independence by building a fleet of his own "ships of Tarshish" at Ezion-geber on the Red Sea. I Kings 22:48-49 and II Chronicles 20:35-37 record that this fleet was destroyed by God because Jehoshaphat trusted in his alliance with Israel's wicked kings.

The Assyrians waged war upon Israel and its surrounding nations during Ahab's reign. An alliance of King Ahab's Israelites, Aramaean kings and Ammonites stopped an Assyrian invasion under Shalmaneser III at the battle of Karkar (or "Qarqar") in about 854 B.C.[26] Werner Keller, in his book, *The Bible as History*, wrote:

Ancient Assyrian Battering-ram supporting a Tower containing Warriors.

> "...King Ahab of Israel...according to the Assyrian account of the battle of Qarqar...assembled 2,000 chariots, the largest force of war-chariots in the anti-Assyrian alliance."[27]

Assyrian accounts refer to King Ahab of Israel as King "Ahabbu," affirming the reality of this biblical king.[28] Israel, Syria, and other nations in the region put aside their rivalries to fight off Assyria, the greater threat from the East. It is remarkable that despite Israel's growing weakness, their alliance still had the strength to fight Assyria to a draw. *The Encyclopedia Britannica* records that more wars between Assyria and Israel were fought in 849 and 846 B.C.[29] The people of Israel surely must have realized that Assyria intended to keep attacking until it conquered Israel, exacting revenge for Israel's subjugation of Assyria under Kings David and Solomon. However, in the middle of the ninth century B.C., Israel was still strong enough to repel Assyrian invasions.

The Encyclopedia Britannica records that the Assyrian annals of the period confirm that many kings mentioned by the Bible, such as Kings Omri, Ahab and Jehu of Israel, and Kings Ben-hadad and Hazael of Syria, were real people.[30] The famous "black obelisk" found in ancient Assyria depicts King Jehu of Israel offering a tribute to Assyria's

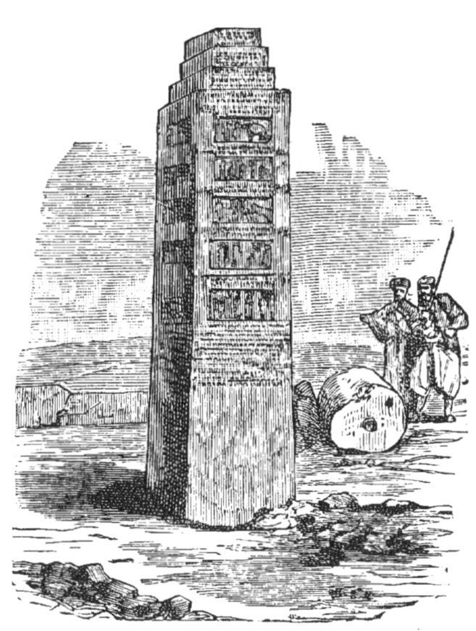

The Black Obelisk.

king. Jehu is referred to as the son of "Khumri," Assyria's name for King Omri of Israel. This further affirms that the term "Khumri," Assyria's name for King Omri, came to designate the Israelites (but not the Jews) in Assyrian references. A clear photograph of the black obelisk *(illustrated to left)* can also be found in C.W. Ceram's book, *The March of Archaeology*.[31]

The Bible records many good things about King Jehoshaphat, who was one of Judah's best kings. I Kings 22:46 and II Chronicles 19 state that he restored the worship of God, rooted out Baalism, appointed impartial judges, and extradited sodomites from Judah. As a direct consequence of these actions, Jehoshaphat and Judah were blessed with wealth, peace and God's protection. However, Jehoshaphat's alliances with Israel's wicked kings weakened Judah after Jehoshaphat's death. The royal houses of Israel and Judah intermarried when Jehoshaphat's son, Jehoram, the next king of Judah, married a daughter of King Ahab of Israel. *(II Kings 8:16-18)* Jehoram departed from God and embraced Baalism. He died eight years later, unmourned and in great agony as his "bowels fell out by reason of his sickness," a curse from God that was pronounced upon him by the Prophet Elijah. *(II Chronicles 21:11-20)*

King Ahab and Jezebel both died violent deaths. Ahab died in combat, and Jezebel died when her servants hurled her out a window. *(II Kings 9:30-37)* Jehu, who instigated Jezebel's death, became King of Israel and led a brief, bloody return to the God of Israel. Besides ordering the death of Jezebel, he slew wicked king Jehoram of Israel, who had the same name as the king of Judah who died with the bowel disease, and Ahaziah, a wicked king of Judah. *(II Kings 9:21-29)* He further arranged the executions of Ahab's 70 sons and all of Ahab's relatives. He executed many of Baal's followers, turned Baal's temple into a public toilet, and expunged Baalism from the kingdom of Israel. *(II Kings 9-10)* Jehu's revival was half-hearted, however, as he permitted the calf-worship of Egypt to continue. However, the cleansing action he took interrupted the deterioration of the Kingdom of Israel.

There is a sober lesson for national rulers here. God sometimes deals personally with national rulers: to bless them for good actions and punish them for evil actions. God killed King Jehoram of Judah via a ghastly illness, ordained the destruction of King Ahab's dynasty (II Kings 10:10-11) and ordained Jezebel's assassination. *(II Kings 9:30-36)* God is patient, but His patience eventually does run out on evil rulers and evil nations.

Jonah, the Misunderstood Prophet

II Kings 14:23-29 records that Israel experienced a resurgence of power during the 41-year reign of Jeroboam II. He brought the Aramaean cities of Damascus and Hamath under Israel's rule and extended Israel's domains. It was during the rule of Jeroboam II that the prophet Jonah lived. While not discussed in the book of Jonah, II Kings 14:25 records that Jonah delivered a prophecy that Israel would be strengthened under Jeroboam II. Jonah was, therefore, personally involved with the restoration of Israel against its enemies. Jonah is known by many as a prophet with a bad attitude, based on events in the book bearing his name. However, Jonah has received a "bum rap" from his modern critics because they have not understood his actions in historical context. Consider this fact: of all the biblical prophets, to which one did Jesus Christ personally compare and link himself? Jesus Christ compared himself to the prophet Jonah. *(Matthew 12, Luke 11)* If Jonah had been a rebel, would Jesus Christ link Himself to Jonah more closely than any other prophet? Obviously, the answer is "no." Here is the truth about Jonah. We certainly cannot excuse Jonah's direct disobedience. However, even in His disobedience he unwittingly became a type of Christ.

Jonah was told by God to deliver a message of imminent doom to Nineveh, the capital of Assyria which was Israel's mortal enemy. *(Jonah 1:2)* Jonah boarded a ship to go to Tarshish instead. Tarshish was in the Atlantic Ocean region, as we have seen earlier, and Dr. Cyrus Gordon has speculated it may have been as far west as Mexico![32] Even though Jonah disobeyed a direct order from God, God went to miraculous lengths to save Jonah's life, creating a huge sea-creature to swallow Jonah and keep him alive for "three days and three nights." Also, Jonah was completely unafraid of death, and he fully expected God to kill him because of his disobedience. *(Jonah 1:4-15)* Jonah's willingness to sacrifice himself for others is evident in the fact that he offered to sacrifice himself to save the ship's crew from a terrible gale. *(Jonah 1:12)* Jonah had an attitude of self-sacrifice, so his motive in refusing to go to Nineveh was not any fear of death. Consider how this attitude is evident in his action of running from his mission to Nineveh.

Jonah likely reasoned that if he were the one selected to deliver the message of God's judgment against Nineveh, he could guarantee Nineveh's destruction (and Israel's rescue!) by refusing to go to Nineveh! Obviously, if he didn't bring God's warning to Nineveh, it could not repent, assuring God's judgment upon Israel's mortal enemy! Therefore, Jonah declined to go to Nineveh to ensure its destruction, and he fully expected God to kill him for his actions. First Kings 13:11-32 records that God had killed an earlier prophet for failing to "follow orders." However, God saw Jonah's motive and had mercy on him because of Jonah's willingness to sacrifice himself in order to save the nation of Israel. This humble attitude of self-sacrifice to save other people is why Jesus Christ directly compared himself to Jonah. Jesus Christ offered himself as a sacrifice for all people by dying for the sins of mankind, and Jonah's willingness to die to save the nation of Israel typified Jesus Christ's mission.

The "great fish" *(Jonah 1:17)* vomited Jonah on dry land *(Jonah 2:10)*, and Nineveh subsequently repented at his message, causing great distress upon the prophet. Jonah's anger at the end of his mission is because he realized he had "outsmarted himself." If he had simply obeyed God and gone to Nineveh, very likely the city would have not repented, and it would have been destroyed by God in like fashion as Sodom and Gomorrah. That would have extended the life of the kingdom of Israel. However, by trying to "outsmart God" Jonah had actually caused Nineveh's repentance — and hastened Israel's doom at the hand of Assyria.

When Jonah was vomited by God's "fish" onto the shoreline, this event surely had witnesses. Jonah would have been a sight to behold! After three days in the stomach acids of what might have been a whale (it must have been huge for its stomach to hold enough oxygen to keep Jonah alive), his skin would have been bleached an unnatural white, and his body hair would have been digested off of him. Jonah's arrival in Assyria, looking bizarre and tumbling out the mouth of a gigantic beached whale, conferred **immense** credibility on his warnings, and the entire city of Nineveh repented at the preaching from this "messenger of the great fish god" which Nineveh worshipped. Jonah 4:2 confirms Jonah declined to go to Nineveh because he wanted God to destroy Nineveh in order to weaken the Assyrian Empire! Jonah didn't want God's mercy to come upon Nineveh, and he was angry that Nineveh repented and that God spared the capital city of Israel's enemy.

One lesson of the book of Jonah is that Jonah's attitude of self-sacrifice for his nation became a model for Jesus Christ's life of self-sacrifice for mankind. However, another lesson is that "you can't outsmart God." While his self-sacrificial attitude was noble, Jonah disobeyed God in order to save Israel and doom Assyria. However, his disobedience actually led to the salvation of Assyria, hastening the doom of Israel. This was the cause of Jonah's deep anguish at the end of the book of Jonah. He learned that one cannot sin, even with a good motive, and expect good to come from it.

The Fall of the Kingdom of Israel

The truce between the two Hebrew kingdoms of Israel and Judah was temporary. The Israelites and the Jews fought another savage war against each other during the reign of King Pekah of Israel. The Israelites killed 120,000 Jews in one day. *(II Chronicles 28:5-6)* This war occurred at a time when Judah had embraced the depravities of Baal worship during the reign of King Ahaz. The Israelites were bringing 200,000 Jewish captives into Israel when God intervened via a prophet, and ordered the Israelites to release the Jewish captives. Remarkably, the Israelites obeyed God, and sent the captive Jews home after feeding and clothing them. Of critical importance is the fact that this decision was not made by the king of Israel, but rather by the elders of the tribe of Ephraim. *(II Chronicles 28:9-15)* Indeed, the prophet did not even go to Israel's king, but rather to the tribal elders. This shows that the monarchy in Israel had become very weak and the tribal leaders were getting stronger shortly before Samaria fell. The willingness of Israel's tribal leaders to make major decisions without even consulting their king had a positive effect on the fate of the Israelites when Samaria fell.

After this war, Judah again had a few good kings, so God allowed the kingdom of Judah to continue. Israel, however, was weakened by another Assyrian invasion, and a final invasion ended the kingdom of Israel when Samaria fell circa 721 B.C. It is a misconception that "all Israel" was carried into captivity when Samaria fell in 721 B.C. As we will see, the Bible and Assyrian records agree that only a small number of Israelites went into captivity when Samaria fell. By then, most Israelites had fled Palestine and were living in new homelands. In fact, most Israelites carried into captivity were taken away circa 745 B.C. during the reign of King Pekah, not when Samaria fell over a decade later.

II Kings 15:29 states that King Tiglath-pileser of Assyria invaded Israel during King Pekah's reign, and took captive the entire tribe of Naphtali, and also the Israelites living in Galilee and Gilead. Gilead was the term for Israelite territory east of the Jordan River, and it was inhabited by the tribes of Reuben, Gad and one-half the tribe of Manasseh. *(Numbers 32:1-33)* I Chronicles 5:26 confirms that Gad, Reuben and half of Manasseh went captive to King Tiglath-pileser.

Besides the above tribes, other Israelites in Galilee were also carried captive at that time. The tribes of Zebulon and Issachar lived in

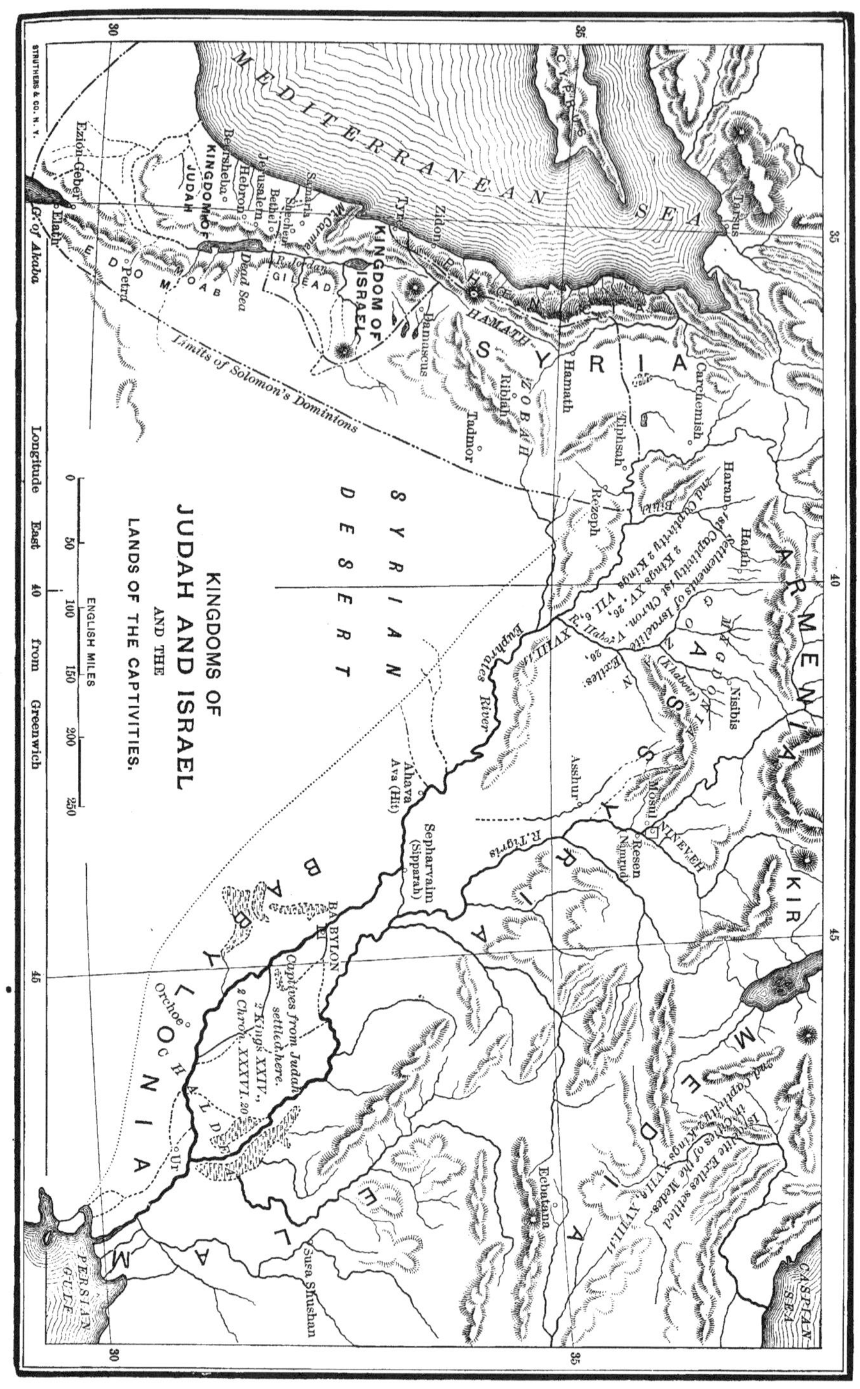
KINGDOMS OF
JUDAH AND ISRAEL
AND THE
LANDS OF THE CAPTIVITIES.
ENGLISH MILES
0 50 100 150 200 250
Longitude East 40 from Greenwich
STRUTHERS & CO. N. Y.
MEDITERRANEAN SEA
CYPRUS
Tarsus
KINGDOM OF ISRAEL
KINGDOM OF JUDAH
Samaria
Shechem
Bethel
Jerusalem
Hebron
Beersheba
Dead Sea
R. Jordan
Mt. Carmel
Tyre
Zidon
Damascus
PHOENICIA
GILEAD
MOAB
EDOM
Petra
Ezion-Geber
Elath
G. of Akaba
Limits of Solomon's Dominions
SYRIA
HAMATH
Hamath
ZOBAH
Riblah
Tadmor
SYRIAN DESERT
Carchemish
Tiphsah
Rezeph
Haran
Halah
Nisibis
ARMENIA
1st Captivity 1st Chron. V. 26.
2nd Captivity 2 Kings XVII. 6.
Euphrates River
R. Habor
(Khabour)
R. Tigris
Ashur
Mosul
NINEVEH
Resen
Nimrud
KIR
Ahava
Ava (Hit)
Sepharvaim
(Sipparah)
BABYLON
BABYLONIA
CHALDEA
Orchoe
Ur
Captives from Judah settled here.
2 Kings XXIV.,
2 Chron. XXXVI. 20.
MEDIA
2nd Captivity 2 Kings XVII. 6.
Israelite Exiles settled in Cities of the Medes
Ecbatana
ELAM
Susa, Shushan
PERSIAN GULF
CASPIAN SEA
30
35
40
45

that region, so contingents of these tribes were likely also carried into captivity. Perhaps a third of Israel's people were carried captive at this time. I Chronicles 5:26 records that these Israelites were resettled in "Halah, Habor, and Hara and to the river Gozan." When Samaria fell in 721 B.C., II Kings 17:6 states that its defenders were also carried captive to those locations and to "the cities of the Medes." Since Samaria was built in the area of the tribe of Ephraim, those Israelites going into captivity when Samaria fell were most likely Ephraimites.

Halah, Habor and Gozan were in the Mesopotamian region of the Assyrian Empire, but "the cities of the Medes," where the Ephraimites of Samaria were placed, were located south of the Caspian Sea in modern Iran. The Assyrians resettled Israelite captives in several places in order to prevent them from consolidating their strength for purposes of a rebellion. According to *Harper's Bible Dictionary*, archaeological finds in ancient Gozan confirm the arrival of captive Israelites in that city as "texts [were found which] mention some of the exiles' descendants."[33] We will also see in the third book in this series that centuries later, the names of the clans of Ephraim resurface in this region when they asserted their power over their captors.

There is secular evidence that the biblical accounts are true. We have already noted that Assyrian records discuss Kings Omri, Ahab and Jehu of Israel, but there is even more evidence. *Halley's Bible Handbook* notes the following about Assyria's annals:

> *"In these annals names of ten Hebrew kings occur: Omri, Ahab, Jehu, Menahem, Pekah, Hoshea, Uzziah, Ahaz, Hezekiah and Manasseh. Many [Assyrian] statements are found which confirm biblical statements."*[34]

Of the above kings, the first six were kings of the northern ten-tribed kingdom of Israel, and the last four were kings of the Jewish kingdom of Judah. Assyrian records also confirm the account of II Kings 15:29 that the entire tribe of Naphtali was taken captive in the Assyrian invasion of Tiglath-pileser over a decade prior to Samaria's fall.[35] The fact that Assyrian accounts mention by name many Israelite and Jewish kings and record the same events described in the Bible demonstrate that the accounts of the Bible are historically accurate.

While perhaps a third of Israel's population was taken captive by Tiglath-pileser by approximately 734 B.C., relatively few people were taken captive when Samaria later fell. II Kings 17:5 states the king of Assyria:

> "went throughout all the land, and went up to Samaria, and besieged it three years." *(KJV)*

Why did the Northern Kingdom of Israel fall to Assyria? The Bible answers that question succinctly, in II Kings 18:12, that the Israelite kingdom fell,

> "Because they obeyed not the voice of the Lord their God, but transgressed his covenant, and all that Moses...commanded, and would not hear them, nor do them." *(KJV)*

The kingdom perished because it chronically disobeyed God's Laws. That is all the epitaph that is needed to explain its demise. If the people had obeyed God, the kingdom would have been blessed and protected by God. Israel trusted in political alliances and its own efforts instead of trusting God. That proved to be a fatal mistake.

Although the Bible declares the Assyrians "went throughout all the land [of Israel]," the only place where any resistance is mentioned was at the city of Samaria. This indicates that while the Assyrians went throughout the whole land of Israel, they found Israelites in significant numbers **only** in the capital city of Samaria. The cuneiform records of the Assyrians claim only 27,290 captives in this final campaign, all of whom came

Assyrians flaying their Prisoners alive, and carrying away Heads of the Slain (Kouyunjik).

from Samaria.[36] The Assyrians claimed no captives other than the residents of Samaria. Since the Assyrian kings were not modest in their victory statements, we can be sure that they would have recorded additional Israelite captives in this conquest if there had been any!

We know that a third or more of the Israelites were taken captive by Tiglath-pileser, and that another 27,000 Israelites were taken captive when Samaria fell over a decade later. A total of 27,000 captives from Israel's capital city is a puny number of captives. The obvious question is: What happened to the rest of the people of the kingdom of Israel? Only a few years previously, the Israelites had been numerous enough to kill 120,000 Jews in a war, and take 200,000 Jewish captives. The Assyrian "catch" of 27,290 Israelites in Samaria was a paltry sum in light of the above numbers. Where did the other Israelites go?

The Bible lists the tribes of Naphtali, Gad, Reuben, half of Manasseh, elements of other tribes, and the residents of the capital city of Samaria as having "gone into captivity." The Assyrians also mentioned the Naphthalites and the Samarians by name as their captives. **But neither the Bible nor the Assyrian records make any claims that the remainder of the Israelite nation went into captivity!** In fact, II Kings 17:5 shows that the Assyrians "went throughout all the land," but found resistance and captives only in Samaria. II Kings 17:25 states that lions had become numerous in the territory of the kingdom of Israel, indicating that the numbers of wild prey species had to be even more numerous, when Assyria settled people from foreign lands to inhabit Israel's abandoned cities. A large increase in wild animals is typical of a land abandoned by its human population.

What happened was that the remainder of the war-weary Israelites finally abandoned their land and cities prior to Assyria's last invasion. Listed above were the Israelite tribes that did go into captivity. Let us now consider the list of tribes unaccounted for in the records of the Bible and Assyria. The "missing" tribes include Asher, Zebulon, Issachar, Dan, Simeon, most of Ephraim and half the tribe of Manasseh. The majority of Israel's tribes are not mentioned as captives, either in Biblical or Assyrian records! The obvious conclusion is that the remaining tribes of Israel fled the land voluntarily, not as captives.

Ancient Assyrian Bowmen and Spearmen.

Put yourself in their place. If you knew another large Assyrian invasion was coming, and you were painfully aware that your homeland of Israel was becoming untenable, what would you choose to do? Would you stay and oppose the Assyrians in a last-ditch effort, knowing that you and your children would become corpses or captives? Or would you rather migrate with your families to new homelands where you could remain free and start over again? Obviously, the latter option was a far better one, and that is what most Israelites chose to do. Only the king's loyalists stayed to withstand a siege in the capital city. Either they were stubborn Israelites who refused to abandon their land, or they were a heroic rearguard who occupied the Assyrian army for three years, allowing their countrymen time to flee without pursuit. What is apparent is that few Israelites remained with the last king of Israel to face the Assyrians. The rest of the nation followed their tribal elders to new homelands.

Israel's Maritime Migrations to Phoenician Colonies

This book is not the first source to realize that there was a great deal of voluntary migration of Israelite people from Palestine to avoid death or captivity. In 1906, the *Dictionary of Christ and the Gospels* stated the following about voluntary migrations of Israelites and Jews from Palestine.

> "Large numbers of **Israelites** had been carried away captive by the Assyrians and Babylonians: and Pompey had taken many **Jewish** captives to Rome. But **a much larger dispersion was due to voluntary emigration**."[37] *(Emphasis added)*

The above quote refers to both "Israelite" and "Jewish" captives and voluntary emigrants from Palestine. The reference to Jewish captives in the time of Pompey belongs to a much later period than currently addressed in this chapter. However, this source does acknowledge the obvious point that many Israelites and Jews voluntarily fled Palestine to avoid captivity, whether it loomed at the hands of the Assyrians, Babylonians, or the Romans still later. To flee imminent death and destruction is a basic self-preservation response of all people. The Israelites were no exception to this rule. They were highly motivated to preserve their lives, fortunes and freedom by fleeing the Assyrians before the final invasion of the ancient kingdom of Israel.

Those who chose to leave the doomed kingdom of Israel had many destinations as options for new homelands. We have seen that the "Phoenician" alliance of Israel, Tyre and Sidon had established many colonies in North Africa, Spain, other Mediterranean locations, the British Isles and even as far as North America. Any of these could have served as new homelands. In the ninth century B.C. so many Israelites had emigrated from Israel via the Phoenician fleets during the drought of Elijah that it was necessary to found a completely new colony (Carthage) to host the refugees. Many people likely had relatives in these mostly Israelite colonies, and they could start afresh with very little "culture-shock" as their customs and language were the same as those of Israel. Carthage, approximately a century old when Samaria fell, was relatively close and probably received the majority of the fleeing Israelites. The fact that Carthage rose to great power in the centuries after the fall of Israel also confirms a major increase in population.

Some might conclude that many Israelites would flee to Judah. However, flight to Judah was not an option. Judah was contiguous to the very area that Assyria's troops were going to invade, so it offered no real security. Also, Judah was not on friendly terms with Israel. What was needed were places of refuge **far away** from Assyrian armies.

Historical evidence has long existed concerning the voluntary migrations of the rest of the Israelites at this time, but such evidence has been ignored or forgotten. We will now reexamine some of that historical evidence to understand what really happened to most of the people in the besieged kingdom of Israel.

The kingdom of Israel was the main engine for the "Golden Age" of what modern historians call the Phoenician Empire. When Israel left Palestine, Phoenician power shifted from Tyre, Sidon, and Israel to their colonies in the west. Because Israel dominated the Phoenician alliance, it had ready access to the large Phoenician fleets to relocate its people to new homelands in Phoenicia's overseas colonies. Before the final Assyrian invasion, Israel was the scene of an ancient equivalent of the Dunkirk operation of World War II. The British sent every seaworthy craft, large and small, across the English Channel to rescue the British army which was besieged by German forces at Dunkirk, on the coast of France. This operation saved the British Empire from defeat.

The ancient kingdom of Israel performed a similar maritime evacuation prior to 721 B.C., evacuating as much of its population as possible to save it from an Assyrian captivity. While the Phoenician-Israelite fleets could not possibly remove a majority of Israel's population, it could remove a significant portion of it. These fleets moved Israelites out of Palestine to Phoenician colonies in Carthage, Spain, the British Isles, etc. for as long as they could. However, even as there was a "last helicopter out of Saigon in 1974," the time came when these ships made their final voyages from Israel's coastline. These last voyages were one-way trips out of Israel. Those Israelites who did not flee Israel via ships had to either face the Assyrian army or find an alternate route out of Israel to preserve their freedom. Most chose the latter option, as will soon be documented.

Judges 5:17 records that the tribe of Dan had a sea-faring heritage as early as four centuries prior to the fall of Samaria, and secular history has confirmed the Danites were part of the Sea Peoples. The tribe of Dan's main homeland was on the Mediterranean seacoast. As a maritime tribe, it was easy for many Danites to sail away from Israel in their ships. Many Danites sailed as far as **Hibernia** (modern Ireland) to seek refuge from Assyria. Their arrival in Hibernia as the **Tuatha De Danaans** is recorded in the early histories of Ireland.[38]

The battles of the Danaans to conquer a new homeland in Ireland are recorded in the annals of ancient Ireland. Emily Lawless' book, *Ireland*, cited an ancient record that after the Danaans fought a victorious, three-day battle against the native Firbolgs at a hill called **Ben-levi**, the Danites fortified ancient Ireland with many stone forts.[39] "Ben-levi" is of obvious Israelite origin as "Ben" means "son" in the Hebrew language and the name of the Israelite tribe of Levi is self-evident. J. H. Allen's book, *Judah's Sceptre and Joseph's Birthright*, records that "the greatest influx of the Tuatha de Danaan to Ireland" occurred around 720 B.C., just after the fall of Samaria.[40]

As an interesting digression, the Irish have not forgotten their Danaan roots: a 1980s Irish band in Minneapolis named itself **"De Danaan."**[41] There was also an intriguing account in *U.S. News and World Report* magazine, noting the presence of then New York Mayor Ed Koch, a prominent American Jew, in a 1987 St. Patrick's Day parade. Mayor Koch "explained his presence at the head of the grand parade thusly:

> 'It's part of my roots. The 10 lost tribes of Israel we believe ended up in Ireland.'"[42]

It is remarkable that New York's Mayor Koch acknowledged that some of the ten tribes of Israel had resettled in Ireland. History confirms he was right and specifically tells us that Danites arrived there after the kingdom of Israel collapsed circa 721 B.C.

Approximately two centuries after the Danaan arrived in Ireland, another tribe called the Milesians conquered Ireland,[43] and merged with the Danaan. Irish histories record the Milesian invasion of Ireland from Europe — sources identify them as coming from ancient Spain. *The Story of Ireland,* published in Dublin by A.M. Sullivan in 1898, states the following:

> "The Milesian colony reached Ireland from Spain, but they were not Spaniards. **They were an eastern people** who had tarried in that country on their way westward...they had passed...across the wide expanse of southern Europe...bearing aloft through all their wanderings the Sacred Banner, **which symbolized to them their origin**...the blessing and promise given to their race...**the "Sacred**

Queen Scota unfurls the Sacred Banner.

Banner of the Milesians," was a flag on which was represented a dead serpent and the rod of Moses..."[44] *(Emphasis added; illustrated to left)*

Sullivan's account also indicates that the Milesians had preserved the story of their ancestors being "**bitten by a poisonous serpent... [who were healed when they] implored the aid of Moses**."[45] The Milesians' ancestors were Israelites who memorialized the following event from Numbers 21:4-9 in their tribal history:

> "And the people spoke against God and Moses...**the Lord sent fiery serpents among the people, and they bit the people**, so that many people of Israel died. And **the people came to Moses, and said 'We have sinned...pray to the Lord, that he take away the serpents from us**.' And Moses prayed for the people. And the Lord said... '**Make a fiery serpent and set it on a pole; and every one who is bitten, when he sees it, shall live**.'" *(RSV)*

There is a perfect match between the Milesians' legends and the events of Numbers 21. The fact that the Milesians had "come from the east" indicates they originated in the eastern Mediterranean, where Egypt and Palestine are located, and history indicates they had wandered across Europe before reaching Ireland. Who were they? There are two options. One is that they were fellow Danites who were wanderers across southern Europe. The serpent is a symbol long associated with the tribe of Dan. *(Genesis 49:16-17)* However, there is a more likely alternate origin for the Milesians.

In the first book of this series, it was noted that most of the tribe of Simeon left the Israelites who were wandering with Moses in the Wilderness. Comparing the census data given for the tribe of Simeon in Numbers 1 and 26, the Simeonite males counted for battle plummeted from 59,300 to 22,200, a 62% decrease. The account of the biting serpents is found in Numbers 21, and soon afterward, census figures in Numbers 26 show a majority of the Simeonites were absent from the camp of Israel. The Milesians recorded that the plague of poisonous serpents stopped by Moses' prayer was the defining event in their ancient history. All the rest of the Israelites would go on to develop centuries of new experiences in their Israelite heritage. But for the group of Simeonites who left the Israelites in the Wilderness, the episode with the biting serpents was their last major experience as Israelites. It became such a defining moment in their history that it was still the theme on their Milesian banner approximately eight centuries later.

Numbers 25 offers us another motive for the Simeonite departure from Israel's encampment. A Levite named Phineas averted God's anger by publicly killing a "prince of a chief house of the Simeonites" *(verse 14)* who was involved in a blatant act of rebellion. The execution of one of their chief leaders may have provoked many Simeonites to leave their Israelite brothers and strike out on their own. The census figures of Numbers 1 and 26 offer revealing information. Many of the tribes had increased their populations: Manasseh had a huge increase and Asher, Benjamin and Issachar had significant increases. However, there are unexplained drops in the populations of the tribes of Ephraim, Reuben, Gad, Judah and Naphthali. This indicates that contingents from other tribes joined the Simeonite-led exodus from the camp of Israel.

In fact, the departure of so many people from the camp of Israel was probably the primary reason for taking this second census. Since all the tribes experienced the same conditions in the wilderness, and since many of the tribes exhibited significant increases in their population — Manasseh exhibited a 63 % increase, for example— there is no reason for a sudden decline in the population of several tribes other than a voluntary departure of some of their people from the camp. Simeon lost 37,100, Ephraim and Naphthali each lost 8,000, Gad lost 5,150, and Reuben lost 2,770. The total change in population of the tribes that decreased comes to 61,020 males. When we add the wives and children of these men to that total, it indicates that perhaps a quarter-million Israelites left the main body.

The Milesians had a legend that there had been a key "departure" in their ancient history that had taken place:

> "... **about fourteen hundred years before the birth of our Lord**."[46] *(Emphasis added)*

If any readers have Bibles with chapter headings giving ancient dates for biblical events, you may want to turn to it to confirm the following statement. The events of the "biting serpents" and the unexplained departure of most Simeonites and contingents of other tribes from the Israelite encampment are described in Numbers 21 and 26. The dates on those chapters are **1410 B.C.** The above account records that a key "departure" in the history of the Milesians occurred "**about 1400 B.C.**" Because the Milesian banner itself proclaimed the event of the biting serpents and the intercession of Moses, it seems evident that they were part of the descendants of the Simeonite-led departure from the rest of the Israelites about 1400 years before the birth of Christ.

John Mitchel's *History of Ireland* adds this fact about the Milesians:

> "Although the Milesians claim the glory of having come **directly from Egypt** to Spain, they do not...lose sight of **their Scythian origin**. They call themselves at all times **the descendants of the Iberians or Scythians of the Euxine [Black] Sea**."[47] *(Emphasis added)*

The Milesians not only claimed an "Egyptian" origin, but also that they were blood relatives of Iberians and Scythians in the Black Sea region. Their origin in Egypt was, of course, with the other Israelites who had come out of Egypt in the Exodus. While the Milesians of Ireland were far from the Black Sea's Iberians and Scythians, they knew they were related to them. We have seen that Iberia, in the Black Sea region, began as a colony of Israelites. We will discuss the Israelite origins of the Scythians in the final chapter of this book. The fact that the Milesians of Ireland knew they were related to tribes living in the Black Sea region indicates that, at least for a time, the dispersed bands of Israelites who left Palestine remained aware of each other's whereabouts.

While the Danaans of ancient Ireland were reputed to be superstitious people who were fascinated with magical things [this Danite trait is manifested in such Irish lore as four-leafed clovers, the mystical powers of the leprechauns, etc.], the Milesians came as soldiers.[48] The Milesians exhibited the martial temperament of Simeonites. Genesis 49:5-7 prophesied the Simeonites would be a warlike people who would be "scattered" among the other tribes. A later book in this series will document where another portion of the tribe of Simeon settled and became renowned for their martial tradition.

Thomas Moore's *History of Ireland,* released in 1843, states the following about the waves of migrants into Ireland and Western Europe:

> "There appears to be **no doubt that the first inhabitants of Ireland were derived from [the] same Celtic stock which supplied Gaul, Britain and Spain** with their original population...there exists...strong evidence of an early intercourse between Spain and Ireland...**which could only have arisen out of her connection with those Phoenician colonies**.[49] *(Emphasis added)*

This verifies that the Celtic migrations into ancient Ireland, Britain and Europe were facilitated via the Phoenician colonial network. The Phoenician colonial network was overwhelmingly Israelite, which explains why early Celtic tribes, such as the **Dan**aans, the **Simon**ii, and the **Bryth**onic Celts, bore obvious Israelite names. This is clear evidence that the ancient Celts were Israelite colonists in the British Isles and Europe. Originally these colonies supplied raw materials to Israel's home kingdom in Palestine, but they eventually became new homelands for Israelite refugees who fled Assyrian captivity by relocating to Ireland, Britain, Spain and other western lands.

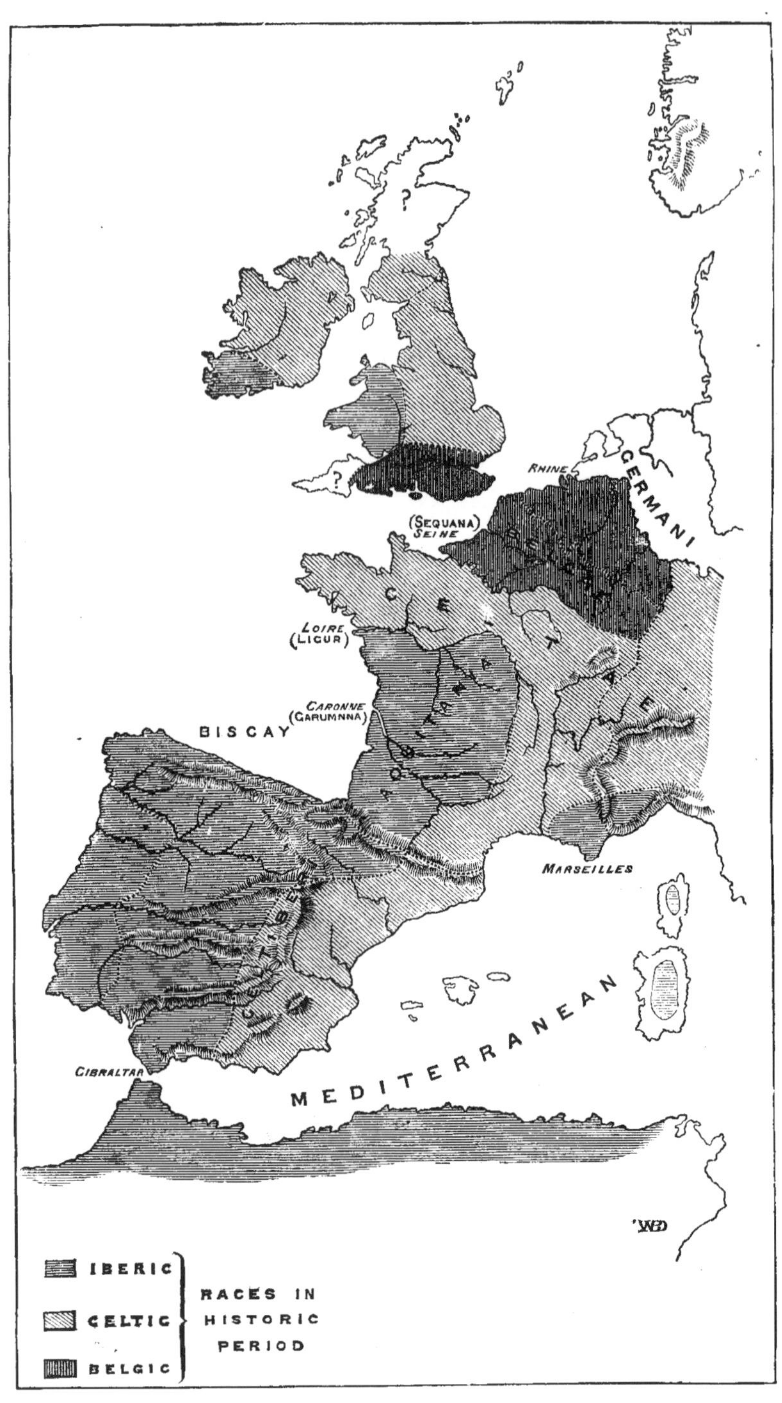
RHINE
GERMANI
(SEQUANA)
SEINE
BELGAE
CELTAE
LOIRE
(LIGUR)
CARONNE
(GARUMNNA)
BISCAY
AQUITANIA
CELTIBERI
MARSEILLES
GIBRALTAR
MEDITERRANEAN
IBERIC
CELTIC
BELGIC
RACES IN
HISTORIC
PERIOD

We also know that Celtic Spain and Portugal were named "Iberia," in honor of "**Eber**," the father of the Hebrews. The Iberians and the Celts were related groups of people. W. Boyd Dawkins, in 1880, wrote in *Early Man in Britain*:

> "the Iberian race extended beyond the boundaries of Spain, and...they were to a great extent intermingled with the Celts in Western Europe."[50]

A map on page 318 of Dawkins' book *(reproduced opposite)* shows the Iberians, the Celts and a related tribe, the Belgae, spread across ancient Spain, Portugal, France, the Benelux nations, England and Ireland. A portion of Celtic France came to be known as "**Brittany**," a name that has endured into modern times. That name also bears witness to the Israelite origin of the European Celts as it preserves the now-familiar consonants, B-R-T, a prime identifier of the "Brit(h)," or "covenant" people of Israel.

There is another name affixed to the ancient Celts that confirms their Israelite origin. Earlier it was documented that the Assyrians called the Israelites the "**Khumri**," a term the Assyrians derived from the name of Israel's King **Omri**, who was greatly respected by the Assyrians. Aylett Sammes, a 17th century historian wrote regarding the ancient British people:

> "The Britains called themselves **Kumero, Cymro and Kumeri**...[and in a later portion of his book]...most of the words of the ancient Britains and Gauls...**proceeded from the Phoenicians**..."[51] *(Emphasis added)*

In other words, the Celtic language itself had a Phoenician-Hebrew origin. The Phoenicians who colonized ancient Britain were Israelites who placed the Hebrew word for "covenant" (B-R-T) on the island of Britain. In addition, they were called Khumri -- the official Assyrian name for Israel (the northern ten tribes ruled by King Omri). This is very strong evidence of the overwhelmingly Israelite origin of the early Celts.

The book, *Celtic Britain*, written by Sir John Rhys in 1882, states the following about the names in ancient Britain and Wales:

> "...both countries of the **Kymry** were for some time called Cambria or Cumbria, the Welsh word on which they are based being, as now written, **Cymru**...pronounced nearly as an Englishman would treat it if spelled **Kumry** or **Kumri**...in the language of the Saxon Chronicle, it became Cumerland or Cumbraland...the land [of]...the **Cumbri** or **Kymry**."[52] *(Emphasis added)*

The Israelite origin of the Celts is well documented. They bore Israelite names both from Phoenician and Assyrian perspectives. Many Celts were descended from Israelites who settled Phoenician colonies in Europe and the British Isles during the Golden Age of Israel-Phoenicia in 1000-720 B.C. Later Celts descended from the many Israelite refugees who fled Palestine to seek new lives in the maritime colonies of Israel. The Bible itself indicates that the British Isles were well-known to the biblical writers, who wrote from a "Phoenician" perspective.

Psalm 72 is dedicated to Solomon, a great king of the "Phoenician" alliance of Israel, Tyre and Sidon. Verses 10-11 state:

> "The **kings of Tarshish** and **of the isles** shall bring presents...all nations shall serve him." *(KJV)*

Earlier we documented that Tarshish was in the Atlantic region and that the most important "isles" in the Phoenician-Israelite Empire were the British Isles, where Phoenicia's key tin mines were located. Isaiah 11:11 prophesied Israel's people would be widely scattered around the world; one such place to which they would migrate was "the islands of the sea." Isaiah 24:15-16 states:

> "Wherefore glorify...the name of the Lord God of Israel in **the isles of the sea**. From the **uttermost parts of the earth** have we heard songs, even glory to the righteous." *(KJV)*

Much becomes clearer when one realizes the Bible is written from the Israelite-Phoenician perspective. The Phoenicians did, indeed, explore and colonize "the isles of the sea" and the "uttermost parts of the earth." It was shown earlier that the "Phoenician" Empire dominated portions of five continents in the ancient world. The above Biblical statements aptly describe the far-flung nature of the Phoenician Empire. The books of Psalms, Proverbs and Ecclesiastes were written primarily by the two greatest kings of the Phoenician alliance: David and Solomon. The books of I and II Samuel, I and II Kings, and I and II Chronicles were written about the rise and fall of the "Phoenician" Empire of ancient Israel. Near the end of Israel's kingdom, Isaiah 23 was written as a warning and lamentation for Tyre, Sidon, the "ships of Tarshish," and verse 6 states: "pass ye over to Tarshish; howl, ye inhabitants of the isle (or coast)." This prophecy correctly predicted where many of the Israelite people would flee when the Assyrians terminated the ancient kingdom of Israel. Many would flee to Tarshish (ancient Spain) or to the "isles" or "coasts" beyond Tarshish: Western Europe and the British Isles. Jeremiah 25 is a warning to many nations in the world and it mentions in verse 22:

> "the kings of Tyre, and all the kings of Sidon, **and the kings of the isles which are beyond the [Mediterranean] sea**." *(KJV)*

The prophet Jeremiah here refers to Phoenicia's empire, including not only Tyre and Sidon, but also "kings of the isles...beyond the sea." This statement confirms Jeremiah knew that there were "kings" with Phoenician origins beyond the Mediterranean Sea — the Celtic areas in the British Isles, western Spain and Europe. There are so many references to distant "isles" and "coasts" in the biblical books of Isaiah, Jeremiah and Ezekiel that the reader is urged to review them with the help of a Bible Concordance. These books were addressed to Israel and Judah at a time when they were disobeying God and falling from God's grace. They warn about the penalties to come because of their national sins. It is noteworthy that these Israelite prophets included so many references to "the isles" in their warnings to Israel. The reason? These distant "isles" and "coasts" were well-known parts of a system of colonies connected to the Israelite homeland by Phoenicia's maritime trade routes. The prophets wrote of them as if they were common knowledge to their ancient audiences -- which they were.

The Celts were descended from a combination of ancient Phoenicia's colonies who were "on their own" after Israel, Tyre and Sidon fell, and Israelite refugees who fled Assyrian captivity. The Celts were not a distinct "empire" or "nation." They were related tribes who developed their own customs, leaders and dialects in new homelands. There were other Israelites fleeing Assyria via the sea that also became known as Celts.

When the kingdom of Israel collapsed circa 721 B.C., a group of the Israelite tribe of Simeon chose a maritime escape from the Assyrians. This group descended from the Simeonites who stayed with Moses, entered the Promised Land and lived there until they fled from the Assyrians. Coinciding with the arrival of the Tuatha de Danaan in Ireland in 720 B.C., the **Simonii** landed in Wales and Southern England at the same time.[53] This date coincides with the fall of Samaria, and the simultaneous arrival of the **Danaan** and the **Simonii** in the British Isles indicates that parts of the tribes of Dan and Simeon apparently sailed there together. Since Britain had been an important Phoenician-Israelite colony for centuries, it is logical that some Israelites would seek refuge there in a time of crisis.

J. H. Allen also notes that:

> "...the people of Wales call themselves, in ancient Welsh, 'Bryth y Brithan,' or 'Briths of Briton,' which means 'The Covenanters' of the 'land of the Covenant.' The first form of this phrase is almost vernacular Hebrew."[54]

The fact that the "**Bry**t**h**onic Celts" who migrated to the British Isles bore the Hebrew word, **B-R-T(H)**, for "covenant" further proclaims their Israelite origin. Israelite immigrants furnished much of the racial stock of early Celtic Britain. The Danaan and the Simonii were only part of the waves of Celtic immigrants that arrived in Briton and Europe over several centuries.

Concerning the Celts in ancient Iberia (modern Spain and Portugal), the *Encyclopedia Americana* states:

> "The Celtic migrations occurred as early **as 1000 B.C. and as late as 600 B.C.**"[55] *(Emphasis added)*

In other words, the period of Celtic migration began during Israel's golden age under Kings David and Solomon, when Israel founded many colonies, continued throughout the time of the kingdom of Israel and concluded just prior to the fall of Judah and Jerusalem. The striking parallels between the timing of Celtic migrations and events in the Israelite kingdoms of Israel and Judah indicate that this relationship is not coincidental. Many of these waves of immigrating Celts were Israelites seeking new homelands. Gerhard Herm's book, *The Celts*, observes:

> "...the first Celtic-speaking tribes came to Ireland as far back as the Hallstatt period. After the beginning of the La Tene era these were followed, via Britain, by other wandering hordes, who spoke a Brythonic, that is a P-Celtic, dialect."[56]

The *Encyclopedia Americana* defines the Hallstatt period of Central Europe as being "about 1000 to 500 B.C...The people of the area were early Celts..."[57] Again, these Celtic migrations began in Israel's Golden Age under kings David and Solomon and ended after the fall of Jerusalem, taking place over several centuries. Some were slow, overland migrations instead of the swift maritime migrations of the Danaan and Simonii. It is not the contention of this book that all ancient Celts were descended from Israel's tribes. Obviously, some came from Tyre, Sidon and the smaller Phoenician cities. But the evidence indicates that most of the migrating Celts were Israelites.

While portions of the tribes of Dan and Simeon fled by sea to the British Isles, other Israelite-Celtic migrants went to Spain and Western Europe. This migration has not gone unnoticed by historians and archaeologists. Richard Harrison's 1988 book, *Spain at the Dawn of History* states the following about the Phoenician migration to its colonies:

> "...during the ninth and eight centuries Assyrian pressure increased steadily upon [the Phoenicians]...forcing them to pay tribute. Then...they were reduced by conquest...beginning with the attacks of Tiglath Pileser III in the 740's and ending finally with the fall of Tyre to the Babylonian king Nebuchadnezzar in 573 B.C. **It is noticeable that the Phoenician expansion into Sicily, Sardinia and Spain in the eighth century coincides with the loss of their residual independence; the conquest of their mother cities probably forced many Phoenicians to become emigrants and seek a new life in colonies and trading stations out in the west.**"[58]
> *(Emphasis added)*

If you change the word "Phoenician" to "Israelite" in the above quote, it is a duplicate account of events recorded in the Bible. The invasion of Tiglath-pileser into Israel in approximately the 740's B.C.

is recorded in II Kings 15:27-29. That account records the Assyrians took captive the tribes of Naphthali, and the "Gilead" tribes, Reuben, Gad and one-half of Manasseh. Nebuchadnezzar's destruction of Jerusalem occurred circa 586 B.C., just prior to the fall of Tyre. The number of Israelites threatened by Assyrian invasions far exceeded the number of Tyrians and Sidonians who were so threatened. Since all these groups were allied in what the Greeks called "Phoenicia," most of the "Phoenicians" migrating to Spain, Sardinia, Sicily and other locations were Israelites! Indeed, with the capture of three and one-half tribes of Israel by the Assyrians in the 740's B.C., the "handwriting was on the wall" that the demise of the kingdom of Israel was imminent. Many Israelites fled by sea to the western colonies of Phoenicia between 740 and 721 B.C. Their own "holocaust" loomed at the hands of the Assyrians, and they left Palestine in huge numbers to save themselves and their children. If you, the reader, were in their ancient situation, would you not have fled as well? The answer for most people would be "yes."

Harrison also wrote the following:

> "...the Phoenicians were the first to discover the far West. Greek sailors arrived centuries after them and then failed, for whatever reason, to maintain the direct contact they had with southern Spain in the seventh century [B.C.]. We can show the dominant influence in the orientalizing period, and afterwards, was Semitic, first Phoenician, then Carthaginian."[59]

The "orientalizing" phase of early Spain refers to the substantial influx of "Phoenician" migrants into Spain after the fall of Israel. The "Semites" pouring into Spain were mostly Israelites fleeing from Assyria, and the later Carthaginians were from a sister colony of Israelites, as will be documented in the next chapter. The reason why Greeks were cut off from ancient Spain at that time is that the Phoenician-Israelites were the rivals of the Greeks. The infusion of Israelites into ancient Spain precluded the arrival of more Greeks, and much of southern Spain became part of the Carthaginian Empire. Carthage and Greece were rivals, so the Greeks were hindered in reinforcing their colonies in Spain by the migrating Israelites, who transplanted Phoenician culture to Carthage and Spain.

Richard Harrison notes that Phoenician activity in its Spanish colony increased markedly in the eighth century B.C.[60] This directly parallels biblical events in Israel. During the eighth century B.C., the Israelites would have been relocating increasing portions of their people and wealth to their western colonies to spare them from the impending Assyrian captivity. Many of the migrating Israelites did not stay in Spain, but used it as a staging point for migrations further north to Britain, Ireland, and Western Europe. Citing the importance of ancient Spain to the Phoenicians, Harrison also asserts that much of the silver given by the Phoenicians (Israel, Tyre and Sidon) to the Assyrians as tribute payments came from the mines of ancient Spain.[61]

Overland Migration of Israelites to the Black Sea Region

Even though Phoenicia's fleets were very large, they could not hope to transport more than a substantial minority of Israel's large population to safety via maritime routes. What happened to the rest of the Israelites who could not flee Palestine via a maritime route to Phoenician colonies? There is historical evidence that most of the remaining Israelites fled via an overland route to conquer a new homeland. They could not go east because of the Assyrian menace, there were not enough ships to take everyone west via the Mediterranean Sea, and there was mostly desert to the south. This left a northern route out of Palestine as the only realistic option, and that is exactly where historical evidence confirms they went.

Colonel J. C. Gawler, a British government official during Queen Victoria's reign in the nineteenth century, cited both Jewish and Armenian historical sources as proof that many refugees from the ten tribes of Israel migrated through Armenia into the region north of the Black Sea, then known by the term "Tartary."[62] Gawler cited this observation about Tartary recorded by Abraham Ortellius, a famous sixteenth century geographer:

> "In his description of Tartary, [he] notes the kingdom of **Arsareth, where the ten tribes retiring...took the name of Gauthei**, because, he says, they were very jealous of the glory of God."[63] *(Emphasis added)*

Gawler also quotes a passage in the apocryphal book of II Esdras, which asserts that refugees of the ten tribes did, indeed, migrate to a new place called "**Arzareth**." This passage in II Esdras 13:40-45 states:

> "...**these are the ten tribes that in the days of King Hoshea** were carried away from their own land into captivity, whom **Shalmaneser, king of Assyria**, made captives, and carried beyond the river...But they formed this plan among themselves, to leave the heathen population, and go to a more distant region...**so that there perhaps they might keep their statutes, which they had not kept in their own country**. And they went in by the narrow passages of the Euphrates River. For the Most High then did wonders for them, for he held back the sources of the river until they had passed over. But it was a long journey of a year and a half to that country...called **Arzareth**."[64] *(Emphasis added)*

This account of the Israelite migration parallels the events of II Kings 17:1-6. The account of II Esdras indicates many Israelites escaped the Assyrian captivity and fled to "Arzareth," in the Black Sea region. Also noteworthy is the account of II Esdras that this group of Israelites was determined to obey God in their new homeland. Such a godly attitude on the part of the ten tribes was foreshadowed in II Chronicles 28:5-15.

CAPTIVES OF WAR; FROM ASSHUR-BANI-PAL'S PALACE.

During the reign of King Pekah of Israel (a few years prior to the removal of all Israelites from Palestine), the ten tribes heeded a prophet of God who told them to release 200,000 Jewish captives taken in a war with Judah. This account, described earlier, offers biblical evidence that the ten tribes of Israel were becoming more responsive to God than to their human king just prior to their leaving Palestine.

II Esdras attributes the escape of the Israelites to divine help in crossing the Euphrates River, and adds that their journey took a year and a half. Some of their escape route was mountainous, and since they had women, children and elderly along, such a journey would be arduous and time-consuming. If God miraculously assisted their escape, it would explain why these migrating Israelites were "very jealous of God" in their new homeland. It would also account for the silence in Assyrian annals about the unexplained disappearance of most Israelites during their final invasion of Israel. Assyria would have been loathe to record that Israel's God supernaturally delivered the migrating Israelites, so they limited their bragging to the small band of Israelites captured in Samaria.

A later chapter in this book will confirm that the Israelites who fled to the Black Sea came to be known by the Greeks as "Scythians" or "Sacae" who did not exhibit evidence of Baal worship. In fact, we shall see that they were known for their wise laws and the avoidance of swine's flesh. The evidence indicates that this group of migrants from the ten tribes of Israel forsook Baal worship and tried to obey God's laws.

Gawler also cited the testimony of the medieval Jewish historian Eldad, who "sent to the Spanish Jews his memoirs of the ten tribes."[65] Eldad stated that these Israelites who migrated via an overland route did so in considerable numbers. He wrote:

> "that many of the people did not go into captivity, but evaded the calamity, going off with their flocks, and turning nomads, and that the chief or prince whom they appointed **could muster 120,000 horse and 100,000 foot.**"[66] *(Emphasis added)*

Because these migrating Israelites had 220,000 armed escorts, one can estimate there were at least a million Israelites in this group of refugees when women, children and elderly are included in the total. Based on biblical and secular accounts of what happened to the other tribes, this body of Israelites likely included the half-tribe of Manasseh which lived west of the Jordan River, many people from the tribes of Ephraim, Asher, Zebulon, and Issachar, and the Danites living in the northern part of Palestine.

As this large group of Israelites resettled in the Black Sea region, many factors identified them as Israelites. The region to the east of the Black Sea and north of Armenia came to be known as **Iberia,**[67] confirming the presence of Hebrews from the ten tribes in that region. The Israelites had given the Phoenician colony in Spain the same name, **Iberia,** after **Eber**, the namesake of the Hebrews. Spain was long called the **Iberian** Peninsula.

The presence of the Hebrew name, Iberia, in the region north of Armenia verifies that this was an area of Israelite resettlement for those migrating there to escape the Assyrians. The previous chapter cited the account of Herbert Hannay that this Asian Iberia "was founded in the Hebro-Phoenician era."[68] This raises the possibility that the Phoenician-Israelites were already familiar with the Black Sea region because they had founded an earlier colony there. Indeed, the migration of these Israelites to the Black Sea region may have been a purposeful effort to link up with a Phoenician-Israelite colony already existing there.

While information about the kingdom of Iberia in the Asian Caucasus region rarely appears in modern histories, it is shown on a map on Armenian history in the *Encyclopedia Americana*.[69] That map represents the dimensions of Iberia's diminished size centuries after most Israelites had migrated out of that area into southern Russia.

Historical evidence provides a positive identification of where most escaping Israelites relocated circa 724-720 B.C. Israel's new homeland was well chosen, as it was in a mountainous region where the terrain greatly favored the defenders. The migration of the Israelites to a defensible region indicates that they purposefully fled to an area where Assyria would be reluctant to pursue them.

The Hebrews relocating to the Black Sea region were Israelites from the ten tribes of Israel; they were not Jews. The Bible records that there was warfare and hostility between the Israelites and the Jews just prior to this Israelite migration. Indeed, since the Jewish kingdom was then allied with Assyria against the Israelites *(II Kings 16:7)*, the Jews had no need to flee. Also, the Bible confirms that the Jews (Judah) remained in Palestine after the rest of the tribes of Israel were gone. *(II Kings 17:18)*

The Fall of the Kingdom of Judah

While Judah remained in the land after Israel departed, their presence in the land was far from secure. Eight years after the Israelites were driven from Palestine, the Assyrians invaded Judah, intending to do to Judah what they had done to Samaria. *(II Kings 18:10-13)* Their initial efforts were successful as the Assyrians "came up against all the fenced cities of Judah and took them." This resulted in much of the tribe of Judah going into captivity at this time. II Kings 18:13-17 and 19:8 state only three Jewish cities (Jerusalem, Lachish, and Libnah) resisted the Assyrians.

Judah was ruled by a righteous king named Hezekiah. The Assyrians mocked Hezekiah's God, asserting that he would be as impotent as the "gods of Hamath, Arpad, Sepharvaim, Hena, Ivah, and Samaria." *(II Kings 18:33-35)* II Kings 18:14 records that Hezekiah gave Assyria's king tribute of "300 talents of silver and 30 talents of gold" in an effort to "buy off" the Assyrians. Assyrian records also mention Hezekiah's tribute of 30 gold talents in a remarkable confirmation of this biblical account.[70] God's judgments are not easily evaded by means of mammon, and Hezekiah finally appealed to God for divine help. An examination of the cuneiform Assyrian records of this invasion shows why Hezekiah and his people were desperate for help.

An Assyrian stone carving depicting the Assyrian siege of Lachish is on display in the British Museum. Werner Keller describes the relief, in his book *The Bible as History*, as follows:

> "On the turrets and breastwork of...Lachish...the Judahite defenders...showered a hail of arrows on the attackers, hurled stones down upon them, threw burning torches...among the enemy...At the foot of the wall the Assyrians are attacking with the utmost violence... Their engineers have built sloping ramps of earth, stones and felled trees. Siege engines, the first tanks in history, push forward up the ramps against the walls. They are equipped with a battering ram which sticks out like the barrel of a cannon...tunnels are being driven into the rock beneath the foundation of the walls...The first captives, men and women, are being led off. Lifeless bodies are hanging on pointed sticks — impaled."[71]

One can imagine the horror of the siege faced by Jerusalem's inhabitants as defenders were terrorized by Assyrian tactics, which included impaling their countrymen on stakes! As extreme as his position was, Hezekiah's prayer did not simply ask God "to save their skins." He laid out before God an Assyrian letter that mocked God's ability to help them. Hezekiah asked God to intervene for his name's sake, portraying the battle as one in which God's own honor was at issue. God responded by sending a death angel to kill 185,000 Assyrian soldiers

Sennacherib besieging Lachish. (Assyrian Monuments.)

in one night! *(II Kings 19:14-35)* Mute testimony to the accuracy of the biblical account is given in the Assyrian records of the siege of Jerusalem. They claim the "30 talents of gold," but include few details why Assyria retreated from Jerusalem without a victory.[72] This indicates that Assyria suffered an unexpected calamity at Jerusalem.

This action of God did not kill all Assyrians in Judah. While God wiped out the Assyrian army besieging Jerusalem, another Assyrian army under Sennacherib himself was besieging Libnah. *(II Kings 19:8)* When they realized that their companion army had been annihilated in one night by divine action, Sennacherib and his army fled in terror to avoid a similar fate. The loss of an entire army severely weakened Assyria, granting a reprieve to the Kingdom of Judah.

Assyrian King Sennacherib, who had defied God at Jerusalem, was killed by his own sons soon after Assyria's debacle at Jerusalem. Significantly, after murdering their father, these Assyrian princes "escaped into the land of Armenia." *(II Kings 19:37)* While the *King James Version* of the Bible uses the term "Armenia" for their place of refuge, the *Revised Standard Version* translates it as "the land of Ararat." Iberia, the region to which a large portion of the Israelites had recently migrated, was in the region of Ararat and Armenia.

After killing Assyria's king, these fugitives fled to a region certain to give them asylum. Their confidence that people in the region of Ararat would grant them asylum supports the conclusion that displaced Israelites were living there. The Israelites would likely grant asylum to anyone who killed the king of Assyria.

After Hezekiah's death, his son Manasseh became the king of the depleted Kingdom of Judah. He was a vile king who caused the Jews to worship Baal and practice astrology and infant sacrifice. He sought the advice of demons via people with familiar spirits, whom we call "channelers," in modern terms. Judah became so degenerate that II Kings 21:1-16 and II Chronicles 33:3-10 record that they became **worse** than the depraved Canaanites whom the Israelites had displaced in the time of Joshua.

Because of Manasseh's degeneracy, God allowed him to become an Assyrian captive. Surprisingly, Manasseh repented! In a testimony to how merciful God can be when one repents, II Chronicles 33:11-20 shows that God reinstated Manasseh as King of Judah, and he afterwards "commanded Judah to serve the God of Israel." *(verse 16)*

Graphically illustrating Judah's spiritual decline, II Chronicles 34 records that years later in the reign of Josiah (a good king), lost scrolls containing God's Laws were found while repairing God's Temple. Imagine! Judah had slipped so far from God that by the time Josiah was king about 639-608 B.C., no one even knew what the laws of God were! When this copy of God's law was dusted off and read, it was the first time that King Josiah had even heard the Law of God!

During Josiah's reign, a message by the prophet Jeremiah gives biblical confirmation that many of the ten tribes of Israel were located near the Black Sea. Jeremiah 3:6-12 contains a divine warning to Judah through the prophet Jeremiah. After restating the sins that caused Israel to be removed from Palestine, God warned Judah that its sins were even worse! Verses 11-12 then state:

> "And the Lord said unto me, The **backsliding Israel hath justified herself more than treacherous Judah**. Go and **proclaim these words toward the north**, and say, **Return, thou backsliding Israel**, saith the Lord; and I will not cause mine anger to fall upon you: for I am merciful... and I will not keep anger for ever." *(KJV)*

When God inspired Jeremiah to direct a message to the ten tribes of Israel, he was told to "proclaim it toward the north." **This message was given to Jeremiah about a century after Samaria fell**. If all the Israelites had been taken captive into Assyria, God would have said to proclaim the message "to the east," since Assyria was east of Palestine. However, the Black Sea is directly north of Jerusalem, and many sources confirm a large body of Israelites migrated to Iberia and the Black Sea region. The Bible's statement, circa 620 B.C., that at least a sizable portion of the ten tribes were living **to the north** of Jerusalem confirms those historical accounts. Also, God's words "...Israel hath justified herself..." gives credence to the historical accounts of Ortellius and II Esdras that many of these resettled Israelites were trying to obey God.

Decades later, the Babylonians conquered Jerusalem and carried the remaining Jews captive in successive invasions. In the invasion of 597 B.C., Nebuchadnezzar took King Jehoiachin, most of the royal family, and much of Judah's leadership into captivity. This first invasion netted over 10,000 captives. *(II Kings 24:8-16)* Nebuchadnezzar made one member of the royal family, Zedekiah, a puppet king over Judah, but nine years later, Zedekiah's revolt triggered the final Babylonian invasion. After a two-year siege, Jerusalem fell, ending the kingdom of Judah. King Zedekiah's sons were killed *(II Kings 25:6-7)*, but this did not terminate the Davidic dynasty. After spending 37 years in captivity, the previous king of Judah, Jehoiachin, was given great favor by a subsequent Babylonian king. *(II Kings 25:27-30)* I Chronicles 3:17-24 shows that Jehoiachin ("Jeconiah") had seven sons who produced numerous descendants, preserving the royal blood of King David in Asia. That the royal Davidic line flourished even through the captivity of Judah will become an important factor later in this history of the tribes of Israel.

There is an important footnote to the fall of the kingdom of Judah. When Judah fell, the Babylonians allowed Jeremiah to go free. *(Jeremiah 39:11-12)* A Jewish contingent fled westward to Tehaphnehes, Egypt, taking Jeremiah, his scribe Baruch, and the daughters of Zedekiah, Judah's last king. *(Jeremiah 43:1-7)* The "king's daughters" were of the royal dynastic line of King David.

—Restoration of the fortress of Tehaphnehes, or Defeneh. The entry is seen at the inner angle, and the pavement of brickwork before it.

While the Bible does not say what became of Jeremiah, Baruch, and Judah's princesses, ancient historical accounts indicate their ultimate place of refuge. J. H. Allen, in his book *Judah's Sceptre and Joseph's Birthright*, cites ancient Irish histories in reconstructing what happened to Jeremiah and his band of Jewish refugees. He states: "About 585 B.C. a 'notable man'...'a patriarch'...came to...Ireland, accompanied by a princess, the daughter of an eastern king, and...Simon Brach..."[73] Allen also states that this princess, Tea-Tephi, married a native Irish king who forsook his old religion and changed his capital city's name to Tara, a Hebrew-Semitic name.

Numbers 33:27-28 states "Tarah" was the name of an Israelite encampment during their wandering in the wilderness, and "Terah" was also the name of Abraham's father. *(Genesis 11:31)* Allen contends that the "patriarch, Simon Brach, and the eastern princess" were Jeremiah, his scribe Baruch, and one of the daughters of King Zedekiah of Judah. Obviously, there is an exact match between the consonants of the Irish immigrant "**Brach**" and the biblical person "**Baruch**."

J. H. Allen further comments that the royal arms of Ireland have long been represented by the "harp of David," which was said to have accompanied Jeremiah, Baruch and Princess Tea-Tephi to Ireland, supporting the idea that the royal daughter from the east was a princess of Judah's royal family.[74]

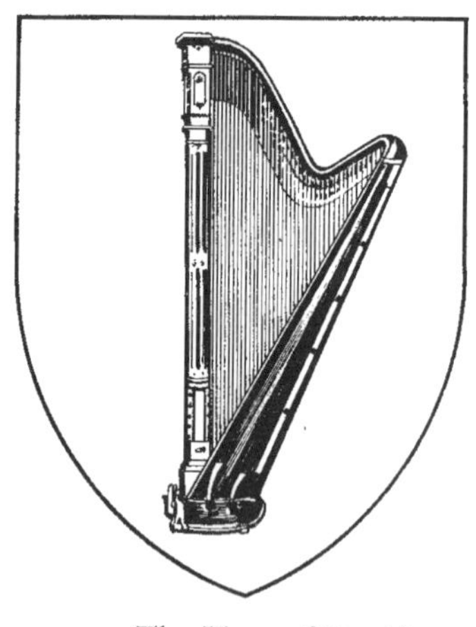

The Harp of David

Jeremiah had been told by God that it would not be safe to stay in Egypt *(Jeremiah 42:13-22)*, so we can be sure he did not remain there. Where did he go? The book of Jeremiah gives us a clue. His own prophecy in Jeremiah 3:11-12 identified the Israelites who had migrated to the Black Sea, and in Jeremiah 23:6, he wrote about "Tyre, Sidon and **the kings of the Isles which were beyond the sea**." Jeremiah mentioned "Tyre and Sidon" and not "Israel" in this account because the kingdom of Israel had ceased to exist by the time he penned those words. "Tyre and Sidon" were all that was left of the mighty Phoenician homeland in the eastern Mediterranean after the Israelites left the area. However, Jeremiah 23:6 confirms that Jeremiah was well aware that there were sovereign "kings" in "the isles" which were "beyond the sea." Jeremiah knew about the long-standing Israelite colonies in the British Isles, which by then had developed into nations with their own kings. His comment that they were "beyond the sea" confirms that these "isles" were beyond the Mediterranean Sea.

Jeremiah and his fellow Jewish refugees apparently sailed to Hibernia (Ireland), one of the old colonies of Israel, and started anew. The reader should be aware that there are many legends about the arrival of Jeremiah and his party of Jewish refugees in ancient Ireland. Some of the legends tell conflicting accounts of this ancient event, but there are core narratives firmly established in the ancient history of Ireland. The great patriarch who arrived there, Jeremiah, became known as the "Ollam Fola" or "Ollam Fodhla," and he became one of the most prominent historical figures in ancient Ireland. One author writes concerning Ollam Fodhla:

> "...his influence caused a national reformation, and the establishment of a new code of law...The famous Four Courts of Dublin...were decorated with large medallions of the world's greatest lawgivers. They included Alfred, Solon, Confucius, Moses and Ollam Fodhla."[75]

Ollam Fodhla established an educational and political center at Tara, in ancient Ireland, and died after a forty-year domination of ancient Ireland's affairs.[76] According to F. Wallace Connon, author of *The Stone of Destiny*:

> "...there is a link in Ireland with Jeremiah; a tomb hewn out of the rock in a cemetery on Devenish Island, in Lough Erne, has been known from time immemorial as 'Jeremiah's tomb.'"[77]

Many legends about Jeremiah and Baruch have them escorting the daughter (or daughters) of King Zedekiah, the last king of Judah, to

Ireland, where one of them, Tea-Tephi, married the ruler of the Irish clans. That ruler was named Heremon Eochaidh I, who was the "head of one of the Danite clans of Ireland."[78] Such an action would have united the royal blood of King David's dynasty with a ruler of the Israelite tribe of Dan, the Danaans who had previously arrived in Ireland. More will be discussed about the significance of this event in a later book in this series, but it was important to note that this event is well established in Irish history.

The harp of David has long been celebrated in Irish history, and has been so prominent in Ireland's heraldry and symbolism that the *Encyclopedia Americana* observes: "...the harp became virtually the national symbol of Ireland."[79] Irish histories also record that Jeremiah and Baruch brought with them to Ireland not only the "harp of David," but also a very famous stone.

The famous stone brought by Jeremiah to Ireland was called the "lia-fail" or "stone of destiny." It was reportedly the very stone on which Jacob rested his head during his famous dream in which God confirmed the Abrahamic Covenant with Jacob and his descendants. After awakening from that dream, Jacob anointed the stone, setting it upright as a "pillar" and it became the symbol of his solemn vow and covenant with God. *(Genesis 28:16-22)* Years later, Jacob still had this stone in his possession when it "witnessed" God's confirmation of the Abrahamic Covenant with Jacob's descendants. Genesis 35:9-14 relates this event in which God confirmed the birthright promises of national greatness given to Ephraim and Manasseh in Genesis 48, and the promise of a dynasty of kings given to Judah in Genesis 49:8-10. The dynasty of kings proved to be King David and the royal dynasty that proceeded from him. When Judah fell, his royal seed was transplanted mostly to Babylon, but Jeremiah transplanted one portion of David's dynasty to ancient Ireland when Princess Tea-Tephi, the daughter of Judah's King Zedekiah, married an Irish ruler.

Joshua set up a special "stone" in Shechem to act as a "witness" between God and the people when the Israelites marched into Canaan. Later, a man named Abimelech was proclaimed as the ruler of Israel in the presence of this "pillar" stone in Shechem. *(Judges 9:6)* The kings of Judah, the dynasty of King David, were enthroned while standing by (or on) a special "pillar stone." II Kings 11:12-14 states that when King Joash was crowned king of Judah, it was done as he "stood by a pillar, as the manner [custom] was." There was a unique "pillar stone" which conferred legitimacy on the royal dynastic kings descended from King David. This "pillar stone" was the stone dedicated by Jacob as a "witness" to the covenant between God and the Israelites, and one of the specific aspects of this covenant affirmed by God and Jacob involved the "kings" which were to descend from Jacob. *(Genesis 35:9-14)*

Given the fact that the royalty of Judah had long been enthroned in the presence of this particular stone, it would have been very appropriate for Jeremiah to bring this stone with him when he brought the daughters of King Zedekiah of Judah to Ireland. It would have been unthinkable to leave behind such a symbol of God's covenant relationship with the "kings" of the Abrahamic covenant. There will be more information about this stone in a later book in this series, which will examine the significance of this stone in the modern world.

Evolutionary skeptics like to cast doubt on the accuracy of biblical narratives, but this series of books is establishing the literal accuracy of the biblical records. Indeed, it is the Bible's narratives that are the real "missing link" in understanding the nature of man and the course of human history. Winston Churchill, the famous Prime Minister of Great Britain, and also a noted historian and author in his own right, wrote the following about the Bible's narratives:

> "We believe that **the most scientific view**, the most up-to-date and rationalistic conception, **will find its fullest satisfaction in taking the Bible story literally...We may be sure that all these things happened just as they are set out according to Holy Writ**."[80] *(Emphasis added)*

You likely have not read this quote from one of the 20th century's greatest minds in your educational courses. The more you read this series of books on Israelite history, the more you will realize Sir Winston Churchill was absolutely correct.

This concludes the narrative about the many ways in which the Israelites and the Jews left the land of ancient Palestine. Had God abandoned them? Of course not. God still had many promises of the Abrahamic covenant to fulfill in their descendants. While the Jews (from Judah) have been traceable throughout history, there is a common misconception that the ten tribes of Israel "disappeared" after they left Israel. That misconception has no support in biblical accounts or secular historical records. There are many accounts documenting their subsequent history, as we will see.

God had not forgotten his Covenant obligations toward the ten tribes of Israel, the "birthright" progeny of Abraham who were destined to inherit the best blessings of God's covenant with Abraham. Indeed, Hosea 1:6-10 prophesied that after the ten tribes of Israel were removed from Palestine, God would so multiply their population that their descendants would be too numerous to count, fulfilling God's promise to Abraham. In the following chapters and books, we shall trace the history of the descendants of the ten tribes of Israel **after** they left Palestine. We shall see that God literally fulfilled the promises He made to Abraham and the ten tribes of Israel!

To set the stage for the next chapters, it is vital to point out that there was a major cultural and religious separation between the various branches of Israelites who left Palestine. We have seen evidence that the Israelites who migrated northward to the Black Sea region tried again to serve Yahweh, the God of Israel. They forsook the Phoenician culture and the evil customs of Baal worship. However, those Israelites who migrated by sea to Phoenicia's colonies in the western Mediterranean retained the Baal and mother-goddess worship that permeated Carthage and the other Phoenician colonies.

Those Israelites who migrated to the Black Sea region had plenty of available room for expansion on the steppes of southern Russia. When these descendants of the ten tribes of Israel reappear in history, they burst forth as a conquering horde! However, that story must wait for chapter four. Chapter three will first examine the history of the largest Mediterranean refuge of the ten tribes of Israel...Carthage!

ENDNOTES: CHAPTER TWO

1.Encyclopedia Americana, Vol. 2, see "Assyria," p. 537
2.Keller, Werner, The Bible as History, p. 230
3.Ibid., p. 230
4.Ibid., p. 230
5.Harper's Bible Dictionary, see "Omri," pp. 729-730
6.Hannay, Herbert, European and Other Race Origins, p. 19
7. The Open Bible, King James Version, I Kings 16:33, p. 350
8.Harper's Bible Dictionary, Heading entitled "Grove," p. 361
9.Young's Analytical Concordance, Heading entitled "Grove," subhead two, p. 439
10.Rawlinson, George, Phoenicia, p. 107-117
11.Ibid., pp. 112-114
12.Fell, America B.C., pp. 261-268
13.Ibid., p. 263
14.Collier's Encyclopedia, Vol. 10, Heading entitled "Iberian," pp. 323-324
15.Fell, America B.C., pp. 262-263
16.Ibid., pp. 219-245
17.Ibid., pp. 236-243
18.Ibid., p. 240
19.Ibid., p. 226
20.Rawlinson, George, Phoenicia, p. 3
21.Ibid., p. 63
22.Church, Carthage, p. 11
23.Ibid., p. 11
24.Rawlinson, George, Phoenicia, p. 116
25.Williams, Larry, The Mount Sinai Myth, pp. 100-101 and photograph 4 (between pages 96 and 97)

26.Encyclopedia Britannica, Vol. 20, Heading entitled "Shalmaneser," p. 454

27.Keller, The Bible as History, p. 212

28.Ibid., p. 231

29.Encyclopedia Britannica, Vol. 20, see "Shalmaneser," p. 454

30.Encyclopedia Britannica, Vol. 13, Heading entitled "Jews," subhead "The dynasty of Omri," pp. 45-46

31.Ceram, C.W., The March of Archaeology, p. 216

32.Gordon, Before Columbus, p. 137

33. Harper's Bible Dictionary, Heading entitled "Gozan," p. 357

34. Halley's Bible Handbook, p. 151

35. Keller, The Bible As History," p. 244

36.Ibid., p. 246

37.Dictionary of Christ and the Gospels, Charles Scribner's Sons, New York, Vol. 1, see "Greeks," p, 692

38.Allen, Judah's Sceptre and Joseph's Birthright, pp. 266-268

39.Lawless, Ireland, pp. 8-9

40.Allen, p. 275

41.Coleman, "De Danaan blends new and old for great Irish sound," Minneapolis Star & Tribune, March 3, 1986, page 2C

42.U.S. News and World Report Magazine, March 30, 1987, p. 7

43.Lawless, Emily, Ireland, p. 9

44.Sullivan, A.M., The Story of Ireland, pp. 12-13

45.Ibid., pp. 12-13

46.Ibid., p. 14

47.Mitchel, John, History of Ireland, p. 62

48.Sullivan, p. 12

49.Moore, Thomas, History of Ireland, p. 3

50.Dawkins, W. Boyd, Early Man in Britain, p. 319

51.Sammes, Aylett, Britannia, pp. 11, 61

52.Rhys, J. Celtic Britain, p. 142

53.Allen, p. 275

54.Ibid., p. 275

55.Encyclopedia Americana, Vol. 6, Heading entitled "Celtiberia," p. 143

56.Herm, The Celts, pp. 251-252

57.Encyclopedia Americana, Vol. 13, Heading entitled "Hallstatt Culture," p. 726

58.Harrison, Richard, Spain at the Dawn of History, p. 10

59.Ibid., p. 15

60.Ibid., p. 41

61.Ibid., pp. 154-156

62.Gawler, Our Scythian Ancestors Identified With Israel, p. 9

63.Ibid., p. 9, quoting M. Sailman's 1818 book, Researches in the East:, an important account of the Ten Tribes

64.Goodspeed, The Apocrypha, (II Esdras), p. 93

65.Gawler, p. 9

66.Ibid., p. 9

67.Rawlinson, The Sixth Great Oriental Monarchy, map between pages 78 and 79

68.Hannay, European and Other Race origins, p. 56

69.Encyclopedia Americana, Vol. 2, Heading entitled "Armenia," p. 331

70.Keller, p. 260

71.Ibid., p. 259

72.Ibid., pp. 260-262

73.Allen, p. 228

74.Ibid., pp. 228-229, 249-251

75.Dobson, The Rev. Cyril C., The Mystery of the Fate of the Ark of the Covenant, p. 77

76.Connon, F. Wallace, The Stone of Destiny, p. 31

77.Ibid., p. 40

78.Dobson, p. 75

79.Encyclopedia Americana, Vol. 13, see "Harp," p. 807

80.Connon, F. Wallace, The Stone of Destiny, p. 17 (citing Churchill's essay on Moses in Thoughts and Adventures)

The City Of Carthage At The Height Of Its Glory
Portion of a painting by Ruth Amelia Lincoln

Chapter 3
Carthage - Israel's Colony that became an Empire

The previous chapter asserted that Carthage was a colony of the kingdom of Israel, founded in the ninth century B.C. during the extreme drought caused by the prayer of Elijah. In this chapter, much evidence will be presented to support that assertion. This chapter will also examine Carthage's history: its rise to empire status, its presence in ancient America, and its eventual decay and collapse. At one point, Carthage's empire included portions of several continents — Africa, Europe and the ancient Americas — and it almost destroyed Rome, its archrival. Carthage was a great empire; its scope and power has not been appreciated in the modern world.

The Israelite Origins of Carthage

In the ninth century B.C., the kingdom of Israel was devastated by a prolonged drought. It came as a result of Elijah's prayer for divine punishment on Isracl's adoption of the libertine and murderous practices of Baal worship. The drought also affected the Baal-worshipping city-states of Tyre and Sidon, which had been allied to Israel since the reign of King David. This alliance was particularly close during this drought, as Israel's King Ahab was married to a daughter of Sidon's king. The Sidonian princess who became the queen of Israel was named Jezebel, and her name still serves as synonym for evil even today. The Bible describes this period of Israel's history in I Kings 16:29 to 22:40.

God did not bring this drought upon Israel in a fit of divine pique. He intervenes personally to punish nations at times in an effort to wake them up spiritually to deliver them from their self-destructive sins. Israel had embraced Baalism, a religion that eventually destroys its adherents by its own excesses. Baalism's sexual hedonism destroys the family units on which the strength of any nation is built, and its grisly rites of human sacrifice were especially degenerate. By using the drought to focus Israel's attention on the national cancer of Baal worship, God was doing Israel a favor.

It is indicative of the stubbornness of King Ahab and Israel's leaders that they endured the ravages of the drought for years rather than forsake their evil practices. As noted in the previous chapter, many Israelites rejected Baalism and relocated to the kingdom of Judah where King Jehoshaphat led his kingdom in obeying God. In order to avoid starvation for its remaining population during the drought, Israel had to export sizeable contingents of its population elsewhere. While Israel, Tyre and Sidon could relocate their citizens anywhere in the Phoenician Empire, which included colonies in Africa, Spain and the British Isles, it would have been difficult and costly to relocate whole

REMAINS OF ANCIENT HARBOURS AT CARTHAGE

communities to distant locations. It was logical to find a closer location that was unaffected by the drought to resettle a large portion of Israel's refugees. Israel, Tyre and Sidon had colonies and trading posts along the North African coast, but none apparently could quickly accommodate so large an influx of people.

Israel needed a new colony, suitable for accommodating large numbers of its hungry population. It needed to be distant enough to be unaffected by the drought, yet close enough to avoid the hardships and risks of long voyages. Since the colony would receive many sea-borne immigrants, it had to include harbor facilities that would accommodate many ships simultaneously. The *Universal Jewish Encyclopedia* states the following about the founding of Carthage:

> "**it was founded about 840 B.C.E...Dido, the Phoenician Queen who is said to have founded the city, was reported to have been the grandniece of Jezebel, the wife of [King] Ahab of Israel**. The native name of the city [was] Karta Hadasha...the language of the inhabitants of Carthage was very close to Hebrew...**the names of important Carthaginians are similar to biblical characters**...Barka, the surname of Hamilcar, is the same as Barak, and Hannibal is of the same formation as Hananiah..."[1] *(Emphasis added)*

It was during the rule of Ahab and Jezebel that the drought of Elijah occurred, and a Jewish record exists that Dido, a relative of King Ahab and Queen Jezebel of the Kingdom of Israel, founded Carthage! The *Encyclopedia Britannica* states:

> "**Carthage was founded about 850 B.C.** by...emigrants led by Elissa, the daughter of the Tyrian king...Elissa subsequently received the name of Dido."[2] *(Emphasis added)*

It would be normal to have a member of the royal house of a founding kingdom to have one of its members, Princess "Dido" or "Elissa," serve as the initial head of a new colony. Carthage began as a "crown colony" of Israel — i.e. "Phoenicia." The above account notes the unmistakable Hebrew nature of the language and names of Carthage. Carthage was likely founded as a temporary camp for refugees from the terrible drought affecting Israel. The need to move many Israelites out of their home country was a very pressing one, and Carthage was much closer to Israel, Tyre and Sidon than the more-distant Phoenician colonies in Spain and the British Isles. The above two accounts date the founding of Carthage to 850-840 B.C., very close to the traditional time of Elijah's drought and the rule of Ahab and Jezebel over Israel. Because the drought in Israel was the singular event requiring the relocation of many Israelites in the middle of the ninth century B.C., this book concludes it was the motivation for the initial founding of Carthage.

Carthage may have been abandoned when Israel's drought ended, and its evacuees were able to return home to their usual lives and ancestral properties. However, as the Assyrian threat loomed larger, Carthage later was developed into a permanent colony, offering ready sanctuary to those who fled from Israel. As repeated Assyrian invasions sounded the death-knell of Israel, the immigration of Israelites into Carthage would have accelerated.

Another traditional date for the founding of Carthage is 814-812 B.C., but it is not known conclusively when Carthage became a permanent colony. Maitland Edey, in *The Sea Traders*, wrote that the earliest known artifacts at Carthage were dated to 735 B.C.[3] This date offers remarkable symmetry with events in the kingdom of Israel. That date corresponds to the time in Israel when the Assyrians had invaded Israel and carried captive the tribes of Naphthali, Reuben, Gad and half of Manasseh. *(II Kings 15:27-29)* Israel's demise was then imminent, and its people began to flee elsewhere to avoid an Assyrian captivity.

This new colony was planted on the north coast of Africa, and given the Hebrew name Kirjath-Hadeschath, which historian Alfred Church translates as "New Town."[4] The name "Kirjath" is a Hebrew word for "city,"[5] and it appears frequently in the Bible. Israelite cities in the Bible included Kirjathaim, Kirjath-arba, Kirjath-jearim, Kirjath-sepher and Kirjath-sannah *(Numbers 32:37, Joshua 15:15, 15:49, 20:7 and I Samuel 7:1).* That this new Israelite colony would be named "New City" or "New Town" was very appropriate. Since the city-states of Tyre, Sidon, etc. were closely allied to Israel, there were undoubtedly Tyrians and Sidonians among the colonizers of Kirjath-Hadeschath as well.

The Israelites who settled "Kirjath" came from the kingdom of Israel, the ten-tribed Israelite nation to the north of the Jewish kingdom of Judah. As discussed in the previous chapter, Judah was then ruled by King Jehoshaphat, who had banned Baalism. Since the drought was on Baal worshippers, and the Bible confirms that Judah sup-

SEVEN-BRANCHED LAMP (*Douimès*)

ported a huge influx of Israelites during the drought, it is clear that Judah was not affected by the drought plaguing Israel, Tyre and Sidon. Judah had no need to join Israel in founding Carthage. Therefore, Kirjath-Hadeschath was an Israelite settlement, not a Jewish one. Since both Israel and Judah spoke Hebrew, it is easy to misunderstand the origins of Kirjath unless it is realized that its founders were Hebrews from the northern kingdom of Israel, not the southern kingdom of Judah.

While the immigrants called their new city by the Hebrew word "Kirjath," the Greeks called it "Karchedon," and the Romans called it "Carthago."[6] Greece and Rome were the enemies of Carthage. Since modern concepts about the ancient world come from Greco-Roman sources, we today refer to this ancient Hebrew city as "Carthage," the name given to it by its enemies.

Many who have written about Carthage's history, such as Alfred Church, Gilbert and Colette Charles-Picard, and B.H. Warmington, have commented that the chief magistrates of Carthage were called the "shophetim," a Hebrew word for "Judges."[7] Gilbert and Colette Charles-Picard make this observation:

> "...the executive power was shared by two shofetim. This title, which the Romans translated as suffetes, means 'judges.' **It was the title borne by the elders of the people of Israel** before institution of the monarchy."[8] *(Emphasis added)*

Another historian, R. Bosworth Smith, adds the following:

> "...two supreme magistrates [were] called by the Romans Suffetes. **Their name is the same as the Hebrew Shofetim**...The Hamilcars and Hannos of Carthage were, like their prototypes, the Gideons and the Samsons of the Book of Judges, not so much their judges, as the protectors and the rulers of their respective states."[9] *(Emphasis added)*

Why did Carthage's leaders have Israelite titles unless they were relocated Israelites? It is significant that Carthaginian leaders called themselves "judges" instead of "kings." This makes sense when one realizes that Carthage began as a "crown colony" of Israel. Hence its true king for at least the first century of its existence was the reigning king of Israel.

Some Carthaginian rulers called themselves "kings" in the years after the fall of Israel. One Carthaginian with the title "king" was named Malchus.[10] Malchus is a Hebrew name, and it was still in use at the time of Christ. *(John 18:10)* The name "Malchus" is clearly based on the Hebrew word "melek," which means, "king." A prominent member of the Hamilcars, a ruling family of Carthage, bore a famous Hebrew name. Historian Alfred Church writes:

> "One of the Hamilcars...bore the surname of **Barca**, and Barca is the same as the Hebrew **Barak**..."[11] *(Emphasis added)*

The fact that some Carthaginian leaders were named after prominent Israelite leaders raises the possibility that they were actually descended from the noble families of ancient Israel. That would explain their hereditary prominence in Carthage.

One observation by Church illustrates how deep is the misconception that all ancient Hebrew-speaking people were Jews. He notes:

> "these resemblances of Carthaginian and Hebrew names are very interesting, and show us how close was the kindred between the Jews and the...Phoenician tribes, enemies to each other though they mostly were."[12]

When it is realized that the "Phoenician tribes" who settled Carthage, with Hebrew names and titles, were not Jews but rather

Israelites of the northern ten-tribed kingdom of Israel, the puzzle is solved. The Bible confirms that Israel and Judah (the Jews) were enemies during most of their common existence. The Jews of the kingdom of Judah were not Phoenician allies. However, the Hebrew-speakers of the Northern Kingdom of Israel were closely joined to Tyre and Sidon in the "Phoenician" alliance. Therefore, the "close kindred" noted above between Carthaginians and Hebrews was because most Carthaginians were Israelites from the northern ten tribes.

Further evidence of the Israelite origins of Carthage is in the name of Carthage's priests. Carthage's priests were called the "**Kohanim**," and the high priest was called the "**Rab Kohanim**" (called "cohen" and "rab cohenim" by B.H. Warmington).[13] In these terms, we can clearly see the Hebrew root word for the term **Rabbi** and such modern Jewish names as Kahn, Cohen, and Kahane. The Hebrew-Carthaginian word **Kohanim** simply means "priests," and the word **Rab** means "great," "mighty" or "elder."[14]

Gilbert and Colette Charles-Picard note that the sacred priestly law of the Carthaginian Kohanim with its instructions on animal sacrifices, libations, and other priestly rites bear **"a very significant resemblance to the Book of Leviticus."[15]** They further note that "the Great God **El** was invoked exclusively under the name of Baal Hammon, which means 'the Lord of the altars where incense burns'...[and many burnt offerings and sacrifices]... **correspond exactly to those of the Hebrews."[16]** The divine name "El" is one of the Hebrew names for the God of Israel.[17] *Daily Life in Carthage*, by Gilbert and Colette Charles-Picard, includes a photograph of a stele depicting Baal Hammon (El) sitting on a throne of winged cherubim.[18] The God of Israel is described as the one who "dwells between the cherubim." *(I Samuel 4:4 and Psalm 80:1)*

That the Carthaginians included the God of Israel in their pantheon is significant. Since the early settlers of Carthage were aware of the divine origin of the drought upon their homeland of Israel, they likely tried to appease a God who had such power. Eventually, "El" became just another name in their pantheon of gods, but for a time, the early Carthaginians paid some homage to the God of Israel.

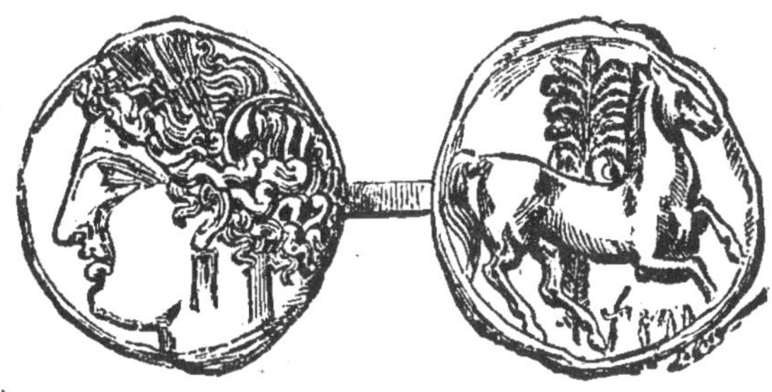

CARTHAGINIAN COIN (ELECTRUM).

Unfortunately, their roots in Baalism were so deep that the laws of God were eventually subordinated to the customs of Baalism. Their sacrificial offerings eventually included human, not just animal, sacrifices due to the contagion of Baalism. Since Baalism was Israel's religion at the time of the great drought and the founding of Carthage, it is not surprising that Baalism became the dominant religion of Carthage.

The historian, George Rawlinson, made the following observations on the unity of the Hebrew and Punic (Carthaginian) languages:

> "...the Phoenicians spoke a Semitic tongue, very closely allied to the Hebrew...the ancients, Jerome, Augustine, and Priscian, state the fact in the clearest terms. The inscriptions that exist confirm it. The ...inscriptions are...readily explicable, if Hebrew be assumed as the key to them, but not otherwise...**A good Hebrew scholar has no difficulty in understanding any legible Phoenician inscription**...the passage in the Poenulus of Plautus, **commonly called Phoenician, belong rather to the literature of Carthage**."[19] *(Emphasis added)*

At times, Carthaginians — the "Punic" people — are referred to as "Western Phoenicians" because they were Phoenicians who resettled in the western part of the Mediterranean Sea. For this reason, Carthaginian inscriptions are at times called "Phoenician," as Rawlinson noted above. The *McClintock and Strong Cyclopedia of Biblical, Theological and Ecclesiastical Literature* adds:

> "**There is no doubt that the Carthaginians and Phoenicians were the same race**...the Carthaginian extract is undeniably intelligible through Hebrew to Hebrew scholars...the close kinship of the two languages is...strikingly confirmed by very many Phoenician and Carthaginian names of places and persons which...become really significant in Hebrew..."[20] *(Emphasis added)*

The above evidence abundantly establishes the Hebrew-Israelite origin of the ancient people we today call the Carthaginians. The *Encyclopedia Judaica* also refers to a Hebrew role in the founding of Carthage,[21] although it makes no differentiation between the two separate Hebrew kingdoms that existed at that time. Biblical accounts of the great drought reveal that the "Hebrew" role in the founding of Carthage came from the Northern Kingdom of Israel, not the Jews of Judah. The *Encyclopedia Judaica* confirms that "there is no evidence of Jews in Carthage during the Punic period (before 146 B.C.E.)."[22] Given the fact that Carthage's early history from the ninth century B.C is permeated with Hebrew names and terms, the avowed absence of a Jewish role during those centuries can only mean that the Hebrew origins of Carthage resulted from its colonization by the ten-tribed kingdom of Israel.

It has been noted that the first two centuries of Carthage were "veiled in obscurity."[23] Part of that time, Carthage (or Kirjath) lived in the shadow of its mother country, Israel. While Carthage was Israel's colony, it did not possess its own sovereignty. It was "obscure" because it was dominated by Israel. It is only after the end of the kingdom of Israel in Palestine that Carthage asserted an independent identity in world affairs.

When the Northern Kingdom of Israel fell, a dispute arose between Judah and Carthage over rights to Israel's former territory. The *Encyclopedia Judaica* records that the "Africans [Carthaginians] are also described as disputing with Israelites the title to the ownership of Erez [the land of] Israel."[24] The *Judaica* account refers to the Jewish residents of Judah as the "Israelites" who disputed with Carthage over rights to the land of Israel. The Jews were Israelites in a racial sense as they were one of the tribes who descended from "Israel," the man whose original name was "Jacob." But in a political sense, the Jews of Judah had not been known by the term "Israel" for centuries. That term referred only to the northern ten tribes of Israel.

Judah's claim to the land of Israel was based on the fact their Davidic dynasty had ruled over that land before Israel and Judah became separate nations. Carthage's claim to Israel's territory was understandable since they were the relatives of the Israelites who had abandoned the land to Assyria's army. Judah's claim was based on dynastic precedent, while Carthage's claims were based on the rights of kinsmen. Both claims were moot, however. Neither Carthage nor Judah could challenge Assyria, and Assyria decided to populate Israel's abandoned land as they saw fit. *(II Kings 17:24-31)*

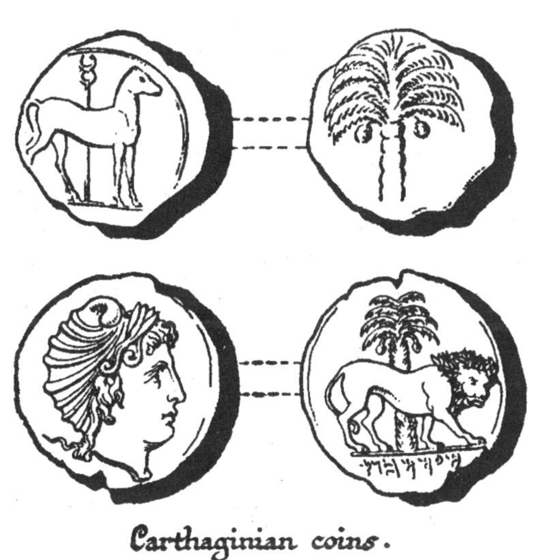

Carthaginian coins.

Carthage Rallies Israel's Colonies To Oppose Greece

After the fall of their mother country, Israel, Carthage had to fend for itself in the world. As the largest Israelite colony in the Mediterranean region, Carthage assumed a leadership position among the remaining "Phoenician" settlements. With Israel's power absent from the Mediterranean, many Phoenician-Israelite settlements soon became untenable and were absorbed by a new power.

The new power in the Eastern Mediterranean was Greece. One account states of this time: "The Greeks took advantage of this eclipse [in Phoenician power] and from 750 to 500 B.C., against little opposition, they drove out the Phoenicians and poured thousands of their own emigrants into Eastern Sicily, into the South of Italy, into Southern Provence and even into Andalusia and Cyrenaica, thus completely encircling the Carthaginian territory."[25] The "eclipse" of Phoenician power coincides precisely with the decline and fall of the kingdom of Israel, which was in its death throes from 750-721 B.C. When Israel fell, Greece filled the void.

The areas vacated by the "Phoenicians" give us an insight into just how widespread was the Israelite dominance of the Mediterranean prior to Israel's demise. Carthage grew in strength, as it became the redoubt to which displaced "Phoenicians" fled. This infusion of refugees into Carthage is described as follows:

> "The Carthaginians...**had already been reinforced on several occasions by refugees from the besieged metropolis of Tyre** and now rallied all the colonists driven from Lixus and Gades, beyond the Pillars of Hercules, to Malta, by way of Sardinia and Western Sicily, in organized resistance to the common enemy."[26] *(Emphasis added)*

Since historians acknowledge Carthage received refugees from Tyre when it was threatened, it is equally apparent that Carthage had also received waves of Israelite refugees from the kingdom of Israel, Tyre's ally, during its calamity at the hand of Assyria.

Due to the influx of many "Phoenician" refugees, Carthage became strong soon after the fall of Israel. Gilbert and Colette Charles-Picard cite Herodotus in asserting that Carthage had attained by 650 B.C. a "rich and powerful....adult status."[27] In other words, Carthage became an independent power within one lifetime of the fall of Samaria. Smarting from their expulsions from former colonies, the Mediterranean Israelites fought back, with allied refugees from Tyre and Sidon. In the 6th century B.C., Carthaginian counterattacks against the Greeks took back Corsica and western North Africa. Sicily became a frequent battleground for Greco-Carthaginian wars.In 409 B.C., the Carthaginians conquered a Greek city in Sicily using classic Assyrian war tactics. The Carthaginians used siege towers and battering rams, and Carthage's mercenaries were as cruel as the Assyrians after their victory. Historian B. H. Warmington wrote the following about this battle:

> "...the Carthaginians had inherited from their Phoenician homeland the techniques of siege warfare which had been a feature of the ancient Assyrian Empire."[28]

Where did Carthage learn about Assyrian battle tactics? The answer is simple. Carthage's ancestors in the kingdom of Israel had been the frequent targets of Assyrian battle tactics. The Carthaginian generals remembered and copied them.

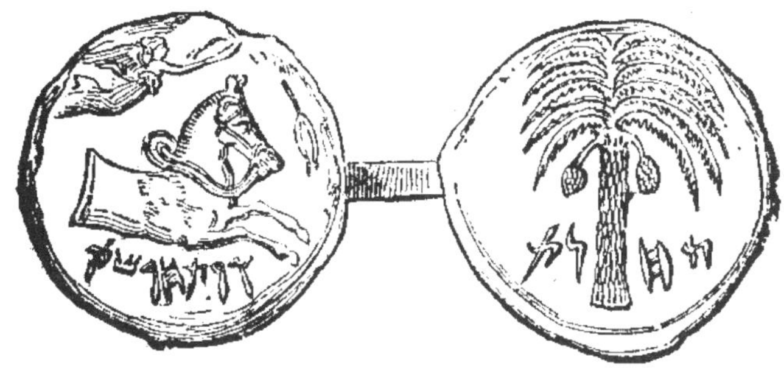

CARTHAGINIAN COIN.

Carthage became so dominant in the Western Mediterranean that they barred Greek passages through the Pillars of Hercules (Gibraltar), making Carthage "the Queen of the Western Seas."[29] Carthage's ability to prevent Greek access to the Atlantic Ocean had a very significant impact on both the ancient and modern worlds, as we shall see later in this chapter.

The Phoenician colony at Gades in Iberia (Spain) allied itself to Carthage when Carthage rescued Gades in a local war."[30] This was a logical alliance as both Gades and Carthage shared a Phoenician-Israelite origin. When Tyre fell to King Nebuchadnezzar in 574 B.C., more refugees migrated to Carthage.[31] For centuries, Carthage served as a refuge for Semitic people who fled Palestine by sea to avoid Assyrian or Babylonian invasions.

The Greco-Carthaginian conflicts divided the Mediterranean Sea into separate spheres of influence, with Carthage dominant in the West and Greece dominant in the East. As the centuries passed, the Romans supplanted the Greeks, becoming the new archenemy of the Carthaginians. In the early centuries of their rivalry, Carthage had the upper hand. Early treaties between the two show the stronger Carthaginians arrogantly dictating terms to the weaker Romans. In a treaty dated 348 B.C., Carthage forbade the Romans even to trade with certain Western Mediterranean areas, and ordered the Romans not to land in Sardinia and parts of Africa unless it was to take on provisions or repair their ships.[32] Carthage could be haughty even with its own allies. Its propensity for arrogance would become a factor in Carthage's undoing.

Carthage continued to blockade the Pillars of Hercules with its powerful navy, permitting neither Greeks nor Romans to sail into the Atlantic Ocean. In fact, when one Greek mariner named Pytheas finally sailed into the Atlantic around 300 B.C., it was an unprecedented event! It has been suggested that the Carthaginians permitted Pytheas to make his voyage in order to placate the Macedonian Empire founded by Alexander the Great.[33] Another explanation is that the Carthaginian ships guarding Gibraltar had left to join an immense fleet of ships supporting an invasion of Sicily. [34] Carthage pioneered the tactic of amphibious invasions of a seacoast from a naval fleet. There is a record that the Carthaginians once invaded Sicily with a force of 100,000 soldiers who disembarked from 1,500 transport vessels escorted by 60 warships.[35] This huge maritime invasion was an ancient counterpart to the sea-borne invasions performed in World War II by the Allies in Normandy and all across the Pacific theater by the American navy.

Whatever the reason for his unusual access to the Atlantic, Pytheas sailed to western and northern European coasts previously unvisited by the Greeks. Pytheas marveled that the positions of the constellations changed as he traveled north, giving the Greeks a hint that the world was a sphere. As Dr. Barry Fell noted: "Never before had any [Greek] navigator been able to sail so far north; Carthaginian commercial interests would not permit it."[36]

In the ancient world, Carthage was so powerful that when a Greek mariner gained access to the Atlantic Ocean, it was an historic event! What was remarkable new knowledge to the Greeks — that the earth was spherical — had been common knowledge to Carthage and to Phoenicia for about a millennium! After the voyage of Pytheas, Greco-Romans were again barred from the Atlantic, and later Greek cartographers came to regard the observations of Pytheas as fictional.[37] Phoenician-Carthaginian knowledge in the fields of world geography, maritime navigation and astral science was approximately one thousand years ahead of the Greeks. Modern history texts teach as fact the ancient Greco-Roman propaganda that they were the "civilized" nations and all others were "barbarians." Our history texts are wrong. In some fields of scientific knowledge, other nations were far superior to Greece and Rome.

Because Carthage long denied Greece and Rome any access to the world's oceans, the Greeks and Romans had a very limited view of the world. The geographical knowledge of Greece and Rome was limited to the Mediterranean region, and those parts of Asia and Europe within marching distance of their armies. This has immense implications for modern perceptions about ancient civilizations.

Modern versions of ancient history are taught almost exclusively from a Greco-Roman perspective. People are taught to assume that no one in the ancient world knew anything until someone in the Greco-Roman world learned it for the first time. This assumption has given the modern world woeful misunderstandings about the ancient world. Since Greece and Rome were land empires rather than maritime empires like Phoenicia and Carthage, the Greeks and Romans were profoundly ignorant of knowledge long possessed by Israel, Tyre, Sidon and Carthage. Greece and Rome were unfamiliar with North America, South America, the northern European region and other places reachable only by long-range ocean travel. Modern history texts teach the false notion that nobody in the ancient world knew about these places until the Greeks or Romans finally learned about them! **In fact, Carthage, and Israel-Phoenicia before them, explored, colonized and exploited the ancient Americas centuries before the Greeks and Romans had access to the New World.**

The Carthaginians did not want the Greeks or Romans to learn about the wealth of North America and other places accessible only to a maritime power. That is why they went to great pains to keep the Greeks and Romans "shut out" of the Atlantic Ocean. They retained the obvious commercial advantages that a monopoly over the Atlantic coastlands gave them. If the ancient Carthaginians could have known that over two millennia into the future, nations would be teaching their schoolchildren that no one in the ancient "Old World" knew about the New World because the Greeks and Romans didn't know about it, the Carthaginians would have roared with laughter! Indeed, if Carthage had defeated Rome, instead of vice versa, later European civilizations would never have inherited the unscientific Greco-Roman belief that the world was flat!

RUINS OF THE TEMPLE OF BAAL HAMMON OR MOLECH

This does not imply that the Greeks and Romans were ignorant or unskilled people. They excelled in many areas. However, modern assumptions about the ancient world have been based on ancient Greco-Roman propaganda rather than on actual physical evidence about the ancient world. This series of books about Israelite history reveals evidence that the truth about the ancient world is much different than has previously been assumed. Let us now examine the real extent of the Carthaginian Empire.

Carthaginian Colonies in Europe and the Ancient Americas

We already know that Carthage was dominant in the western Mediterranean regions of Spain and North Africa. Sardinia, Western Sicily, and other areas of the western Mediterranean were frequently under their control. However, the maritime commercial empire of Carthage extended far beyond Gibraltar. Carthage had inherited Phoenician commercial contacts in Europe, and they were involved with the British tin trade, and the amber trade of the Baltic Sea area.[38] This would place the Carthaginian traders as far north as Poland and the Baltic States. While this was not a part of their physical empire, it shows that Carthage's commercial empire included the regions of northern and western Europe. One historian wrote in 1878 that:

> "The Celtic harbors teemed with the craft of...Carthage ...For several centuries, the Carthaginians...used the harbors of Spain, of Gaul, even of Erin [Ireland] and Britain, as their own. The Celtic inhabitants of those countries allowed them to settle peacefully among them, to trade with them, to use their cities as emporiums... [Carthage] does not appear to have made war on the inhabitants in order to occupy it...they always lived on peaceful terms with the [native Celts] whom they benefited by their trade..."[39]

This highlights a stark contrast between Carthaginian and Roman priorities. While the "business" of Rome was to build an empire founded on military conquest, the "business" of Carthage was "business" itself. Carthage was intensely capitalistic and sought commercial profit with other nations, attempting to link them to their commercial empire. Rome sought to conquer people militarily, but Carthage sought to dominate people economically!

TOWER OF ERYX AT CARTHAGE

PORT OF CARTHAGE (FROM SARCOPHAGI).

Carthaginian commercial pursuits led to an ancient predecessor of the paper money of the modern world. It was called "leather money" and Alfred Church, in his 1890 book, *Carthage*, cited a Greek disciple of Socrates for this information:

> "'The Carthaginians...make use of the following kind of money: in a small piece of leather a substance is wrapped...After this it is sealed and issued for circulation; and he who possesses the most of this is regarded as having the most money...' The seal was a State mark. We have, in fact, here a kind of clumsy banknote."[40]

Carthage also had a strong presence in an area that few modern readers would ever have guessed: ancient America! In his book, *Atlantic Crossings before Columbus*, Frederick Pohl cites ancient Greek accounts of a land beyond Gibraltar, which can only be ancient America. The first account cites the writings of Aristotle:

> "In the sea outside the Pillars of Hercules...an island was found by the Carthaginians, a wilderness having wood of all kinds

> and **navigable rivers**...**many days' sailing distance away**. When the Carthaginians [the] **masters of the Western Ocean**, observed that many traders and other men, attracted by the **fertility of the soil and the pleasant climate**, frequented it...and some resided there, **they feared that knowledge of the land would reach other nations**...Therefore, lest the Carthaginian Empire itself should suffer injury, and the dominion of the sea be wrested from their hands, the Senate of Carthage issued a decree that no one [else], under penalty of death, should thereafter sail thither..."[41] *(Emphasis added)*

Aristotle's reference to an important Carthaginian colony "many days sailing distance" across the "western ocean" could only indicate ancient America! Aristotle lived in the fourth century B.C., a time when Greek knowledge of the world beyond Gibraltar was limited to whatever Carthage wanted them to know or whatever Greek spies could ascertain from Carthaginian sources — perhaps drunken Carthaginian sailors on shore leave. The only land many days sailing time west of Gibraltar, the Pillars of Hercules, large enough to have navigable inner rivers, fertile soil, forests, and a pleasant climate was ancient America. To safeguard their monopoly on such a rich territory, Carthage used every means at its disposal to keep others away from it. Carthage was determined to keep the Greeks and Romans out of the Atlantic; they did not wish those nations to find out about (or tap) the riches of North America. The second account is from Diodorus, a Greek historian of the first century B.C. It is as follows:

> "Over against Africa lies a **very great island in the vast ocean, many days sail from Lybia westward**. The **soil there is very fruitful**, a great part whereof is **mountainous**, but much likewise is a **plain...watered with several navigable rivers**...the mountainous part of the country is clothed with **very large woods**, and all manner of fruit trees and springs of fresh water... there you may have game enough **in hunting all sorts of wild beasts**..."[42] *(Emphasis added)*

This Greek writer lived after Carthage fell so Greek awareness of the New World had become more detailed. The "very great island" westward in the same latitude as Lybia was ancient North America, with its forests, mountain ranges and a vast inner plain with navigable rivers. When one follows the same latitude as Libya westward across the Atlantic Ocean, one comes to the southern portion of North America. A Roman writer of the second century A.D., Claudius Aeliannus, also commented that the existence of a marvelous land to the west was "a definite tradition of the Carthaginians or Phoenicians of Gades."[43]

When Carthage fell, many Punic cities survived in North Africa by cooperating with the Romans in attacking Carthage. These Punic cities likely provided the navigators for the few Roman ships which did attempt the Atlantic crossing. Rhys Carpenter's book, *Beyond the Pillars of Heracles*, states:

> "...with the utter collapse of the Carthaginian empire...in 146 B.C., the western seaways were open to all...Yet little or nothing is recorded of any Greek or Roman explorer taking advantage of this opportunity to navigate the open Atlantic..."[44]

Some Roman coins and artifacts have been found in the New World, and even in Iceland,[45] but it is apparent Rome made no serious effort to develop the New World. The Roman coins and artifacts found in the Americas may have been brought by Roman expatriates or dissidents who had to flee the Old World for their own safety. We will see evidence later in this chapter about one such group.

The late Dr. Barry Fell's book, *Saga America*, documents the finding of Carthaginian coins, artifacts and inscriptions in the American states of Alabama, Connecticut, New York, Colorado, Kansas, Oklahoma and Nevada.[46] Dr. Fell, a Professor Emeritus of Harvard University and the founder of The Epigraphic Society, notes that Carthaginian coins found in America date primarily to the period of the fourth and third centuries B.C., prior to the First Punic War with Rome.[47] He postulates that, during the above period, Carthage's gold and much of the timber for the construction of its naval vessels came from ancient North and South America.[48] A previous chapter documented that Phoenicia and Carthage tapped the iron ore resources of ancient Brazil, which even today is known by the word "barzel" (B-R-Z-L), the Hebrew word for "iron." Symbols of Carthage included a horse's head and a palm tree. Carthaginian coins preserving both themes have been found in Alabama and Connecticut, and a Carthaginian horse-head sculpture was unearthed in North Salem, New York.[49]

During the final Punic Wars, ancient America likely became the refuge for some Carthaginians fleeing the Romans. The discovery in Georgia of an atlatl stone (a spear-hurling device) with a Punic (Carthaginian) inscription from the second century B.C. supports the view that more Carthaginians arrived then. Dr. Fell confirmed the Hebrew roots of the Carthaginian inscription by writing:

> "As no adequate Punic dictionary exists, we are always obliged to deduce the sense from corresponding words in Hebrew."[50]

Dr. Fell further observed in *Saga America* that:

> "The Punic language can be read without difficulty, as it is similar to ancient Hebrew..."[51]

Carthage was famous for its wealth! R. Bosworth Smith's book, *Carthage and the Carthaginians*, states that "Carthage was, beyond doubt, the richest city of antiquity."[52] No wonder! They exploited the resources of the New World while shutting out all rivals. Carthage monopolized the resources of the New World and the maritime commercial routes, so it profited from an ancient "global economy" in which Greece and Rome did not share.

We cannot know the full extent of the Carthaginian presence in ancient America. It was certainly wide-ranging, given the locations of Carthaginian artifacts found on American soil. We know that they thoroughly explored ancient America as Greek accounts of North America — accurately listing such features as mountain ranges, plains, forests, and navigable rivers — were based on Carthaginian records. Carthage did not "occupy" ancient America to expand their empire. They explored America to locate natural resources they could exploit for their commercial advantage. They also had a monopoly on commercial relations with New World cultures.

Another Greek account gives an insight into the size of Carthage's presence in ancient North America. Dr. Nigel Davies, in his book *Voyagers to the New World*, cites an account of Herodotus that the Carthaginians mounted an expedition of 30,000 men and women in 60 ships in 500-480 B.C., and sent them westward into the Atlantic toward an unknown destination. Dr. Davies observes aptly that this "resembles a migration more than a mere expedition."[53] The above data indicates that this Carthaginian expedition averaged 500 persons per ship, but Dr. Davies offers the minimalist view that this massive Carthaginian fleet never left the Old World. However, the presence of Carthaginian coins, artifacts and inscriptions in ancient North America reveal where ancient Carthaginian expeditions such as this one headed!

Dr. Davies attacks Dr. Barry Fell for daring to conclude in his book *America B.C.* that the presence of Phoenician and Carthaginian inscriptions, artifacts and coins in North America resulted from Phoenician and Carthaginian ships crossing the Atlantic in ancient times.[54] Yet in the same book, Dr. Davies has no problem proposing that ancient Polynesians sailed across the much larger Pacific Ocean and reached North America in outrigger-canoes holding only forty to one hundred men.[55]

If one can accept that Polynesians could have crossed the Pacific to North America in large canoes, why is it so hard to accept that the Carthaginians (with much larger vessels holding hundreds of people each) crossed the smaller Atlantic Ocean to North America? Unfortunately, modern academia has all too often ignored pre-Columbian Old World artifacts and inscriptions in the Americas. Rather than applying the scientific method to these discoveries (which would expose errors in current dogmas about the ancient world), many are in a state of denial about the voluminous evidence of trans-oceanic travels in the ancient world. Not all modern academics put dogma ahead of truth. The late eminent archaeologist, Dr. Cyrus Gordon, wrote in his book, *Before Columbus:*

> "The Atlantic was crossed long before the Vikings, by different peoples during different centuries."[56]

The Carthaginians crossed the Atlantic in vessels so huge that ocean-going Polynesian canoes would seem like mere lifeboats in comparison. If the English on the Mayflower could make a trans-oceanic voyage with a ship of only 180 tons, the Carthaginians — with much better nautical skills — could easily have done so with ships much larger than the Mayflower!

Dr. Davies' assertions typify a strange academic dogma that may be paraphrased as: "We cannot admit that anyone could have crossed the Atlantic before Columbus no matter what evidence exists to the contrary." Given the immense weight of evidence that pre-Colombian crossings of the Atlantic were made over many centuries by several Old World civilizations, that attitude represents an unwillingness to accept reality. Where did such a prejudicially unscientific approach originate? A possible answer is provided by Roberta Smith in an article published in the *Epigraphic Society Occasional Publications*:

> "When the early settlers of Plymouth Colony and the first French missionaries arrived in this country they found curious stone structures and the native Americans using scripts. These facts were duly reported to their superiors, but...the reports remained in the mother countries and the burgeoning new nation quickly forgot about them. **In the late 1800's the Smithsonian issued a pronouncement that Columbus had been the first to discover America, and archaeologists and historians who disagreed with that view were politely asked to resign their positions in the universities.** Thus, for several generations American archaeologists...have been so thoroughly conditioned to the idea

> that no pre-Colombian contact was possible that now they find it exceedingly difficult to recognize significant data when it is encountered..."[57] *(Emphasis added)*

It is significant that this early form of "political correctness" was imposed on the American educational community not by scientific evidence, but rather by intellectual intimidation. It is unfortunate that many academics continue to cling to the erroneous view that Columbus was the first European to discover America. History would be a much more fascinating subject to American students if they were taught the truth about ancient Israelite and Carthaginian commercial and mining operations in the New World.

It is noteworthy that the Carthaginians, in the middle of the first millennium B.C., launched larger New World expeditions than the colonial efforts of the European powers after Columbus rediscovered America some two thousand years later. American archaeologist, Dr. E. Raymond Capt has noted the following about the ships of the Phoenicians and Carthaginians:

> "During the 7th and 6th centuries B.C., the Phoenicians sailed large ocean-going vessels called "hippos" which could remain at sea for a year or more."[58]

These "hippos" give us an indication of the size of the Israelite-Phoenician ships in the days of Kings Hiram and Solomon whose fleets in the tenth century B.C. undertook three-year voyages. *(I Kings 10:22)* Because Carthage inherited Phoenicia's nautical skills, and because both Phoenicians and Carthaginians sailed across the Atlantic Ocean, Israelites were present in ancient America through most, if not all, of the first millennium B.C.

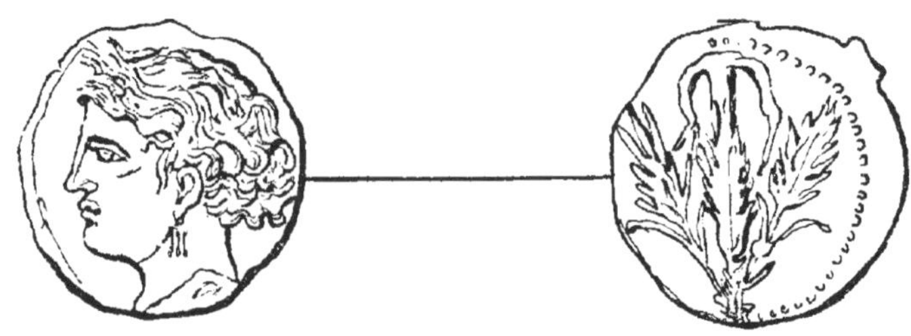

Carthaginian Coin.

Carthaginian Society and Customs

Baal-Hammon
(Perrot and Chipiez.)

Earlier, it was shown that the people of Israel referred to themselves as the "covenant" people, and used the Hebrew word **berith (B-R-T)** as a national identifier. The Carthaginians also placed this Hebrew word **(B-R-T)** on their coins,[59] attesting to their awareness that they were descendants of the "covenant" kingdom of Israel.

While Carthage eventually degenerated into the depravities of Baal worship, their culture began at a higher level. We have already seen evidence of Levitical priestly customs in the early religion and culture of Carthage, and that they at first honored **El**, a common name for Israel's God. The Carthaginians initially continued the biblical customs of making "small monuments which were at first just plain stones" and avoiding "graven images."[60] Later, they built large temples for their "gods." It is also apparent that the Carthaginians were not always degenerate, orgiastic Baal-worshippers. Gilbert and Colette Charles-Picard note the following about them:

> "...little indulgence was shown to the weaknesses of the flesh. The religious reform of the fifth century ...had purified religion of most of its sexual practices, which had their origins in fertility rites...the structure of the family and the status of women did little to encourage masculine license. Monogamy was generally, if not universally, practiced, and many tombs contain the skeletons of married couples...The women of the aristocracy...received an extensive education [and] were able to exercise considerable political influence...There appears to have been little homosexuality in Carthage."[61]

The above account makes the early Carthaginians sound like "Bible Belt" Republicans! A "fifth" century, B.C., dating for this description of Carthaginian values applies to the time prior to the famous Punic Wars with Rome. When Carthage's moral fiber was shaped by "religious reform," it was a strong empire that had nothing to fear from Rome. When their society deteriorated amidst the debauchery of Baal worship, Carthage's power declined until its collapse at the end of the Third Punic War.

The Carthaginians used the same Hebrew word for a place where the dead bodies of human sacrifices were placed.[62] This word was "**tophet**" or "**topheth**,"[63] and it is used five times in Jeremiah 19 in a discourse against human sacrifices in the kingdom of Judah. Jeremiah 7:31-32 also decries Judah's custom of infant sacrifice. King Josiah of Judah stopped the practice of human sacrifice for a time (II Kings 23:10), but the grisly custom of Baal-worship caused the declines of Judah and Israel as well as Carthage. There is an account that the Carthaginians once sacrificed 500 children in an effort to appease the "gods" during a military crisis.[64]

After the fall of Carthage, other Punic cities and the Punic language survived in North Africa for another half-millennium. Their inscriptions were written "in a language very like Hebrew,"[65] and St. Augustine and St. Jerome commented on the Hebrew nature of their language as late as the fourth century A.D.[66]

One of the groups of people identified as living in the region of Carthage were the "Massaesyli."[67] Might their original Hebrew-Carthaginian name have been "Manasseh," one of the "birthright" tribes of Israel which dominated the kingdom of Israel which founded Kirjath (Carthage)? Given the Israelite origins of the Punic people, such an identification would be logical.

After the fall of Judah, one group of Jews apparently settled near their Carthaginian-Israelite relatives. This band of people, known as the "Pharusians," lived south of Spain in North Africa.[68] Since the Carthaginians were fellow Semites, it is unsurprising that some Jews would seek refuge in North Africa. The Pharusians bore the name of that branch of the tribe of Judah that descended from Phares (or "Pharez"), the same bloodline that produced King David, the kings of Judah, and Jesus Christ.

We will now examine other aspects of Carthaginian culture. Like its parent nation of Israel, Carthage was a food exporter. It was one of the wheat kings of the ancient world, controlling nine million bushels of exported wheat per year.[69] Interestingly, some Carthaginian wheat exports went to Greece and Rome. Carthage was willing to feed her enemies if there was money to be made in the process. North Africa is now mostly desert, so it is a sobering commentary on what can happen to fertile land when it is misused and overworked for a prolonged period of time. The agricultural region of Carthage was still productive when the city fell, because the Carthaginians were good custodians of the soil. North Africa supplied Rome with much of its wheat long after Carthage fell, so the responsibility for turning North African wheat regions into deserts lies either with the Romans or later people.

The Carthaginians were inventive people, harvesting their wheat fields with "a fairly advanced threshing-machine — a kind of sledge fitted with small toothed wheels, which the Romans called the 'Punic cart.'"[70] Carthaginian agriculture was varied, as they were also bee-keepers and methodical cattle-breeders.[71] Livestock breeding is a classic Israelite trait that was present in their ancestor Jacob, whose name was changed to Israel. *(Genesis 30:37-43)* It is no surprise that his descendants also possessed that skill.

Strabo, a Roman writer, wrote that the population of Carthage was 700,000 people, and some estimates record a population of 1,000,000 people![72] One account records that the circumference of Carthage and its related suburbs was 23 miles![73] Alexander Tytler, a former professor of Greek and Roman antiquities in the University of Edinburgh, wrote the following about Carthage in his 1854 book, *Universal History*:

The smaller cisterns of Carthage

AN AQUEDUCT OF CARTHAGE

> "...in the days of its splendor [Carthage]...was one of the most magnificent and most populous cities in the universe. The number of its inhabitants is said to have amounted to 700,000, and it had under its sovereignty about three hundred towns along the Mediterranean coast."[74]

Since Carthage's agricultural land was very productive, it could easily have supported a large number of people. We discussed earlier that Herodotus recorded that the Carthaginians sent colonizing expeditions of 30,000 men and women westward into the Atlantic. If it was large enough to send fleets of colonists of that size into the Atlantic region, Carthage itself had to have had a very large population, and the entire Punic culture must have numbered in the millions.

However, Carthage's own power and wealth led it to become arrogant toward its Punic allies. When Rome finally destroyed the city of Carthage, many of Carthage's fellow Punic cities, including the prominent city of Utica, allied themselves with Rome.[75] This action by the other Punic cities led to the prolongation of the Punic people and language in North Africa for many centuries, albeit as Roman subjects.

Hannibal and the Punic Wars with Rome

The story of the Punic Wars between Rome and Carthage is available in history books; however, some aspects of the Punic Wars will be discussed in this book, as modern audiences are largely unaware of many important historical facts.

Before the Punic Wars, Carthage's army fought with:

> "...iron breastplates and brazen helmets, bearing great white shields covering most of their bodies...this suggests a phalanx formation. They were supported by four-horse chariots — the invention of which weapon is attributed to their Canaanite [i.e. "Israelite"] ancestors."[76]

After losing their initial battles with Rome in the First Punic War, Carthage reorganized its military forces and changed its battle tactics. The source of these changes? His name was Xanthippus, and he was a Spartan. He replaced the chariots with battle-elephants, and

RESERVOIRS OF CARTHAGE

The Walls Of Carthage

rearranged how the Carthaginians deployed their cavalry and infantry. After his changes were implemented, Carthage began winning battles with the Romans.[77] It is noteworthy that the Greek city-state, Sparta, deserves credit for much of Carthage's military success against Rome. Greece was the old enemy of Carthage; why would a Grecian city-state aid Carthage against Rome? Sparta did not have the same ethnic origins as the rest of the Greeks, as will be documented in a later book in this series. When Sparta's ethnic origins are understood, it is no surprise that they assisted Carthage.

In the Second Punic War, the famous Carthaginian general, Hannibal, almost succeeded in destroying Rome. Hannibal's Hebrew name, according to the *McClintock and Strong Cyclopedia*, meant "the grace of Baal," but was formed from the same root word as Hanniel, "who is mentioned in Numbers 34:23 as a prince of the tribe of Manasseh."[78]

HANNIBAL

After original bust in National Museum, Naples

Hannibal led his army in a famous march over the Alps and warred against the Romans on their home soil of Italy for approxi-

HANNIBAL CROSSING THE ALPS

The march from Spain to Italy, across rivers and through unknown mountain passes, took five months

mately twelve years. He destroyed entire Roman armies, and pillaged Italy almost at will. Significant portions of Italy switched sides and became Hannibal's allies! Hannibal's high point came in 216 B.C. when his army slew up to 70,000 Romans in a single battle at Cannae.[79] It has been estimated that in the battle at Cannae, Hannibal annihilated one-sixth of Rome's total military forces![80] Rome was "on the ropes," and it is amazing that Rome survived Hannibal's campaign in Italy. It is a tribute to Rome's tenacity that it did not collapse. Even the Roman historian, Livy, wrote: "No other nation in the world could have suffered so tremendous a series of disasters and not been overwhelmed."[81]

Hannibal was one of the greatest military tacticians in history, but he inexplicably did not press home his advantage and capture Rome after his total victory at Cannae. If he had quickly marched into Rome after Cannae, the course of history would have been altered with Rome becoming a mere province of the Carthaginian Empire. However, this opportunity slipped away, and Rome recovered to win the Second Punic War.

It may have been divine intervention which saved Rome from destruction at the hand of Hannibal's Carthaginians. Centuries before the Second Punic War, the prophet Daniel interpreted a divinely-inspired dream given to Babylon's King Nebuchadnezzar which predicted a series of four empires, beginning with Babylon and ending with Rome. *(Daniel 2)* Many Biblical scholars recognize that the "legs of iron" of this great image represented the Roman Empire, which was destined to split into two sections, the Western and Eastern Roman Empires, even as the image's "iron" split into two legs. *Halley's Bible Handbook* expresses this viewpoint.[82] During the Second Punic War, Rome had not yet fulfilled its biblically prophesied destiny, and because God promises that He will implement His prophecies in world events *(Isaiah 41:21-26)*, this author believes that God prevented a Carthaginian triumph over Rome.

When Hannibal later had to flee for his own life, he sought refuge for a time in Armenia.[83] It is interesting that Hannibal viewed Armenia as a place of refuge. Since Hannibal had descended from the Israelites who founded Carthage, and since the region of Armenia included the Israelite kingdom of Iberia, Hannibal may have sought refuge there because the people in that region shared a common ancestry with the Carthaginians.

As mentioned above, the Punic culture and language survived in North Africa until 400 A.D., when its Hebrew roots were still recognizable by early Christian writers. Many Punic Israelites were, therefore, in North Africa at the time of Christ. Acts 2:10 states that people from North Africa (Libya) were present among the devout who attended the Feast of Weeks, which Christians later renamed Pentecost. These North Africans may have been scattered Jews, but they could also have been Punic Israelites who still worshipped the God of Israel. During the life of Jesus Christ, Simon of Cyrene (a North African), was made to carry the cross of Christ on his way to Golgotha. *(Mark 15:21)* Simon was apparently making a pilgrimage from North Africa to Jerusalem to attend the Passover that coincided with Jesus' crucifixion. Acts 11:20 and 13:1 also indicate that some early Christians were either Jews or Punic Israelites from Punic North Africa (Cyrene).

Where did most of the Carthaginians go when Carthage fell to Rome after the Third Punic War? Many did not stay in Carthage for the last futile war against the Romans. Since Carthage had a network of colonies, many likely fled the Romans in the same way the Israelite-Phoenicians had earlier fled from Assyria. Many Carthaginians with the means to do so could evade the Romans by relocating elsewhere. The Celts of Western Europe could have received many of them, and there is a 19th century account that a large group of Carthaginian refugees did relocate to the coast of northern France:

> "M. de Penhouet, the greatest antiquarian...in Celtic lore in Brittany, has proved that the Veneti of western Gaul were not really Celts, but rather a colony of Carthaginians ...in the time of Caesar."[84]

If the Veneti were displaced Carthaginians, one would expect them to exhibit the nautical skills of Carthage, and so they did! The *Encyclopedia Britannica* calls the Veneti: "the most powerful maritime people on the Atlantic,"[85] during the time of Caesar.

The Carthaginian Presence in Ancient America

Historical evidence indicates some Carthaginians sought refuge in ancient America via Carthage's old maritime routes across the Atlantic Ocean. We have already seen that Carthaginian coins, artifacts and inscriptions have been found in a wide area of North America. Petroglyphs honoring the Carthaginian goddess, Tanith, have been found in Colorado, Oklahoma, Kansas and North Carolina.[86] Dr. Fell was

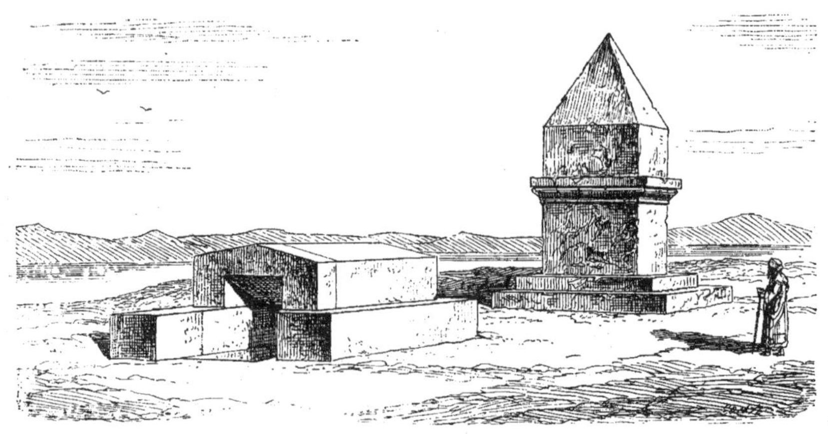

–Tomb at Amrit restored. From Renan.

earlier cited as noting that the Carthaginian coins in ancient America date to the "fourth and third centuries B.C.,"[87] a time including the First and Second Punic Wars between Rome and Carthage. The presence of Carthaginian coins from that period confirms that Carthage was still linked to its North American colony, and many could have sought it as a place of refuge from the Romans.

A stone was found in Massachusetts with an ancient Punic inscription, which Dr. Fell translated as:

> "A PROCLAMATION of annexation. Do not deface. By this Hanno takes possession."[88]

Hanno was a common name of the Carthaginian nobility, but there was a famous Carthaginian explorer (circa 520 B.C.) named Hanno who led large exploration fleets into the Atlantic Ocean. Nineteenth century historian, Alfred Church, wrote of this expedition:

> "It was decreed by the Carthaginians that **Hanno should sail beyond the Pillars of Hercules and found cities**...Accordingly he sailed with sixty ships of fifty oars each and a multitude of men and women to the number of thirty thousand, and provisions and other equipment."[89] *(Emphasis added)*

This was likely the same voyage of 60 ships and 30,000 men and women cited above by Nigel Davies. Dr. Davies dates the voyage to 500-480 B.C. while Church assigns it to 520 B.C. Church suggests that the "sixty ships" were military escort vessels (military ships were "oared" ships) and that the 30,000 colonists sailed on a separate fleet of transport vessels. What is known is that the Carthaginians did send huge fleets of colonists westward into the Atlantic Ocean toward destinations unknown to the Greeks. Obviously, the Carthaginians would not send thousands of families into the Atlantic to new colonies unless they had already explored and secured the sites to be settled.

Perhaps the "Hanno" who claimed possession of America was the very "Hanno" who led this ancient Carthaginian fleet into the Atlantic Ocean; it cannot be known for certain. **However, this does give physical evidence that a Carthaginian named Hanno claimed North America for Carthage two thousand years before later European explorers claimed portions of America for "king and country."**

Earlier, it was shown that the Israelite-Phoenicians had founded the "Adena" culture in the Ohio River region of ancient America. Carthage and the Adena colony were both founded by Israel-Phoenicia, so the Adena culture served well as a refuge for Carthaginian refugees. The Adena colony in North America received a major infusion of new immigrants known as the Hopewell People in 300-200 B.C.[90] The *Encyclopedia Americana* states the Hopewell culture "reached its peak between 200 B.C. and 400 A.D."[91]

MOUNDS (MISSISSIPPI VALLEY)

The above dates for the infusion of new people into the Adena colony coincides with the First and Second Punic Wars (264-241 B.C. and 218-201 B.C.), and the period of time in which Carthaginian coins were infused into North America as cited by Dr. Fell. Who else could the Hopewell People have been but Carthaginians merging with the Adena Colony (of Phoenician origin)? Even as Carthage was founded by Israelites seeking refuge from successive Assyrian wars, the New World received refugees from Carthage who fled the Roman wars. The Adena/ Hopewell people were mound builders. A tablet found in their Grave Creek Mound of West Virginia was inscribed in:

> "...**Punic written in the form of an alphabet used in Iberia** in the first millennium B.C. The Grave Creek Mound is believed to be the largest of the Adena [mounds] and according to Don W. Dragoo in Mounds for the Dead, was of the late Adena period **coincident with the arrival of the Hopewell People, 300 to 200 B.C.**"[92] *(Emphasis added)*

That a large burial mound in West Virginia dating to the time of the Punic Wars included a Punic (i.e. Carthaginian) inscription supports the view that the Hopewell infusion into the Adena Culture of North America was comprised of Punic refugees. The fact that it was Iberian-Punic indicates the maker of the inscription was from the Spanish portion of the Carthaginian Empire.

Also, numerous gravestones have been found in Pennsylvania with Carthaginian inscriptions. Dr. Barry Fell states the following about one gravemarker:

> "It is written **in Carthaginian script of about the first or second century A.D**...It carries four rows of **neatly-executed Punic letters**...The grave-marker makes it clear also that **he was also an early Christian** [who died]...lacking the rites of the church."[93] *(Emphasis added)*

This confirms not only that Carthage's Punic culture survived among the Hopewell culture, but also that Christianity, an Old World religion, later followed them across the Atlantic Ocean to the New World! A Punic gravestone "with neatly-executed Punic letters" indicates that the Punic culture in North America was still well established three or four centuries after the fall of Carthage and in the second century after the birth of Christ. The presence of Christianity in the late Hopewell culture also confirms that the maritime routes between the Old and New Worlds were still active at that same time.

Strong evidence has been found that at least one group of Jews traveled to the New World to seek refuge from the Romans. Dr. Cyrus Gordon wrote the following:

> "Other contacts with the Roman Mediterranean of the second century A.D. have...come to light in Kentucky, where inscribed Hebrew coins of Bar Kochkba's rebellion against Rome (A.D. 132-135) were dug up in Louisville, Hopkinsville and Clay City...There is no difficulty in identifying these Bar Kochkba coins."[94]

Dr. Gordon's book offers photographed samples of these ancient Hebrew coins found in Kentucky, and he adds that they were found over a period of time from 1932 to 1967. Dr. Gordon notes additional evidence of this Jewish enclave of refugees in ancient America.

In the 19th century, a stone with a Hebrew inscription was found in Tennessee along with nine skeletons. Called the "Bat Creek Stone," it was documented in a report to the Smithsonian Institution by the U.S. Government Printing Office. It was originally misinterpreted as being in Cherokee script because the script was published upside down. Skilled linguists later identified it as a Hebrew inscription, and Dr. Gordon writes that the inscription could date to Jewish refugees "from either the first (A.D. 66-70) or second (A.D.132-135) rebellions"[95] against Rome.

Dr. Gordon warns others against denying the obvious facts of this pre-Columbian contact with ancient America as follows:

> "Trying to explain away the Bat Creek evidence as anything other than American contact with Palestine around the second century A.D. can only amount to obscurantism that no sensible scholar or layman should elect...**The significance of the excavations at Bat Creek is that they attest inscriptionally and archaeologically to a migration in early Christian times from Judea to our Southeast**."[96] *(Emphasis added)*

Since Jews of the first or second century, A.D., could find their way from Judea to North America to flee the Romans, it is even easier to grasp that the Carthaginians, with a strong maritime tradition, could also have journeyed to ancient North America to flee the Romans a few centuries earlier.

Carthage, the Mayans and Ancient American Mines

Evidence that Carthaginians sought refuge in the New World also exists in the Mayan ruins of Mexico. Neil Steede, a President of the Mexican Epigraphic Society, notes that many inscribed bricks found at the Mayan site of Comalcalco indicate that speakers of Old World languages were present at that ancient site. He writes:

> "...Some 58% of the inscribed bricks are in Maya hieroglyphs while...**18% are in what appear to be Old World languages**.[he adds] in 1983 Dr. Fell had already recognized **[a] Punic calendar inscribed on one of the bricks in a late Punic script dating to the period 100-300 A.D**..."[97] *(Emphasis added)*

It is significant that the Carthaginian Punic culture of North Africa interacted with the Mayans of Mesoamerica. This inscribed Punic calendar, found at Comalcalco in 1977-78 under the auspices of the El Instituto Nacional de Antropologia de Historia de Mexico, is described by Dr. Barry Fell as follows:

> "...they [the letters] can be recognized as belonging to the extremely degenerate Neopunic...in use at Carthage after the first century A.D...study of the letters shows that they form in sequence, from right to left, the initial letters of the names of the Phoenician and Hebrew months, taken in the order of the Civic Year...The manner in which the Calendar is set out, showing the astronomical basis of the succession of months, suggests that it was made for the purpose of explaining a concept of a [Hebrew calendar] to a person unfamiliar with the notion, such as a Mayan...Both the degenerate Neopunic script, therefore, and the use of weeks, with an evident need for an intercalary 13th [month] every 3 or 4 years, indicate that this calendar belongs to the first to third centuries A.D."[98]

The fact that the Punic language was represented in a "degenerate form" in Comalcalco, but was inscribed in "neatly-executed Punic letters" on a gravestone in ancient Pennsylvania shows that the Carthaginians who fled to the New World did so to different locations and with different levels of educational skills. It is a well-established fact that soldiers from many nations served as mercenaries in Carthage's military. The multi-racial composition of Carthage's army included native Carthaginians, Celtiberians from Spain, Celts from Europe, Libyans and Numidians from Africa, Greek mercenaries, etc.[99] Because Carthage's refugees in the New World included both native Carthaginians and people who knew just enough of the Punic language to "get by" as mercenaries, it is not surprising that Punic inscriptions in ancient America reflect different levels of writing skills among their makers.

Another inscribed brick excavated from Comalcalco offers additional evidence that the Christian religion had reached the Mayan region of the New World. Dr. Fell writes:

> "Some [inscriptions]...are decidedly foreign, and their presence, incorporated into the structure of Mayan temples and mounds implies contact between the Mayan builders and foreign

> nations...Tablet AP-480 is of North African origin or, at least, is the work of a North African...[and it contains] letters of the Libyan (Numidian) alphabet...the letters are understood as spelling the name Y-S-W that is to say, Yoswa=Hebrew Joshua...that is Jesus. The next letters...evidently spell the Berber-Arabic word H-M-N, Hamin, meaning 'Protector.' The crude figure of a robed man... apparently represents Jesus the Protector, and the tablet was made for, or by, a North African of the Christian faith."[100]

The above North African inscription in a Mayan structure dates to the very early Christian era. It is of Numidian origin, and Numidians served in Carthage's army. The presence of Punic, Numidian and Berber-Arabic inscriptions in Mayan Comalcalco confirms that several of Carthage's racial groups interacted with the Mayans. Dr. Barry Fell also wrote that a Christian inscription of the Micmac Indians in Maine was based on the Egyptian hieratic script,[101] and that a Christian prayer-stick of the Kikapu Algonquins in Wisconsin was inscribed with "the dextral script of the late Punic language of Carthage."[102] The presence of such Christian inscriptions confirms that transatlantic voyages were still occurring in the early centuries of the Christian era.

Since Christian inscriptions dating to the first few centuries A.D. have been found in Pennsylvania, Maine, Wisconsin and the Mayan city of Comalcalco, it is evident that Christianity was widely diffused in the New World at a very early time. The Phoenicians and Carthaginians had known the sailing routes between North Africa and the New World throughout the first millennium B.C., so it is hardly surprising that Punic North Africa maintained contact with the New World into the early Christian era. (Isle Royale ancient mine below.)

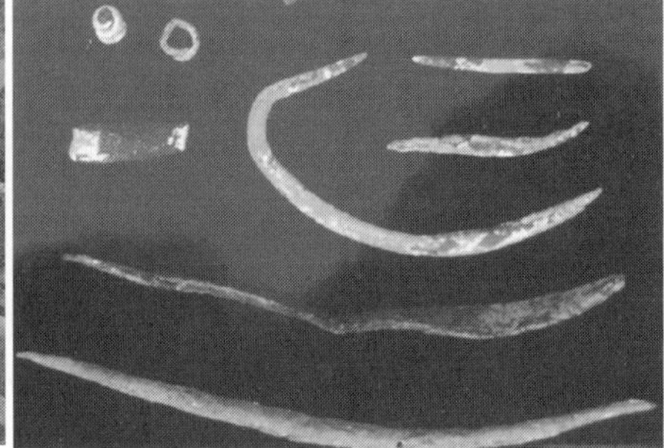

Michigan's Keweenaw Peninsula: The Site of Ancient Copper Mining by a Long-Vanished People!

The Old Clark Mine was the site of extensive ancient mining

THE COPPER COUNTRY
AN ANCIENT VANISHED RACE MINED NATIVE COPPER HUNDREDS OF YEARS AGO IN COUNTLESS PITS AND TRENCHES SCATTERED AMONG THE HILLS FROM COPPER HARBOR TO ONTONAGON AND ON ISLE ROYALE.
THE EXPLORER, JACQUES CARTIER, REPORTED IN 1536 THAT INDIANS ON ST. LAWRENCE RIVER TOLD HIM OF GREAT HILLS OF NATIVE COPPER FAR TO THE WEST.
THE JESUIT, FATHER CLAUDE ALLOUEZ, WAS THE FIRST WHITE MAN TO REPORT SEEING COPPER ALONG THE SOUTH SHORE OF LAKE SUPERIOR. THIS WAS IN 1666.
IN 1771 A COMPANY WAS ORGANIZED IN LONDON, ENGLAND WHICH SENT AN UNSUCCESSFUL EXPEDITION TO THESE SHORES TO MINE COPPER.
A TREATY BETWEEN THE U.S. GOVERNMENT AND THE CHIPPEWA INDIANS ON MARCH 12 TH. 1843 OPENED THE DISTRICT TO MINING.

Overlooking Copper Harbor

Quincy Mine modern entrance

Isle Royale in Lake Superior was the site of much ancient mining by an unknown and now-vanished people. (left: Isle Royale from the air)

Above: the over-grown remnant of an ancient mine

Above and below right: Isle Royale's eastern shoreline reveals evidence of many ancient mines visible today.

Below: close-up view of a now-flooded ancient mine near the central coast of Isle Royale

There is additional evidence that colonists from the Carthaginian Empire settled in the New World. Iberian Punic gravestones were found in Michigan,[103] as were many other evidences of ancient Old World civilizations. In the first book in this series, it was documented that the ancient copper mines of Michigan were exploited by the Israelites of Kings David and Solomon to amass copper for the Temple of God and other building projects. A Michigan author, Betty Sodders, wrote a book entitled *Michigan Prehistory Mysteries*, documenting much evidence about the presence of Old World civilizations in ancient Michigan and eastern North America. Her book documents the widespread ancient mining activities, dolmens, stone-circles and inscriptions left behind by ancient civilizations in North America. There is evidence of the presence of Phoenicians, Celts, Iberians and Carthaginians. After mentioning the presence of Phoenicians and Iberian Celts in ancient America, Sodders writes:

> "...a strong possibility exists that **early people from the Celtic race** traveled from Beaver Island in northern Lake Michigan, up the Escanaba River towards Lake Superior. **These routes tie in dramatically with the copper culture ore trade**...all major rivers and tributaries as well as shoreline across the United States, have turned up **evidence of a long-gone seagoing race of people**...One must tend to agree these facts are not fiction...followers of [Dr. Barry] Fell believe after the Celtic pioneers arrived in this country, **they were followed by Phoenician traders from Spain. This ancient race of people spoke a language called Punic**."[104] *(Emphasis added)*

An earlier chapter showed that the Celts lived in Israel's European colonies, so they would have inherited the knowledge of America's mineral wealth. The "Phoenicians" Sodders refers to were the people who spoke "Punic," the language of the Carthaginian Empire. Carthaginians are often called "Phoenicians" because they continued the Phoenician-Hebrew culture after Israel fell. Sodders also comments on how extensively these ancient civilizations sought for minerals and natural resources in ancient America:

> "...members of a long vanished race had mined every productive copper-bearing vein in the region, from Isle Royale...in Lake

> Superior, to the copper ridges of the Keweenaw Peninsula...**even hidden copper veins that did not directly surface as mineral outcroppings were previously tapped by these people from the past...one can but speculate as to this early race's inscrutable method of ore detection**...while our home state of Michigan was 'THE' copper mining center of the New World, still **other prehistoric diggings for various minerals became clearly evident across our entire nation...mica** was mined in North Carolina, **serpentine** in Pennsylvania, and **lead** mines were found in Kentucky, just to name a few...along the Mississippi Valley **prehistoric oil wells** were actually discovered. Additional oil operations can be noted in Ohio, Pennsylvania and Canada."[105] *(Emphasis added)*

It is noteworthy that the ancient race, which sought and mined the natural resources of ancient America, had a sophisticated technology to locate copper veins buried in the earth! They could have burned the oil from America's ancient mines to light their open-pit mines, buildings, homes and ships. They could have used burning oil for ship and signal beacons. When Rome destroyed Carthage, an immense amount of knowledge vanished with the Carthaginians. Their sophisticated nautical and astral sciences, their scientific knowledge of the earth, their maps of the continents and the best sea-routes for oceanic travel were lost to the Old World. Some knowledge survived in the remaining Punic cities, but arrogant Carthage kept the best secrets for her own commercial advantage. Some of this knowledge lived on in Carthage's American colonies for a time, but eventually was lost as these colonies were cut off from the main repository of such knowledge: Carthage itself.

Iberian Punic inscriptions also were found in Massachusetts.[106] Furthermore, striking parallels have been found between the currency (copper ingots), pottery and adornments of the mound builders of ancient America and the Iberian-Punic civilization of the Old World.[107]

A "Creation Chant" of the Pima Indians of the American southwest, found to be "an ancient Semitic hymn," was preserved by the Pima tribe in an archaic form of the Punic language.[108] The language of the Zuni Indian tribe was based on a variety "of Afro-Asian tongues of mixed Semitic-Hamitic origin."[109] An article in the 1998 issue of the *Epigraphic Society Occasional Publications* entitled "A Curious Element in Uto-Aztecan," by Brian Darrel Stubbs, documents that many Uto-Aztecan languages are partially based on an archaic form of the Hebrew language. The Uto-Aztecan family includes Native American languages in tribes located from Central Mexico to the American Southwest and Rocky Mountain region. Such Native American tongues as Ute, Paiute, Shoshone and Pima are included in this broad linguistic family. Stubbs writes that the Hebrew on which some of Uto-Aztecan is based is from "Northwest Semitic forms more archaic than those found in the Masoretic text (the Hebrew Old Testament text, voweled by the Masoretes about 700 A.D.)"[110]

The Hebrew tongue of ancient Israel was exported throughout the Phoenician colonies, including Carthage. The Hebrew origin of Carthage's language is well documented. Carthaginian refugees who emigrated from the Old World to flee the Romans brought with them the Hebrew-Punic tongue many centuries before the time of the Masoretes. Given the widespread Carthaginian-Punic artifacts and inscriptions in the ancient Americas, and the Punic inscriptions in Mayan areas, Carthage had to be the source of the Hebrew-Semitic portion of Uto-Aztecan. In discussing how the Semitic language reached the New World, Stubbs notes:

> "In looking at a globe, one can see that the shortest distance from Africa to the Americas is shorter then the length of the Mediterranean Sea."[111]

It is not difficult to realize that the Carthaginians could easily sail the short distance from Africa to South America and follow the coast up to the Gulf of Mexico. Stubbs continues:

> "A considerable amount of Hebrew morphology is apparent in UA [Uto-Aztecan]...the lexical, morphological, and root-specific similarities seem rather numerous to attribute to chance...the fact that some UA forms depict the very archaic voweling patterns of proto-Northwest Semitic is stunning."[112]

Stubbs offers many specific cognate words between Hebrew and the Uto-Aztecan languages in his article. The conclusion is clear:

the Phoenician-Carthaginian connection with the ancient Americas is supported by firm archaeological, epigraphic, historical and linguistic evidence.

The *Encyclopedia Americana* states the Mayan Civilization lasted for almost two millennia until its demise at the hands of the Spaniards in the sixteenth century A.D.[113] Therefore, **the Mayans were contemporary with Carthage during the Punic Wars and the fall of Carthage**. Given the presence of Punic inscriptions on the bricks that built some Mayan buildings, it is evident that the Carthaginians interacted with the Mayans. A remarkable ancient American engraving from Spiro Mound, Oklahoma shows oarsmen, dressed in a Mesoamerican style, seated in a ship carrying three images of the Carthaginian goddess, Tanith.[114] Such a drawing preserved the Carthaginian interactions with Mesoamericans as it depicts a Carthaginian deity and the fact that ancient fleets arrived with oared-vessels. Remember the account that Carthage sent 30,000 colonists westward into the Atlantic in a fleet escorted by 60 warships "of fifty oars each?" Carthage built many thousands of oared vessels (biremes, triremes, etc.), and this engraving apparently depicts an oared Carthaginian ship. The presence of a Carthaginian goddess on the engraved ship confirms such a conclusion.

The Carthaginians practiced human sacrifice and came from North Africa, the home of Egypt's pyramids. Carthage was familiar with the Egyptian pyramids, as there were "close economic and cultural ties between the new Tyre and the capital of the

Ptolemies."[115] Carthage was the "New Tyre" of this quote and Alexandria, Egypt was the capital of the Ptolemies. The Carthaginians came to the ancient Americas in considerable numbers and stayed for centuries. **The Mayans also practiced human sacrifice and built large pyramids.** The conclusion seems obvious that the Mayans learned the customs of human sacrifice and building pyramids from Carthaginians.

In 1900, an "alabaster egg carrying the cartouche of the Egyptian Pharaoh Tutankhamen" was discovered in Idaho, and Dr. Fell opined in his book, *Saga America*, that it was brought to America with trade goods by the Carthaginians or Iberians.[116] Indian tribes also had relics of the Old World in their possession. When the renowned Nez Perce Chief Joseph surrendered to American troops in Montana in 1878, he had in his possession a small tablet with an inscription on it. This tablet was placed in a West Point Museum, and it was later realized the inscription was a Sumerian one from ancient Mesopotamia. Are you ready for the result?

> "Translated by Prof. Robert Biggs of Chicago, it...was a receipt for a lamb, dated in the year that Enmahgalanna was installed as high priestess of Nanna, or about 2042 B.C. The tablet was presumed to have been made in southern Iraq."[117]

A lead tablet with a Sumerian cuneiform inscription from ancient Mesopotamia was unearthed in Georgia in 1963 when a homeowner was digging a flowerbed. It was a receipt for sheep and goats to be sacrificed to "Utu the sungod and the goddess Lama Lugal...in the 37th or 38th year of the reign of King Suigi of Ur...about 2040 B.C."[118] Ur of Mesopotamia is where Abraham's family originated *(Genesis 11:31)*, and these Sumerian tablets found in ancient America date to a time preceding the birth of Abraham!

Given the extreme antiquity of these last two tablets, it seems apparent that the ancient Sumerians explored the Americas about a millennium before the Phoenicians of King David and Solomon arrived and about two millenniums before the fall of Carthage. It begins to appear that the "Dark Ages" of roughly 500-1500 A.D. may have been the only time in the last four millennia when the Old World mostly lost track of the New World.

The African-based Carthaginians also brought Negroid people to the ancient Americas. Some may have served in Carthage's army as mercenaries and others may have been captured slaves. Many huge, sculpted "Negroid" heads were discovered at Oaxaca, Mexico, confirming that black Africans were well known in ancient America. A photograph of one of the gigantic heads appears in the book, *In Quest of the Great White Gods*, by Robert Marx.[119] Norman Totten of Bentley College wrote the following about these huge Negroid heads:

> "...the colossal stone heads, weigh[ed] 20 to 30 tons each. Their unmistakably Negroid features would seem to indicate some kind of migration from Black Africa to Middle America early in the first millennium BC."[120]

Dr. Cyrus Gordon's book, *Before Columbus*, includes photographs of many Negroid statutes from Mesoamerica as well as a bearded Semite carved onto a Mayan incense burner.[121] Concerning these Negroid faces and the Semitic face from Mayan locations, Dr. Gordon wrote:

> "The implication is simply that **early America was the meeting ground of various races of men from the Old World who were eventually absorbed into the modern Indian populations**...[and] we have **a specific link between preclassical Mesoamerica and the ancient Mediterranean**."[122] *(Emphasis added)*

Dr. Gordon's observations are insightful and accurate. During the 1st millennium B.C., Phoenicia and Carthage had a monopoly on Old World voyages to the New World. We know they brought many colonists from Africa and Europe to populate their colonies located beyond the Atlantic Ocean. The great fleet of 30,000 colonists recorded by the Greeks was surely just one such voyage undertaken by Phoenicia and Carthage. They brought the people from the Old World who, as Dr. Gordon observed, were "eventually absorbed into the modern Indian populations" of the ancient Americas. These were the people already in North America many centuries later when Europeans again began to make trans-Atlantic voyages to the New World.

Dr. Barry Fell's book, *Saga America*, has a photograph of an ornate urn excavated in the state of New York. It depicts the Phoenician goddess, Astarte, with "African rain-dancers" amidst obviously

Egyptian themes.[123] That one urn indicates the New World had to be aware of Semitic, Egyptian and Black African cultures.

Aztec drawings of human sacrificial rites depict people of what appear to be several races participating in a grisly ritual of sacrificing fair-skinned Semitic captives.[124] The Mesoamerican civilizations retained the knowledge of fair-skinned people from the east, as the Spaniards arriving from across the eastern ocean were first regarded as returning "gods" by the Aztecs.

Few examples of the wheel are found in ancient American sites, leading to speculation that Ancient Americans did not invent or use the wheel. That assertion is nonsense. Phoenicians and Carthaginians, as well as people from other Old World nations who served as mercenaries in Carthage's army, were very familiar with chariots and carts. When they came to the ancient Americas, they brought the knowledge of the wheel with them. Ancient Americans knew about the wheel. Wheeled animals (with two axles and four wheels) have been found in Mexican tombs, and Jonathan Leonard shows one such example in the book, *Ancient America*.[125]

The apparent lack of draft animals to pull carts or chariots in the ancient Americas has been noted both by Jonathan Leonard's book and by Dr. Cyrus Gordon.[126] The Carthaginians were skilled cattle-breeders, so it is inconceivable that they did not attempt to bring cattle and horses to the Americas. Perhaps they tried to do so, but the transport ships carrying their breeding stocks sank at sea. It is also possible animal diseases wiped out their herds. If such an event happened, Punic refugees could not return to the Old World to restock their herds after Carthage fell. Given the mathematical skills it took to build the pyramids of Mesoamerica, they certainly understood the applications of the wheel.

Carthage fell in 146 B.C. at the end of the Third Punic War. Historian Alfred Church wrote:

> "The wall of Carthage had a circumference of 18 miles. It was about 46 feet high, and 34 feet thick...with towers four stories high and much higher...Within the casements of the main wall there

> was room for 300 elephants, 4,000 cavalry and 20,000 infantry...In the inner harbour were kept ships of war [with] slips in which 220 vessels could be placed."[127]

AFTER THE DESTRUCTION OF CARTHAGE
Romans plowing the ground where the city had stood

Carthage's defenses were impregnable for centuries, but the city finally fell to Rome. As an indication of Carthaginian wealth, the pillaging Romans were said to have stripped 1000 talents of gold from Carthage's temple of Apollo alone.[128] Rome took 50,000 Carthaginians captive,[129] a paltry total compared to earlier accounts of Carthage's population being 700,000 people or more. It seems apparent that many Carthaginians chose the rigors of migrating elsewhere rather than face death or a Roman captivity. Carthage had exploited the ancient Americas for centuries, and the New World could easily have received a number of Carthaginian refugees.

After the fall of Carthage, Roman access to the New World was no longer blocked. As noted above, Roman coins and artifacts from the period after the fall of Carthage have been widely found in the New World. Coins minted under four Roman emperors were found in Massachusetts, a large cache of Roman coins "from the reigns of all the emperors of the first three centuries after Christ" was found in Venezuela, and individual Roman coins have been unearthed in Tennessee, Georgia, Texas, and North Carolina.[130] Roman oil lamps have been found in Alabama and Connecticut.[131] The Romans could have come themselves or traders from the surviving Punic cities — part of Rome's Empire after the fall of Carthage — may have transported Roman goods and coins to the New World. While some Roman artifacts and coins were brought to the New World, Rome manifested no major interest in the Americas.

Earlier, it was documented that Punic inscriptions can be deciphered by consulting the Hebrew language. To illustrate this point, we will examine Dr. Fell's translation of a Carthaginian inscription at Massacre Lake, Nevada, as reading "may the clouds spew forth rain."[132] The inscription reads from right to left in the normal Hebrew fashion and Dr. Fell wrote that the inscription consists of the letters "Q, M-T-R, I-B." Any reader can confirm that these Carthaginian words are Hebrew root words by consulting a Hebrew lexicon. The Hebrew words involved are "QO" (or "QI"), "MATAR", and "AB" (vowels being absent).[133] The Hebrew words "QI" or "QO" mean "spew out," or "vomit out;" "MATAR" means "rain," and "AB" means "cloud." Clearly, the Carthaginian vocabulary was based on the Hebrew language of its Israelite founders.

When Rome sacked Carthage, the priceless knowledge in Carthage's libraries was lost. Apparently, only one literary work survived: a 28-volume Carthaginian work on the "breeding and management of cattle, the care of poultry and bees, the planting of forest trees and the treatment of the vine and olive."[134] If the Romans had heeded the agricultural knowledge in these volumes, North Africa might still have wheat fields instead of deserts. The Carthaginian agricultural volumes included "the planting of forest trees" in its subject matter, indicating they understood the need for "planting forests" and the agricultural damage posed by deforestation.

Carthage began as an Israelite-Phoenician colony, and its library would have contained the history of the Israelite, Hebrew-speaking people. Had it survived, the modern world would have a vastly different, and more accurate, perspective on ancient history than we have inherited from the ethnocentric accounts of the Greco-Romans. When Carthage fell, it was the Romans who were the "barbarians," destroying the preserved, cumulative knowledge of the Phoenician and Carthaginian Empires. We can only imagine what global nautical maps and texts of scientific knowledge were destroyed at that time.

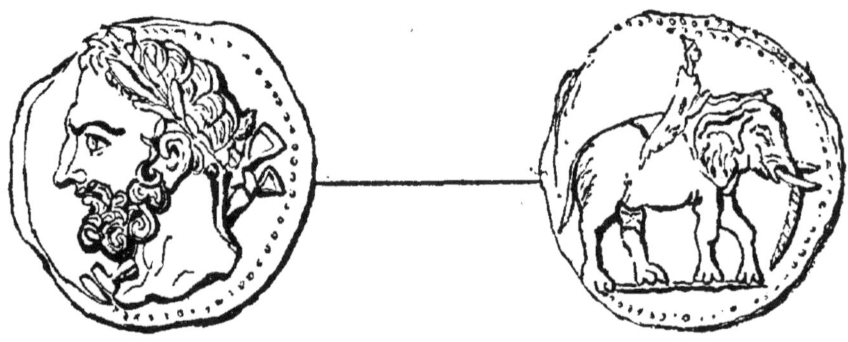

Carthaginian Coin.

Carthaginian Elephants in the Americas?

There is an unusual, but fascinating, piece of evidence about the Carthaginian presence in ancient America. This evidence involves the possibility that elephants were introduced into the Americas by Carthage, and that they were present in the New World until almost colonial times. George Carter, Professor Emeritus of Texas A & M University, has written in the *Epigraphic Society Occasional Publications* that a number of American Indian tribes preserved legends of elephants living in North America. He wrote:

> "The most striking ones [elephant legends] were told to Cotton Mather in New England and to Thomas Jefferson in Washington...the Indians told Jefferson that elephants could still be seen in the Great Lakes region."[135]

Professor Carter also wrote:

> "There are other accounts amongst the eastern United States Indians that mention the tusks, the trunk, the immense size, the size of the tracks that the elephant left and other details."[136]

Historians tend to condescendingly discount such Indian tribal legends, but that was not always so. President Thomas Jefferson believed elephants lived in ancient America. He was fascinated by the subject and wrote to Robert Livingston from Washington, D.C., on December 14, 1800:

> "I have heard of the discovery of some large bones, supposed to be of the mammoth, at about 30 or 40 miles distance from you...The bones I am most anxious to obtain, are those of the head and feet, which are said to among those found in your State...If they are to be bought, I will gladly pay for them..."[137]

President Jefferson called them "mammoth" bones instead of "elephant" bones, but the historical evidence indicates they were African elephant bones. The American Indian legends of elephants in ancient America deserve more respect than they have received.

Professor Carter comments on the ample evidence of elephant motifs in ancient America. He writes:

> "...America is liberally sprinkled with pictures of elephants. Painted on a cave in Washington State, in the rock art of the West, in Mayan glyphs where elephant heads appear as affixes at least 14 times, in a Mexican codex [it]...was noted that a priest sacrificing a man wore an elephant headdress."[138]

Dr. Barry Fell's book, *America B.C.*, also notes elephant motifs in both North and South America. His book shows an Ecuadorian engraving depicting an elephant (and identified as such in a North African script) from the "latter half of the third century before Christ."[139] At that time, Carthage still existed. Dr. Fell's book also shows a carved African elephant unearthed in a mound near Davenport, Iowa.[140] Ancient rock carvings and petroglyphs depicting elephants have been documented in New Mexico, Utah and Oklahoma, confirming that ancient Americans were widely familiar with elephants.[141]

Additionally, the actual bones of elephants that lived in ancient America have been found and dated. Carter records that:

> "In Florida one set of extinct animals that included the elephant tribe, carbon dated to 2000 years"...[and] "a mammoth skeleton in the Mississippi River valley was once dated at about 2000 years."[142]

These dates (2000 years ago) place elephants in ancient North America at the approximate time of Christ. There is a question of whether the elephants in ancient North America were African or Asian elephants or surviving mammoths from ice-age times. The artifacts shown in Fell's book clearly indicate African elephants were present, as they are described in North African scripts and Old World contexts. However, Carter notes evidence that an Asian elephant-headed god was worshipped in the ancient Americas, and Dr. Fell added that: "California tablets...employ the ancient Sanskrit word, Gaja, used in India even today for the Asiatic elephant."[143] Ancient Americans were aware of both African and Asian elephants, confirming global commerce and travel were far greater in the ancient world than generally realized.

There is even an eyewitness report from the American colonial period. An English sailor named David Ingram was marooned in Mexico after a naval battle with the Spanish but walked through much of North America before returning to Europe from New England with the help of French fishermen. The late American novelist, Louis Lamour, was familiar with his account and wrote concerning Ingram's walk through North America: "He said he saw elephants and I have his account right before me."[144]

The evidence indicates there were elephants in ancient, and not-so-ancient, America. The North American elephant bones carbon-dated to the time of Christ are particularly significant, as they date to the known period of the Hopewell Culture, which sprang up in America as Carthage declined in the Old World. Where did these elephants originate? Were they surviving mammoths or modern elephants imported from the Old World? To this author, the obvious answers are that they were African elephants and that they were brought to America by Carthaginians.

We know that Carthage specialized in the use of elephants, deploying hundreds of them at a time in battles, and elephants accompanied Carthaginian troops even under arduous conditions. For example, Hannibal's army brought African elephants across southern Europe and over the frigid Alps into Italy during the Punic Wars. How did Hannibal's forces transport the elephants from Africa to Europe? Obviously, they crossed the Mediterranean Sea in Carthaginian ships adapted to transport elephants! The remains and reports of elephants in the ancient Americas indicate that the same method was used to transport African elephants to ancient America.

The American elephant motifs depict elephants, not mammoths. The presence of elephants in ancient America indicates that descendants of Carthaginian elephants survived in the New World until the early colonial period in America. Who but the Carthaginians, with their large ships and unique skills in handling elephants, could have transported African elephants to America?

This concludes the narrative on Carthage ("Kirjath"), Israel's colony which became an empire. The record of history indicates that when Carthage possessed at least some respect for the God of Israel and had strong social and family values, it was blessed with expanding power and influence. When Carthage grew great, it became arrogant and deeply infected with the self-destructive religious practices of Baal worship. The same evils (sins) that destroyed ancient Israel and Judah also brought down Carthage.

God promised that Abraham's and Israel's descendants, when obedient to God's laws, would inhabit the fatness, or best places, of the earth, possess the gates of their enemies, have agricultural abundance and be militarily victorious (Genesis 22:17, 27:28-29, Leviticus 26:4-8). Like Israel, Carthage received all those blessings in its early centuries. They possessed excellent agricultural regions, a monopoly on the wealth of the Americas, the critical sea-gate of Gibraltar, and military power. Carthage's possession of many of the "covenant" blessings of Abraham upon Israel helps confirm their Israelite heritage.

Fleeing Carthaginians who migrated to North America apparently founded a civilization — the Hopewell Civilization — which lasted till 400-500 A.D. We do not know what caused their demise. It is possible that warfare depleted their numbers. Epigrapher Gloria Farley documented an inscription in a North African script which claimed victory in an ancient battle in Oklahoma. She writes that the Old World script and the presence of "Amerindian sign systems" in the inscription "suggests that the battle...may have occurred

Signum.

Medallion Face of Baal (on the Temple at Rükhleh).

after the time of Christ."[145] This supports the viewpoint that competing groups descended from Old World colonists were fighting pitched battles with each other.

The ancient American Punic civilization may have been destroyed by disease. The Baal-worship that Carthage brought to America included promiscuous sex-rites providing an ideal environment for spreading venereal diseases. Our modern world is experiencing a venereal disease plague, called AIDS, which will kill millions of people all over the globe. Since modern man has been unable to stop the spread of AIDS despite all our modern technology, it can easily be seen how a similar disease could wipe out a more primitive culture. Dr. Fell broached one other possibility. He noted that one sculpture found in a burial mound in Ohio depicts a Nubian (a Black African), indicating the Hopewell culture was multiracial. This would be consistent with the known fact that Carthage's army included mercenaries from many nations. Dr. Fell postulated that the literate aristocracy of the Hopewell civilization might have been eliminated by a "slave revolt" of non-Punic people.[146] It is also possible that the Punic culture gradually lost its identity via intermarriage with other races. Since the Carthaginians practiced human sacrifice, and taught this evil practice to the Mayans, their North American descendants likely did so as well. This practice depleted their own gene pool. Most likely, several of the above factors gradually destroyed the last remnants of Carthaginian civilization in North America.

If Carthage, a mere colony of ancient Israel, grew to become an empire which came very close to crushing Rome, what became of the larger body of Israelites who migrated into Asia in 740-720 B.C.? As the reader will see in the next chapter, they also developed into powerful nations of their own. Then in the third book of this series, *Parthia: The Forgotten Ancient Superpower And Its Role In Biblical History,* we will learn that one of their nations became an ancient "superpower" empire, which rivaled the empire of Rome.

ENDNOTES: CHAPTER THREE

1.The Universal Jewish Encyclopedia, Vol. 3, see heading "Carthage," p. 52

2.Encyclopedia Britannica, Vol. 4, see "Carthage," p. 945

3.Edey, p. 131

4.Church, Carthage, p. 11

5.Young's Analytical Concordance to the Bible, see word "Kirjath," p. 574

6.Church, p. 11

7.Warmington, Carthage, p. 140; Charles-Picard, Daily Life in Carthage, p. 98, and Church, Carthage, pp. 11, 103

8.Charles-Picard, Daily Life in Carthage, p. 98

9.Smith, Rome and Carthage: The Punic Wars, pp. 11-12

10.Charles-Picard, p. 71; and Church, p. 12

11.Church, p. 11

12.Ibid., p. 11

13.Charles-Picard, Daily Life in Carthage, pp. 71 and 76; and Warmington, Carthage, p. 150

14.Young's Analytical Concordance to the Bible, see words "Priest," p. 772, and "Rabbi," p. 791

15.Charles-Picard, pp. 76-77

16.Ibid., p. 77

17.Young's Analytical Concordance to the Bible, see word "God," subhead two, p. 411

18.Charles-Picard, plate between pages 48 and 49

19.Rawlinson, George, Phoenicia, pp. 327 and 332

20.McClintock, John, and Strong, James, Cyclopedia of Biblical, Theological, and Ecclesiastical Literature, Vol. VIII, see "Phoenicia," p. 161

21.Encyclopedia Judaica, Vol. 5, Heading entitled "Carthage," p. 214

22.Ibid., p. 214

23.Charles-Picard, p.18

24.Encyclopedia Judaica, Vol. 5, heading entitled, "Carthage," p. 215

25.Charles-Picard, p. 18

26.Ibid., p. 18

27.Ibid., p. 19

28.Warmington, Carthage, p. 87

29.Charles-Picard, p. 19

30.Ibid., p. 173

31.Ibid., p. 173

32.Ibid., p. 178

33.Ibid., p. 179

34.Fell, Saga America, p. 53

35.Church, Carthage, p. 29

36.Fell, Saga America, p. 60

37.Encyclopedia Britannica, Vol. 18, Heading entitled "Pytheas," p. 804

38.Church, p. 122

39.Thebaud, Rev. Aug. J., The Irish Race, p. 6

40.Church, Carthage, p. 123

41.Pohl, Atlantic Crossings before Columbus, p. 20

42.Ibid., p. 21

43.Ibid., p. 22

44.Carpenter, Rhys, Beyond the Pillars of Heracles, p. 101

45.Fell, Barry, Saga America, pp. 54, 124-132; Boland, Charles, They All Discovered America, pp. 54-78

46.Fell, Saga America, pp. 55-58, 65-67, 84

47.Ibid., p. 56

48.Ibid., pp. 77-87

49.Ibid., pp. 56-59

50.Fell, "A Punic Inscription on an Atlatl-Weight From Georgia," Epigraphic Society Occasional Publications, Vol. 18, 1989, pp. 321-325

51.Fell, Saga America, p. 237

52.Smith, R. Bosworth, Carthage and the Carthaginians, p. 28

53.Davies, Voyagers to the New World, p. 151

54.Ibid., pp. 152-156

55.Ibid., p. 208

56.Gordon, Cyrus, Before Columbus, p. 187

57.Smith, Roberta, "Ancient Celtiberian and Mediterranean Peoples in the New World," Epigraphic Society Occasional Publications, Vol. 7, Part 2, 1979, p. 190

58.Capt, The Traditions of Glastonbury, p. 23

59.Waddell, The Phoenician Origin of Britons, Scots & Anglo-Saxons, p. 9, and Church, Carthage, p. 116

60.Charles-Picard, p. 35

61.Ibid., p. 153

62.Warmington, p. 147

63.Young's Analytical Concordance to the Bible, see words "Tophet" and "Topheth," p. 995

64.Charles-Picard, p. 67

65.Ibid., p. 64

66.Warmington, p. 239; and Charles-Picard, p. 64

67.Smith, R. Bosworth, Carthage and the Carthaginians, see map following p. 14

68.Charles-Picard, map on p. 16

69.Ibid., p. 183

70.Ibid., p. 89

71.Ibid., pp. 92-93

72.Wise, Terence and Healy, Mark, Hannibal's War With Rome, p. 13

73.Smith, R. Bosworth, Carthage and the Carthaginians, p. 8

74.Tytler, Alexander, Universal History, Vol. 1, p. 357

75.Charles-Picard, p. 125

76.Wise and Healy, Hannibal's War With Rome, p. 14

77.Ibid., p. 14

78.McClintock and Strong, Cyclopedia of Biblical, Theological and Ecclesiastical Literature, Vol. VIII, see "Phoenicia," p. 161

79.Church, pp. 218-224

80.Wise and Healy, Hannibal's War With Rome, p. 121

81.Ibid., p. 137

82.Halley, Bible Handbook, see "Daniel, Chapter 2," p. 266

83.Church, p. 269

84.Thebaud, p. 6

85.Encyclopedia Britannica, Vol. 23, see "Veneti," p. 46

86.Fell, Saga America, pp. 58 and 67; and article "Tanith in North Carolina," Epigraphic Society Occasional Publications, Vol. 18, 1989, p. 259

87.Fell, Saga America, p. 56

88.Fell, America B.C., pp. 95 and 160

89.Church, pp. 95-96

90.Lenhart, "The Adena Tablets," Epigraphic Society Occasional Publications, Vol. 13, 1985, pp. 206-208

91.Encyclopedia Americana, Vol. 14, see "Hopewell Culture," p. 370

92.Lenhart, "The Adena Tablets," Epigraphic Society Occasional Publications, Vol. 13, 1985, pp. 206-208

93."Interview with Barry Fell," Epigraphic Society Occasional Publications, Vol. 7, Part 2, 1979, pp. 162-163

94.Gordon, Before Columbus, pp.175-179

95.Ibid., p. 185

96.Ibid., p. 187

97.Steede, "Inscribed Bricks from Comalcalco," Epigraphic Society Occasional Publications, Vol. 17, 1988, p. 278

98.Fell, "A Punic Calendar from Comalcalco," Epigraphic Society Occasional Publications, Vol. 17, 1988, pp. 284-286

99.Wise and Healy, Hannibal's War With Rome, pp. 11-27

100.Fell, "A Christian North African Inscription from Comalcalco," Epigraphic Society Occasional Publications, Vol. 17, 1988, pp. 283-284

101.Fell, Barry, "The Micmac Manuscripts," Epigraphic Society Occasional Publications, Vol. 7, Part 2, 1979, pp. 146-150

102.Fell, Saga America, p. 174

103.Moore, E.R., "Inscribed Stones from Kent County, Michigan," Epigraphic Society Occasional Publications, Vol. 7, Part 2, 1979, pp. 182-185

104.Sodders. Betty, Michigan Prehistory Mysteries, p. 111

105.Ibid., pp. 28-29

106.Fell, America B.C., pp. 81 and 89

107.Ibid., pp. 164-167

108.Fell, America B.C., pp. 169-173

109.Ibid., pp. 174-175

110.Stubbs, Brian Darrel, "A Curious Element in Uto-Aztecan," Epigraphic Society Occasional Publications, Vol. 23, 1998, p. 109

111.Ibid., p. 109

112.Ibid., pp. 110, 112

113.Encyclopedia Americana, Vol. 18, Heading entitled "Maya," p. 539

114.Fell, Saga America, see illustration on p. 67

115.Charles-Picard, p. 51

116.Fell, Saga America, p. 78

117.Farley, Gloria, "The Shawnee Creek Stone of Oklahoma," Epigraphic Society Occasional Publications, Vol. 18, 1989, p. 260

118.Ibid., p. 260

119.Marx, Robert, In Quest of the Great White Gods, p.

120.Totten, Norman, "South to Eldorado," Epigraphic Society Occasional Publications, Vol. 7, Part 2, 1979, pp. 151-152

121.Gordon, Before Columbus, pp. 23-27

122.Ibid., pp. 22 and 26

123.Fell, Saga America, p. 79

124.Ceram, The March of Archaeology, p. 266

125.Leonard, Jonathan, Ancient America, p. 83

126.Ibid., p. 83 and Gordon, Cyrus, Before Columbus, p. 147

127.Church, pp. 280, 282

128.Ibid., p. 296

129.Ibid., p. 297

130.Fell, Saga America, pp. 31-32, 54, 124-132, 153

131.Ibid., pp. 124-128, 132

132.Fell, Saga America, p. 65

133.Young's Analytical Concordance to the Bible, Hebrew Lexicon Section, see words: "Ab, Matar, Qi, and Qo," pp. 1, 25, and 37

134.Smith, pp. 35-36

135.Carter, "A Note on the Elephant in America," Epigraphic Society Occasional Publications, Vol. 18, 1989, p. 90

136.Ibid., p. 90

137.Jefferson's Letters, Arranged by Willson Whitman, p. 199

138.Carter, "The Mammoth in American Epigraphy," Epigraphic Society Occasional Publications, Vol. 18, 1989, p. 213

139.Fell, America B.C., p. 184

140.Ibid., p. 188

141.Epigraphic Society Occasional Publications, "An Elephant Petroglyph," Vol. 17, 1988, p. 195

142.Carter, "A Note on the Elephant in America," and "The Mammoth in American Epigraphy," Epigraphic Society Occasional Publications, Vol. 18, 1989, pp. 90, 213

143.Carter, "A Note on the Elephant in America," Epigraphic Society Occasional Publications, Vol. 18, 1989, p. 90; and Fell, America B.C., p. 184

144.Carter, "The Mammoth in American Epigraphy," Epigraphic Society Occasional Publications, Vol. 18, 1989, p. 214

145.Fell, America B.C., p. 181

146.Ibid., p. 189

THE CARTHAGENIAN CONQUEROR, HANNIBAL, CROSSING THE RHONE ON HIS INVASION OF ROME 218 B.C.

Chapter 4
The Scythian "Sacae"
The Asian "Sons of Isaac"

There is a common misconception that the ten tribes of Israel "disappeared" when they migrated into Asia. Nothing could be further from the truth! For many centuries, ancient historians knew both who the Israelites were, and where they went. They were not "lost" at all.

Consider one such example. Flavius Josephus was a Jewish military commander, a Pharisee, and an historian of the first century A.D. He wrote this about the ten tribes of Israel who were in Asia:

> "...there are but two tribes in Asia and Europe subject to the Romans, while **the ten tribes are beyond Euphrates till now, and are an immense multitude, and not to be estimated by numbers**."[1] *(Emphasis added)*

Eight centuries after the ten tribes of Israel migrated to their new Asian homelands, Josephus knew that their population had become too numerous to estimate, and that the Euphrates River served as their western border.

Ezra 4:1 records that contingents of only three tribes (Judah, Levi and Benjamin) returned to Palestine in the time of Ezra and Nehemiah. They were the forebears of Judean Jews living in Judea at the time of Christ and Josephus. Judah, Levi and Benjamin were part of the former kingdom of Judah (II Chronicles 11:1, 14), not the

SCÜTH-LAND,
Illustrating Israel's Escape from Media, and first Settlement in Europe
Israelite Migrations shewn thus --------
Scale of English Miles.
0 100 200 300
BALTIC SEA
Lithuania.
Moscow
Prussia
R. Vistula
Poland
Germany
Great Russia
R. Dniepr, Dan-apris, or Borysthenes
R. Don, Tanais
SCÜTHIA at its largest.
B.C 450 - 400
S Russia
Country of the Cossacks.
Victory over Darius B.C. 507
Carpathian
Sereth
Kimmerians ber B.C. 655
Arsareth
R. Dniestr
R. Pruth
R. Hypanis
B.C. 654
Tyras
Ok-sakow
Hungary
R. Drave
R. Danube, Ister
Getai after B.C. 350
Isakchi
Servia
Getai, B.C 508
Balkans
Thrace
Turkey
BLACK SEA
Crimea
Sauro-matai
(Under this name were included tribes of Assyrians and Medes)
Caucasus
CASPIAN SEA
SAKAI
settled E of the Caspian in the 7th Centy B.C
R. Kür
Massagetai ber B.C. 655
R. Araxes
Scüths ber B.C. 685
Paphlagonia
Bithynia
Asia Overrun by Israel
Phrygia
Sardes
Lydia
Ephesus
Minor
Cilicia
R. Euphrates
Assyria
L. Van
Media
B C 650 - 600

kingdom of Israel (i.e. the "ten tribes of Israel"). Josephus affirmed that while contingents of Jews lived in Palestine, the ten tribes of Israel stayed in Asia. This is important because it refutes the misconception that the ten tribes migrated back to Palestine and were included with the Jews at the time of Christ.

The Ten Tribes of Israel Become "the Scythians"

Josephus asserts that **the ten tribes of Israel were still in Asia in the first century A.D.** His comment that the ten tribes were an "immense multitude" indicates we should expect to find very large masses of Israelites in Asia in the first century A.D., not isolated little remnants. An inevitable result of nations having very large populations in the ancient world was the achievement of political and military power, and we will see that the Asian Israelites had attained such power long before the time of Christ. Josephus' comment that the Israelites were "beyond Euphrates" tells us that the Asian Israelites were then located north and east of the Euphrates River. As the reader will see, it is not difficult to locate the Israelites in Asia.

The Bible contains promises concerning the Israelites that must be mentioned before the historical evidence is examined. A prophecy in Hosea 1:6-10, stated that although God would "utterly take away Israel [from Palestine]," he would, thereafter, make their population "as the sand of the sea, which cannot be measured or numbered." This prophecy about an innumerable population for the ten tribes had been fulfilled by the time of Christ, as Josephus confirmed. This illustrates an important lesson: God always keeps His promises and fulfills His prophecies.

Also, the Bible promised that the descendants of Abraham, Isaac and Jacob (Israel) would perpetually be known by a particular name. Genesis 21:12 records God's promise to Abraham that:

> "**through Isaac shall your descendants be named**." *(RSV)*

God's "covenant" blessings upon Abraham were inherited by Isaac and Jacob, whose name was changed to "Israel." Genesis 48:14-20

Ancient Egyptian Representation of the People of Samaria.

shows that Jacob-Israel passed on these blessings to the tribes of Ephraim and Manasseh. Therefore, while the name of "Isaac" could generally apply to any of the Israelite tribes, the term would most specifically identify the descendants of the tribes of Ephraim and Manasseh. Therefore, we should look for the Israelites in Asia or elsewhere to be known by various forms of the word "Isaac." As we shall see, secular history confirms that many large population groups in Asia did come to be known by variations of the name "Isaac."

Chapter two discussed several waves of migrations into Asia by the ten tribes of Israel. The captivity of the Israelites who withstood a three-year Assyrian siege in Samaria is the most famous, but it is actually the least significant of the Asian migrations. Assyrian cuneiform records state that a mere 27,290 Israelite captives were taken from Samaria.[2] The other two migrations involved far more people.

About twenty years before the fall of Samaria, the tribes of Gad, Naphtali, Reuben, and one-half the tribe of Manasseh were carried captive into Assyria (II Kings 15:29, I Chronicles 5:26). While the captives from Samaria represented only one city in the territory of the tribe of Ephraim, this earlier captivity involved the entire populations of at least three and one-half tribes. The Israelites taken in this captivity can be conservatively estimated in the hundreds of thousands. Also, as we learned in chapter two, many Israelites fled the final Assyrian invasion, voluntarily migrating into the region of the Black Sea and the Caucasus Mountains. Since this body of Israelites had a military escort of 220,000 soldiers as they migrated,[3] it easily numbered over one million people.

Many inhabitants of Israel's capital city, Samaria, were taken to the cities of the Medes (II Kings 17:6). We will begin our search by looking for a group of people who were not physically present in Media before the fall of Samaria. One historical account records that Assyria's King Esarhaddon in 674 B.C. was confronted by an alliance of "Mannaean, Median, and **newly-arrived Cimmerian forces**."[4] *(Emphasis added)* The "newly-arrived" Cimmerians were the Israelite Samarians who had been settled among the Medes only a few decades earlier. *Webster's New World Dictionary* states that "Cimmerian" is pronounced "Si-mer-e-en;"[5] the consonants of "**S**a**m**a**r**ia**n**" and "**S**i**m**e**r**ee**n**" are a perfect match. That these "Cimmerians" were "recent arrivals" in Media adds weight to their identification as Israelite captives from the city of Samaria.

The Israelites who migrated to the Black Sea region became known as "Scythians." The *Encyclopedia Britannica* records the Scythians as first being present in Eurasian locations in the seventh century B.C.[6] The *Encyclopedia Americana* adds:

> "The Scythians...are those tribes that occupied this territory [the region north of the Black Sea] from **about 700 B.C.**"[7] *(Emphasis added)*

Another account of the Scythian arrival in the Black Sea region is found in *The Scythians*, by Tamara Talbot Rice, which states:

> "The Scythians did not become a recognizable national entity...before the **eighth century B.C**...By the seventh century B.C. they had established themselves firmly in southern Russia...**Assyrian documents place their appearance...on the shores of Lake Urmia [just south of Armenia] in the time of King Sargon (722-705 B.C) a date which closely corresponds with that of the establishment of the first group of Scythians in southern Russia.**"[8] *(Emphasis added)*

These accounts are all consistent with the historical records cited in chapter two that the Israelites migrated to the Black Sea area toward the end of the eighth century B.C. Rice's account indicates **the Black Sea Scythians arrived in southern Russia via a route that included territory south of Armenia in 722-705 B.C.** That is

Ancient Representation of a Scythian Family.

exactly the time period the Israelites were migrating from their homeland, and **it also indicates the Scythians originated in a former homeland south of Armenia**. That place was Palestine, the location of the old kingdom of Israel.

Later in this chapter, we will see other Scythians came to live far to the east of the Black Sea Scythians. Tamara Rice's book includes a map showing that the burial sites of these "related clans" of the Scythians have been found as far eastward as the Pazirik/Altai region where the old Soviet Union joined the western edges of China and Mongolia.[9]

The opening of a burial mound of these eastern Scythians was the subject of an article in the October, 1994 issue of *National Geographic* magazine. It had the following commentary:

> "The Pazyryks thrived in these steppes...in the sixth through the second centuries B.C. They were horsemen ...[and] shepherds...Dozens of such tribes rose on the steppes of Eurasia in this era, creating a deceptively uniform culture labeled Scytho-Siberian...The Greek historian Herodotus faithfully detailed much of the life of the Scythians, a powerful, semi-nomadic people who lived north of the Black Sea between 800 B.C. and 100 B.C."[10]

A female mummified in the burial vault must have been a prominent Scythian as she was buried with several horses and gravegoods

1. A Scythian Footman; 2. A Scythian General.

with gold ornamentation. An earlier excavation in the area had yielded "two skeletons with European features" who were buried with weapons and ten horses. These eastern Scythians were one of many clans on the steppes related to the Scythians of the Black Sea region. The fact that some of their burial mounds yield skeletons "with European features"[11] will become increasingly important later in this chapter and in the next book in this series.

The Scythians were frequently called the "**Saka**," or "**Sacae**." The *Encyclopedia Britannica* states that the terms:

> "**Saka [Sacae] and Scyths...were regarded as synonymous**."[12] *(Emphasis added)*

The Greek story of Xenophon mentions the "Sacians" of Asia had "suffered very severely" at the hands of the Assyrians,[13] and a Roman writer, Pliny, stated the Scythians were "descended from slaves."[14] These accounts can only describe the Israelites: they bore the name of "Isaac" ("Sac"-ians), the Israelites truly were descended from a race of slaves (freed from Egypt in the Exodus), and they had suffered the complete destruction of their old kingdom of Israel at the hands of Assyria.

It is very significant that the Scythians were known as Sacae or Saka. As cited earlier, Genesis 21:12 promised that Abraham's future descendants would be known by the name of Isaac. The ancient Hebrew language did not list vowels; therefore, the name Isaac would be represented by the consonants S-C or S-K. Sac-ae is the word Isaac with the Latin plural "ae" attached. That these "Sacae" are recorded as living near the Black Sea soon after many Israelites migrated there supports the contention that they were relocated Israelites.

Speculation that the Scythians originated in the interior of Asia is clearly refuted not only by the above account of Tamara Rice, but also by the images found on Scythian artifacts. A Russian art book translated into English) reproduces many examples of Scythian artwork showing Scythians with bearded, Semitic features, not Mongoloid features.[15] The *McClintock and Strong Cyclopedia* reproduces images of a Scythian family and a Scythian horseman, footman and general.[16] All depict Scythians with obvious Caucasian and Semitic features, indicating their origin was in the Fertile Crescent, not the interior of Asia.

Not all ancient people bearing the name "Scythian" were descended from the ten tribes of Israel. The term "Scythian" was sometimes used generically to describe any tribe with a nomadic or semi-nomadic lifestyle. Some "Turanians" were also called "Scythian" or "Sacae." The Turanians may have had a Japhetic descent, with the term "Turanian" perhaps based on Tiras, one of the sons of Japheth. *(Genesis 10:2)* The Dniester River, which empties into the Black Sea, was anciently called the "Tyras" River, further supporting such a conclusion. It is possible to confuse the "Sacae Scythians" and "Turanian Scythians," as George Rawlinson observed:

> "The term 'Scythic' is not...ethnical. It designates a life rather than a descent, habits rather than blood. It is applied by the Greeks and Romans to Indo-European and Turanian races indifferently, provided they are nomads, dwelling in tents...living on the produce of their flocks and herds..."[17]

Two races were called Scythians: the Indo-European "Sacae" and the "Turanians." The terms "Sacae" and "Saka" do indicate an Israelite ethnicity, but the term "Scythian" can sometimes include non-Israelites as well.

In 653 B.C., the Medes and Cimmerians allied with the Scythians under a leader named "Phraortes" against the Assyrians. They lost their war with the Assyrians (and Phraortes died),[18] but it is significant that the Scythians were anti-Assyrian. Once it is understood that these Scythians were Israelites, their antipathy toward Assyria is understandable. **The Scythians and Cimmerians were kinsmen**; the

A Scythian Horseman. (From the sculptures at Kertch.)

Encyclopedia Britannica calls the Cimmerians a "Scythian tribe."[19] Here we see Israelite tribes joining the Medes to fight the Assyrians mere decades after they left Palestine.

Their leader's name, "Phraortes," was a Hellenized form of "Phares," a name of the tribe of Judah. Genesis 49:10 promised that dynasties of kings would come from Judah, and Jeremiah 33:17-22 prophesied that the descendants of King David, also of the Phares line, would become very numerous and would perpetually rule over descendants of "the house of Israel." Jeremiah prophecied this **after** the house of Israel (the northern ten tribes) had migrated to Asia. The name "Phraortes" indicates that descendants of King David were ruling Asian Israelites soon after their removal from Palestine, showing that God had not forgotten His promise to David's progeny. *(II Samuel 7:8-17)* One of the last kings of Judah, Jehoichin, was taken to Babylon as a captive *(II Kings 24:8-15)*, but a later Babylonian king "set his throne above the throne of the kings that were with him in Babylon." *(II Kings 25:27-30)* Jehoichin, David's descendant, became a high vassal king in the Babylonian Empire. He fathered many sons *(I Chronicles 3: 16-24)*, making the royal seed of King David numerous in Asia. The kings of Babylon apparently placed these royal descendants over captive Israelites, fulfilling God's promise to King David that his seed would rule over the ten tribes of Israel! Almost from the beginning, these royal descendants were the kings of the Asian nations and empires of the Israelites.

What happened to the Israelites — the tribes of Reuben, Gad, Naphthali and one-half of Manasseh — who were carried captive by the Assyrians about twenty years before Samaria fell? It is recorded that the "Scythians" were not only located in the Black Sea region, but also in Mesopotamia, just east of Assyria. The *Encyclopedia Britannica* states that: "A Scythian power had grown up in the old kingdom of

SIEGE OF SAMARIA. KHORSABAD.

Ellip, to the east of Assyria...[by] Ecbatana."[20] History records that Scythian powers developed in two locations: one by the Black Sea and the other east of Assyria.

The Scythians located east of Assyria in modern Iran were descended from Israelites taken captive by the Assyrians, while the Sacae Scythians in the Black Sea region were descended from Israelites who fled there to avoid Assyrian captivity. The captive Israelites soon displaced the nation of Ellip into whose region they had been placed. What nation had been displaced by the Israelites who migrated to the Black Sea and Caucasus Mountains? This region was previously called Urartu. William Culican's *The Medes and the Persians* states that Urartu was "enfeebled by Scythian incursions."[21] Tamara Rice's book, *The Scythians*, records:

> *"in the area roughly corresponding to present-day Azerbaijan, the kingdom of Urartu had crumbled. The Scythians, under their king Partatua...firmly established themselves in...Urartu itself, where they set up their capital at **Sak**iz..."*[22] *(Emphasis added)*

A Scythian capital was named "**Sak**iz," honoring the Israelite patriarch, I**saac**. Who else but the relocated ten tribes of Israel would name an Asian city in honor of Isaac? Their territory was in the modern region of Armenia and Azerbaijan, between the Black and Caspian Seas. One of their first kings was named "Partatua." Ancient languages often interchanged the letters "p" and "b." Try saying these letters yourself; they have very similar sounds and are called "labial consonants." When you change the first "p" in the Scythian king's name to a "b," you have "Bart-atua." The first syllable of his name "Bart-" preserves the root word of "B-R-T," the Hebrew word for "covenant." As the reader knows from previous discussions in this series on Israelite history, the consonants "B-R-T" are a distinctive identifier of the tribes of Israel.

The *Encyclopedia Britannica* refers to the Scythians as "newcomers" to the area in the seventh century B.C.,[23] and William Culican's book, *The Medes and the Persians*, states that Scythian numbers and influence grew in the seventh century B.C.[24] Since the Israelites migrated into Asia at the end of the eighth century B.C., their rise to prominence in the seventh century B.C. is very consistent with biblical accounts.

Scythian Culture and Society

Historians tell us the Scythians were agriculturists who both planted crops and followed their herds (hence the word "nomads"). The old Israelite lifestyle from the days of Abraham revolved around agriculture, and they both planted crops and were herdsmen. Ezekiel 27:17 records the Israelites had been food exporters in the kingdoms of Israel and Judah. A Jewish historian cited by Col. Gawler in an earlier chapter stated that the Israelites fled through Armenia from the Assyrians, and went "with their flocks, and turned nomads."[25] The Scythians carried on the Israelite traditions of being agriculturists, food exporters and "nomads" dwelling in portable dwellings as they followed their flocks and herds. Zenaide Ragozin's book, Media, records:

> "Some seventy years after the time of Herodotus we find from contemporary evidence that 600,000 bushels of Scythian corn went to Athens alone each year."[26]

If 600,000 bushels of grain went to one Greek city each year in the fifth century, B.C., one wonders how much the Scythians exported to the world as a whole. Herodotus confirmed that the Scythians grew corn for use as an export crop,[27] and the production of a voluminous grain crop shows the Scythians were skilled farmers, not "hunter-gatherers."

Scythian agriculturists had civilized tastes. William Culican, in *The Medes and the Persians*, states:

> "...it was to the Scythians that Achaemenid objects had greatest appeal. The dinner services, upholstered beds and thrones designed for the mess tents of Persian officers on field duty admirably suited the...nomadic Scythian leaders. Scythian tombs were elaborately furnished and...the Scythians not only had a close relationship with the Medes and Persians but supplied from their Ural territories much of the gold on which Persia depended."[28]

Tamara Rice also wrote concerning the Scythians:

> "...their wealth and love of finery won them the good will of the great Hellenic merchants established along the shores of the Black Sea...the Scythians already displayed an extraordinary ability to appreciate and assimilate the best in the art of their day."[29]

The above accounts are significant. A nation that possessed wealth, enjoyed fine tableware and upholstered beds, and exhibited an "extraordinary" appetite for the fine arts is one that prizes the material comforts of a civilized society. The fact that Scythia had a well-developed gold mining, refining and exporting industry indicates that not all Scythians were farmers or ranchers. Their gold mines indicate that some Scythians were involved in industrial pursuits, and their success in the gold trade confirms that they possessed the technological expertise to process gold ores into beautiful finished products. These Scythians had originated in the kingdom of Israel's "Phoenician" homeland. The Israelite-Phoenicians were a very civilized, prosperous people who enjoyed a civilized society and excelled in international commerce. It is not surprising that their Asian descendants exhibited these same attributes. Like their Scythian progeny, the Phoenicians had been excellent goldsmiths. The *McClintock and Strong Cyclopedia* states that the Phoenicians:

> "...manufactured all kinds of beautiful vessels and ornaments in gold, silver and ivory..."[30]

The Scythians manufactured some of the ancient world's most elegant works of gold art. Books have been written which display their artistic abilities.[31] Their civilized tastes and sophisticated skills

confirm their origin was in the Mesopotamian/Mediterranean region, not the wild steppes of deepest Asia. A comment by Georges Charriere, author of the bok, *Scythian Art: Crafts of the Eurasian Nomads*, also confirms the Scythians migrated into the Russian steppes from the south, not from the north. Speaking of the "characteristic animal style of Scythian art," Charriere wrote:

> "There is no ground for concluding that this style had its birth in the Altai or in any other region of Siberia. Along with the other elements of the Scythian culture, it was derived from the cultural heritage of the ancient East and **originated in the peripheral regions of Assyria, among the Iranian-language tribes settled in the north of Iran**."[32] *(Emphasis added)*

Charriere is speaking specifically of the Scythians who lived east of the Caspian Sea. While the Black Sea Scythians descended from Israelites who fled to that region to avoid Assyrian captivity, the eastern Scythians evidenced an origin in "the peripheral regions of Assyria" and "the north of Iran." The Bible records that the Israelites who did go into captivity were settled "in Assyria" *(II Kings 15:29)* and in the "cities of the Medes." *(II Kings 17:6)* The "cities of the Medes"

Close-up of figures on the Behistun Rock

were in "the north of Iran." Here we see strong cultural evidence that the eastern Scythians were originally subjects of the Assyrian and Medo-Persian Empires, and moved into the Russian steppes from the south. These Scythians were the Israelites who had, indeed, been captives in the Assyrian Empire and were transplanted to the north of Iran. When the Assyrian and Medo-Persian Empires fell, these Israelites were freed from their captors, and they migrated into the steppes east of the Caspian Sea. II Kings 15:29 and 17:6 identify these captive Israelites who became the eastern Scythians as the tribes of Naphthali, Gad, Reuben, one-half the tribe of Manasseh, and the Ephraimites who had been besieged in Samaria.

Georges Charriere also notes linguistic evidence that the Scythians migrated into the Russian steppes from the south, not from northern Asia. He wrote:

> "...the steppes as far as the Altai Mountains were inhabited by **Scythians** or **Sac**ian tribes — **Persian-speaking peoples** of Central Asia, similar to the Scythians in their economic organization, way of life and culture."[33] *(Emphasis added)*

Obviously, if these Scythians had originated in the northern, interior regions of Asia, they would not have been a "Persian-speaking" people. The fact that their many tribes spoke a language of the Persian Empire confirms not only that the Scythians had once lived within the Persian Empire, but that they had lived there for a considerable period of time. This would be an expected trait of the Israelite captives who had lived within the Assyrian and Medo-Persian Empires for centuries.

It was mentioned earlier that the "Scythians" included both the Sacae and the Turanians. In addition to the civilized Scythians, there were ignorant and uncouth tribes on the steppes. Herodotus, a Greek historian of the fifth century B.C., affirmed that the civilized Scythians lived close to some very uncivilized tribes, which he described in these words:

> "the Man-Eaters, a tribe that is entirely peculiar and not Scythian at all...[and] the Black Cloaks, another tribe which is not Scythian at all."[34]

Herodotus confirms the civilized qualities of the Scythians and the backwardness of "non-Scythian" tribes in the following blunt words.

> "The Euxine Pontus [the Black Sea]...contains — **except for the Scythians** — the stupidest nations in the world."[35] *(Emphasis added)*

In these accounts, Herodotus used the term "Scythian" in an ethnic sense to designate the civilized "Sacae." However, as noted above, other writers sometimes used the term "Scythian" to describe all the tribes living in the Russian steppes.

Colonel Gawler cites Epiphanius as stating "the laws, customs, and manner of the Scythians were received by other nations as the standards of policy, civility, and polite learning."[36] He also cites the following from book viii, iii, 7 of Strabo's *Geography:*

> "Aeschylus too...says, 'but the Scythians governed by good laws...' And this is still the opinion entertained of them by the Greeks; for we esteem them the most sincere, the least deceitful of any people, and much more frugal and self-relying than ourselves."[37]

Strabo was a Greek writer during the first century B.C. Modern students are taught to think the Greco-Romans were the most civilized people of the ancient world, yet Strabo's account offers the opinion that the laws, frugality and self-reliance of the Scythians excelled that of the Greeks! Strabo even declares that the Scythians excelled all nations in their sincerity and honesty. Strabo, a prominent Greco-Roman, seems to assert that the Scythians were the most civilized people of his time.

There is an additional record that the Scythians of South Russia had their origins among the Semitic nations of the Mideast. Zenaide Ragozin's *Media* states:

> "...Scythians was not a race name at all, but one... used for all remote, little known, especially nomadic peoples of the north and northeast, denoting tribes...of Turanian as of **Indo-European stock: to the latter the Scythians of Russia are now universally admitted to have belonged**."[38] *(Emphasis added)*

The term "Scythian" came to represent a lifestyle as well as a racial group. However, the highly civilized Scythians of South Russia were known to be "Indo-European," not "Turanian." This adds more confirmation that their origin was among the Indo-European nations south of the Black Sea, not among the uncivilized nomads in the interior of Asia.

The evidence clearly indicates that the Scythians moved into the Russian steppes from the south, not from the north! A large body of the ten tribes of Israel moved from Palestine to the Black Sea region of south Russia when Samaria fell. Even as the Israelites were herdsmen and exporters of grain, so were the Scythians. Even as the Israelites had been skilled in metallurgy from the time of Solomon, so were the Scythians. Even as the Israelites had civilized tastes, so did the Scythians. The Israelites were descendants of Isaac, and the Scythians bore the name of Isaac ("Sac-ae" or "Sak-a"). The Israelites fled into the Black Sea regions in about 721 B.C., and the "Scythians" were first noted in the Black Sea regions soon after this date. There is no doubt about the origin of the Scythians: They were displaced Israelites building a new homeland in the Black Sea region and in parts of the Russian steppe.

Herodotus records that the Persians called all the Scythian tribes "Sacae."[39] Latin writers substituted an "x" for the "c" or "k" in Sacae/Saka and called them the "Saxoi" or "Saxones."[40] This provides even more evidence that the Sacae Scythians were the descendants of the ten tribes of Israel. The Israelites were known by these names before they ever left Palestine!

Assyrian records mention the rebellion of the Esakska, who called themselves "Beth Sak" or "House of Isaac" in their own

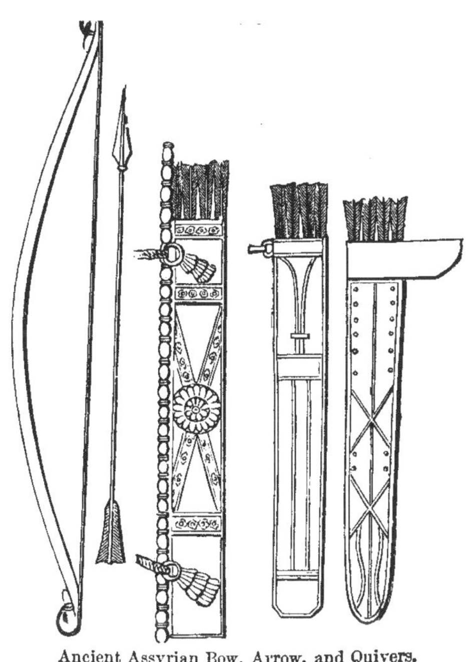
Ancient Assyrian Bow, Arrow, and Quivers.

country.[41] Here we have an Assyrian confirmation that the Israelites were known by the name of Isaac (the root word: "**Sak**") prior to their migrations into Asia. The word "beth" is a Hebrew word meaning, "house."[42] The Israelites continued to bear the Hebrew racial names "**Saka**" or "**Sacae**" after their migration into Asia. The prophet Amos cited the term "House of Isaac" (i.e., "Beth Sak") as describing the ten-tribed northern kingdom of Israel just decades prior to the fall of Samaria and the Israelites' migrations to Asia. *(Amos 7:16)*

The biblical book of Jeremiah confirms that many of the ten tribes of Israel migrated to the Black Sea region. Jeremiah 3:3-12 contains a message from God to both the Jews (Judah) and the ten tribes of Israel. This message was given a century **after** the ten tribes of Israel were conquered by the Assyrians. In verses 6-10, God warned that Judah was repeating the sins that had caused the kingdom of Israel to fall. In verse 11, God states: "Backsliding **Israel** hath justified herself more than treacherous **Judah**." This confirms that the Jews and the northern ten tribes were still separate entities, and that the ten tribes were in a better standing with God than were the Jews at the time of this message! That is consistent with accounts presented in an earlier chapter that the people of the ten tribes who migrated to the Black Sea region had implemented religious reforms. Jeremiah 3:12 directs this statement to the ten tribes of Israel:

> "...**proclaim these words toward the north**, and say, Return, thou backsliding **Israel**, saith the Lord; and I will not cause mine anger to fall upon you: for I am merciful..." *(KJV)*

If all ten tribes of Israel were taken captive to Assyria, this message to the Israelites would have been sent "to the east" since Assyria was located east of Jerusalem. **Jeremiah 3:12 acknowledges that most of the ten tribes of Israel were then located not to the east but to the north of Jerusalem**. If you check a map or globe, you will confirm that the Black Sea region is located due north of Jerusalem. Jeremiah's message to the ten tribes ("Israel") was directed toward the Black Sea region where the Scythians (the "Sacae") lived.

Many have the mistaken impression that God forsook the ten tribes of Israel when they migrated from Palestine. Not at all! Jeremiah directed a favorable message from God to them about a century after Samaria fell. Hosea 1:10 records that God promised to vastly increase the population of the ten tribes of Israel **after** he expelled them from Palestine. Josephus' quote at the beginning of this chapter indicates God had fulfilled that prophecy by the first century A.D. In Jeremiah 51:5, it is also stated:

> "For **Israel hath not been forsaken**, nor **Judah** of his God, of the Lord of hosts..." *(KJV)*

This was written circa 595 B.C., long after the ten tribes went into captivity. God was still guiding the destinies of **both** the ten tribes of Israel and the Jews even after the ten tribes left Palestine. How could he forsake them? They were the "birthright" seed of Abraham, and God's covenant with Abraham's descendants was unconditional! In greatly expanding the ten tribes' population, God was keeping His promise to Abraham! *(Genesis 13:16 and 48:14-16)* God also kept His promise in Genesis 21:12 and Genesis 48:14-20 that Abraham's descendants would be known by the name of Isaac. Because this promise primarily applied to the tribes of Ephraim and Manasseh, many of the Scythians known as the "Sacae" would be from those tribes.

God did not give the great "birthright" blessings of the Abrahamic covenant to the tribe of Judah (the Jews). These birthright blessings were permanently given to the tribes of Ephraim and Manasseh in Genesis 48. The one Abrahamic blessing specifically given to the tribe of Judah was the promise that dynasties of kings would emerge from that tribe. *(Genesis 49:10)* This was fulfilled when King

David's descendants founded many dynasties of kings, as will be examined more extensively in the next book in this series.

The famous "Amarna Tablets" are very ancient records of letters from Canaanite rulers to Egypt's Pharaoh desperately calling for help against the powerful invasions of a people called the "Haberi," "Habiru," etc. These invaders were the **Hebrews**, as documented in David Rohl's book, *Pharaohs and Kings. (see the first book in this series)* Mrs. Sydney Bristowe, in *Oldest Letters in the World*, wrote the following about the Amarna Tablets:

> "The great importance of the Amarna Tablets has not been recognized because apparently, the translations have been unwilling to admit that the Israelites are mentioned upon them...the name Haberi...is hardly seen in these translations, yet that name, appears frequently in the tablets and leading philologists certify that it stands for the Hebrews (Israelites)... Another name mentioned upon the tablets is **Saga** which is said to be identical with Haberi (Knudtzon, Die El-Amarna Tafeln, p. 51), and is proved to be so by the fact that it occurs upon the Behistun Rock in Persia where, according to Sir Henry Rawlinson, it represents the Israelites (the **Sakai** or 'House of Isaac')."[43] *(Emphasis added)*

Mrs. Bristowe's book cites a German book and Sir Henry Rawlinson in support of the conclusion that the Amarna Tablets identify the Israelites. Dr. H. R. Hall, a former Keeper of the British Museum's Department of Egyptian and Assyrian Antiquities, wrote in his book, *The Ancient History of the Near East:*

> "It seems very probable that **the 'SA-GAZ'...and...the Khabiru who devastated Canaan in Akhenaton's time are no other than the invading Hebrews**...In my own view, the probabilities are all in favor of the identification."[44] *(Emphasis added)*

Both the above authors agree with David Rohl that the Habiru were the Hebrews, and that the Amarna tablets record a Hebrew invasion of Canaan. Bristowe and Dr. Hall favor the time of Joshua for this invasion, while David Rohl assigns it 400 years later to the time of King David's conquest of all the cities of Canaan. This author finds Rohl's evidence persuasive. Accounts that the Hebrews were known as "**Saga**" or "**Sagaz**" indicate an obvious similarity to "**Saka**" or

"**Sacae**" ("g" and "k" are closely related guttural consonants). This confirms that the name of Isaac, so firmly stamped on the Scythians, had also been applied to the Israelites in Palestine at least since the time of King David.

Israelite Customs among the Scythians

The inscriptions on the Behistun Rock also link the Scythians to the Israelite/Phoenicians. The Persian ruler, Darius, proclaimed a victory (circa 516 B.C.) via a huge inscription on a mountain near Behistun (or "Behistan"). It depicts Darius receiving the leaders of captive nations who are being led before him via ropes tied around their necks.[45] The *Encyclopedia Britannica* states that the last captive in line is "a Scythian wearing a tall, pointed cap."[46] Herodotus was cited above as stating that the Persians called all the Scythians "Sacae," so a cultural characteristic of the Sacae was the wearing of tall, pointed caps.

That only the Scythian captive wore this hat identifies it as a trait unique to the Scythians. Herodotus commented on this Scythian headgear:

> "The Sacae, who are Scythians, have high caps tapering to a point and stiffly upright, which they wear on their heads."[50]

Wearing a tall, pointed cap was also a cultural trait of the Israelite-Phoenicians. Evidence of this Phoenician trait has been found in both the Old World and in ancient America. In the Old World, an example of Phoenicians wearing such caps is found on a relief from Persepolis as shown in the *Encyclopedia Americana*.[47] Dr. Barry Fell's *America B.C.* shows a terra-cotta figurine found in an American burial mound depicting a Phoenician with a tall cap, the "characteristic high-crowned hat, the hennin, worn on formal occasions."[48] Israelite high priests wore tall hats called miters. *(Exodus 28:37-29:6)* The miter had a "forefront" *(Exodus 28:37)*, and a blue decoration "high upon the miter" *(Exodus 39:31)*, verifying that it was a tall cap. This type of headgear was adopted by Israelites in leadership positions. *Harper's Bible Dictionary* shows tall, pointed hats as an example of "Hebrew royal attire."[49]

The matching headgear of the Israelite-Phoenicians and the Sacae-Scythians is one more cultural factor supporting the conclusion that the Scythians were the displaced ten tribes of Israel. Further evidence of the Israelite origins of the Scythians is found in this comment of Herodotus about them:

> " They make no offerings of pigs, nor will they keep them at all in their country."[51]

Such a prohibition is very consistent with the well-known Hebrew custom of forbidding the use of swine for either consumption or sacrifice because it was an "unclean" animal. *(Deuteronomy 14:7-8)* Who else but displaced Israelites would be observing — if readers will pardon the oversimplification — a "kosher" lifestyle in the Russian steppes? Herodotus also records that one of the Scythian kings was named "**Saulius**."[52] Given the Hebrew-Israelite background of the Scythians, the namesake of this Scythian king was **Saul,** the first Israelite king. *(I Samuel 9)*

Herodotus also records that "The Scythians themselves say that their nation is the youngest of all the nations...[and] from their first king...to the crossing of Darius into Scythia was, in all, one thousand years..."[53] Col. Gawler analyzed Herodotus' record as follows:

> "Now Darius' expedition against the Scythians was about 500 B.C., and 1000 years before that brings us to the time of Moses."[54]

Significantly, the Scythians traced their origin as a nation to the approximate time of Moses. It was after the Exodus, under Moses, that the Israelites truly became a nation with their own distinct culture, sovereignty and laws.

Additional evidence that Scythia was a new Israelite homeland is the appearance of the name of the Israelite tribe of Dan in the Black Sea area. The tribe of Dan was known for giving its tribal name to geographic locations (Joshua 19:47). The rivers emptying into the Black Sea were formerly known as the Ister, Tyras, Borysthenes, and Tanais, but, after the Scythians migrated into the region, their names were changed to the **Danube, Dniester, Dnieper, and Don** Rivers.

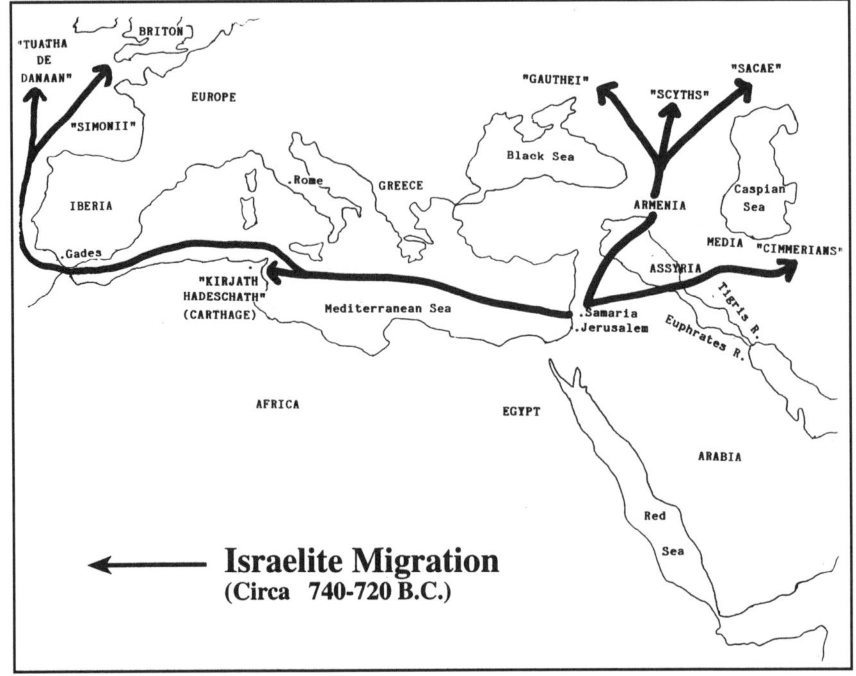

Collier's Encyclopedia states:

"The names of the...rivers Danube, Dnestr, Dnepr and Don are Scythian..."[55]

The tribe of Dan was split into two homelands in Palestine: one on the seacoast and one in a land-locked area in the north of Israel. In a previous chapter, we saw evidence that many Danites migrated to Ireland when Israel fell, but the prominence of the name **Dan** in Scythian areas indicates that other Danites joined the migration into the Black Sea regions. A major Scythian tribe was named the Dahai or Dahae, which may also indicate the tribe of Dan.

One of the most prominent Scythian tribes was the Massagetae, most likely indicating the Israelite tribe of Manasseh. Note the similarity between the Scythian **Massa-getae**, and the **Massae-scyli**, a tribe that lived in Carthaginian territory (the Israelite origin of Carthage was discussed in the previous chapter). Manasseh was one of the largest tribes of Israel, so large that it received two territories for its population when Joshua conquered Canaan. As one of the largest tribes,

Manassehites logically would have been among the Israelites who founded Carthage, as well as being one of the more recognizable tribes in Scythia.

Scythia Conquers the Assyrian Empire

We will now reconstruct the widely ignored history of the Scythians. We have seen that the Cimmerians and Scythians were allied against the Assyrians in 653 B.C., but were defeated. In approximately 624 B.C., the Scythians launched a massive invasion to the south, and occupied Asia Minor, Syria, Media, Palestine and much of Assyria. They marched as far south as Egypt, but spared that nation when the Egyptians offered them tribute money.[56] Assyria was not so fortunate. In the words of Werner Keller, the Scythians "inundated the Assyrian Empire."[57] The *Encyclopedia Britannica* states:

> "The Scythians penetrated into Assyria and made their way as far as the borders of Egypt. Calah was burned, though the strong walls of Nineveh protected the relics of the Assyrian army which had taken refuge behind them..."[58]

The Scythian attack upon the Assyrian city of Calah (Kalakh) is noteworthy. The *Encyclopedia Britannica* notes that Calah "was the headquarters of the army in Assyria."[59] By directly attacking the headquarters of the Assyrian army, the Scythians were "going for the jugular" of Assyria. Though Assyria struggled on for a few years, the Scythians dealt Assyria a mortal blow. Babylonia soon revolted against Assyria, and the eastern Scythians joined this revolt. As the reader will recall, there were "northern Scythians" from the Black Sea region and "eastern Scythians" who lived east of Assyria. It was the northern Scythians who conquered most of the Assyrian Empire and burnt Calah, but it was (apparently) the eastern Scythians who joined Babylon to administer a "coup de grace" to Assyria. The *Encyclopedia Britannica* records:

> "the Scythian king of Ecbatana [a city east of Assyria])...came to the help of the Babylonians. **Nineveh was captured and destroyed by the Scythian army**."[60] *(Emphasis added)*

Some accounts credit "the Medes and Babylonians" with destroying Nineveh, but the *Encyclopedia Britannica* states that it was the Babylonians and Scythians who conquered Nineveh. It explains that the Babylonians referred to Scythians as "Manda,"[61] and that Greek writers missed the Scythian role "through a confusion of Mada or 'Medes' with Manda." The Babylonian term **Man-da** may also have been derived from **Man-asseh**, one of Israel's chief tribes.

The northern Scythians from the Black Sea occupied Asia Minor, Mesopotamia, Syria and Palestine for a short time, just twenty-eight years according to Herodotus.[62] Why did Scythia attack the whole territory of the Assyrian Empire, and then leave the region after so short a time? Both answers come clearly into focus when one understands that the Scythians were the descendants of the ten tribes of Israel.

The motive for the Scythian invasion was likely two-fold. One primary motive was the desire for revenge against the Assyrians who had driven them from their former homeland in the kingdom of Israel. It was poetic justice that after Assyria invaded and destroyed the kingdom of Israel, Assyria was itself invaded and defeated by Scythia, the offspring of the Israelites that had originally fled from Assyria. Indeed, the desire to liberate their fellow Israelites who were still Assyrian captives may have served as a further motive for the Scythian invasion of Assyria.

A second reason for Scythia's invasion was apparently the reoccupation of the territory of the old kingdom of Israel in Palestine. The fact that the Scythians charged straight south through Asia Minor and Syria into Palestine gives weight to this conclusion. In the century that had passed since the ten tribes were forced out of Palestine, old-timers reminiscing about their homeland had probably referred it to as "the land of milk and honey." The Scythian Israelites may have originally intended to reoccupy Palestine permanently when they reconquered it.

Scythian victories were so widespread that Herodotus observed:

> "...the Scythians took control of all Asia."[63]

While the Scythians waged war against the Assyrians in Mesopotamia, Herodotus records that on their march through Palestine:

> "...the majority of the Scythians marched by, doing no harm to anyone."[64]

It is significant that while marching through Palestine, the Scythians did not attack or harm the Jewish capital of Jerusalem. The kingdom of Judah was still in existence at that time. If the Scythian motive was simple conquest, why did they spare the Jewish capital? Since the entire Assyrian army could not stand before the Scythian onslaught, Judah had no might to resist them. The obvious conclusion is that the Scythians **chose** to spare Jerusalem. This makes sense only if the Scythians were the descendants of the ten tribes of Israel who knew the Jews were actually a "brother" tribe. This argues that while the Scythians were determined to destroy Assyria, their purpose was to "liberate" Palestine. One city in Palestine, Beth-Shan, was renamed "Scythopolis" in honor of the Scythians, and the local population retained that name even after the Scythians left the area. Werner Keller notes that there is no evidence that the Scythians ever occupied or garrisoned Beth-Shan,[65] so the reason for changing the name of Beth-Shan to Scythopolis is a mystery. There is a logical answer for this "mystery." When a city is renamed, it is usually done to honor the memory of someone or something. Since the Scythian presence among the Jews was a gentle one, and they freed them from the Assyrian Empire, Beth-Shan was likely renamed Scythopolis to honor the Scythian liberation of the region.

That the Scythians devastated Assyria while sparing Jewish cities confirms that the Scythians looked upon the Jews favorably. **This would make no sense whatsoever if the Scythians were wild Asian nomads in Palestine for the first time. However, it is completely logical when one realizes that, as descendants of the ten tribes of Israel, the Scythians were blood relatives of the Jews!**

The fall of Nineveh has been dated as follows:

> "...the Assyrian capital [Nineveh] fell after a long war conducted by the Medes, Babylonians and Scythians in 612 B.C..."[66]

Scribes Writing down the Number of the Slain. (Koyunjik.)

With the Assyrian Empire eliminated, Herodotus observed:

"For twenty-eight years, then, the Scythians were masters of Asia..."[67]

King Josiah of Judah and the Scythians in Palestine

The Scythian occupation of the entire region of what is today called "the Mideast" occurred during the reign of King Josiah over Judah, circa 639-608 B.C. The Bible does not mention "Scythians" being in Palestine at that time because "Scythian" was a Greek term. **The Bible does refer to the "Scythians" who were in Palestine during Josiah's reign, but it refers to them by their Israelite tribal names.** There is an interesting account in the reign of Josiah that involved the Scythians. II Kings 22:3 states that Josiah issued a decree to restore the Temple of God "in the eighteenth year" of his reign, circa 621 B.C.

During the reigns of previous evil kings, the Jews had lost their awareness of God's laws. When a copy of God's laws was found in Josiah's Temple restoration project, Judah again realized what God's laws actually commanded. *(II Chronicles 34:8-33)* When he learned what God's laws stated, Josiah was aghast at his nation's degeneracy. Josiah embarked on a national crusade to "clean house." II Kings 23:4-20 records that King Josiah's reforms included the destruction of sun-god and mother-goddess images, forbidding human sacrifices, tearing down "the houses of the male cult prostitutes which were in the house of the Lord" *(RSV)*, the execution of pagan priests and even the destruction of the altars for pagan gods which King Solomon had built for his foreign wives. It is shocking to realize that for over three centuries, King Solomon's altars to foreign gods had been standing in Jerusalem! Josiah finally destroyed them. Josiah even commanded the destruction of the pagan altar at Bethel, built by Jeroboam, the first ruler of the kingdom of Israel.

Josiah also reestablished the observance of God's Holy Days: the Passover and the Days of Unleavened Bread. *(II Chronicles 35:17-18)* However, notice the curious account of who kept these festivals along with Josiah and his nation. Verses 17-18 add:

> "And the **children of Israel that were present** kept the Passover... and the feast of unleavened bread seven days. And there was no Passover like to that kept in Israel from the days of Samuel...as Josiah kept... and all Judah **and Israel that were present**..." *(KJV)*

This records that "all Judah" and "the children of Israel that were present" kept these Holy Days of God. This account affirms that descendants of the ten tribes of Israel were keeping this festival along with Josiah and Judah as a clear distinction is made between "Judah" and "Israel." One's first impression is that this seems to be an impossibility, as II Kings 17:18 states that when the Israelites were deported from Palestine, God "removed them" and that "none was left but the tribe of Judah only." Since all the tribes of Israel were earlier removed from Palestine, how was it possible that not only were portions of the ten tribes again in Palestine at the time of Josiah, but that they were also devout enough to participate in observing God's Holy Days?

The answer is simple. The "Israelites" from the ten tribes "who were present" in Palestine during king Josiah's revival were the Scythians (the "Sacae") whose armies were then occupying everything from Palestine to Mesopotamia! We have seen that Herodotus recorded that the Scythians were known for good laws, avoided idols and pagan ceremonies and even avoided swine's flesh. Herodotus has preserved for us the fact that the Scythians were known for keeping key aspects of the Law of Moses. Since it is known that the Scythians were already practicing key aspects of the biblical laws of God, it is not surprising that Scythian Israelites joined Josiah and Judah in celebrating God's Holy Days. If the Greeks had written II Chronicles 35:17-18, it would have stated "all the Jews and the Scythians that were present...kept the Passover."

Now consider II Chronicles 34:3-9 for even more evidence. Verse 3 records that Josiah began his religious reforms in the eighth year of his reign. Verses 6-7 tell us:

> "And so did he in the cities of **Manasseh, and Ephraim and Simeon, even unto Naphthali**...And when he had... cut down all the idols **throughout the land of Israel**, he returned to Jerusalem." *(KJV)*

Any Scythians then present in Palestine would have supported Josiah's reforms as Scythian laws banned idols. Ten years later, Josiah took up a collection for the restoration of the Temple, and verse 9 states:

> "...they delivered the money that was brought into the house of God, which the Levites...**had gathered of the hand of Manasseh and Ephraim, and all the remnant of Israel**, and of all Judah and Benjamin and they returned to Jerusalem. *(KJV)*

For years, contingents of the ten tribes were present in Palestine and living in their former tribal homelands. Biblical accounts clearly state that these members of the ten tribes were separate and distinct from the tribes of "Judah and Benjamin," who comprised the nation or "house" of Judah. These members of the ten tribes of Israel were both willing and able to donate money to restore God's Temple! In fact, the Israelites were able to donate far more for the Temple than the Jews. The Israelite Scythians had conquered "all Asia" and were flush with war booty out of which to make donations.

The Bible mentions that Israelites from the tribes of Manasseh, Ephraim, Naphthali, Simeon and others were present in their old tribal lands and cities during the reign of King Josiah. Scythia's military power dwarfed what was left of Judah by that time, so it is apparent that

Josiah's reforms were implemented with the support of the Scythians. The fact that the tribes of Israel were then reoccupying their old tribal lands in Palestine argues that their initial intention was to resettle the land and make it a part of the Scythian Empire. The grandparents of these Scythians were the ones who fled to the Black Sea to escape the Assyrians. Their grandchildren had not only destroyed the Assyrian Empire, but were likely familiar enough with their history to identify which Scythian families had claim to the old tribal estates in Palestine!

Reconsider the prophecy of Jeremiah 3:8-12 that stated the ten tribes of Israel were "more justified" than the Jews at that time, and that their new homeland was located "to the north" of Judah. Jeremiah lived in the reign of King Josiah. *(Jeremiah 3:6)* Bibles including dates for chapters in the Old Testament likely date this chapter to "circa 620 B.C." No wonder God inspired Jeremiah to give a message to the Israelites of the ten tribes during King Josiah's reign. The Scythians had sent contingents of the ten tribes' descendants to reoccupy the territory of the kingdom of Israel. The descendants of the ten tribes were at that time spiritually closer to God than were the Jews of Judah, as the Prophet Jeremiah's words above indicate. This biblical account is supported by Herodotus' account that the Scythians were known for avoiding idols, pagan practices and unclean meats.

In Jeremiah 3:10-11, God states that while "Israel" (the Scythians) was genuinely observing God's laws, Judah had "feignedly" turned to God. The Bible makes it clear that the prophet Jeremiah and King Josiah genuinely served God, but the rest of the nation of Judah did not do so. After Josiah's death, Judah quickly reverted to idolatry and rebellion against God's laws, and their condition became terminal. Jerusalem fell to the Babylonians in 604 B.C., just a few years after Josiah's great revival. Given the fact that the people of Judah did not really agree with Josiah's and Jeremiah's reforms, what was it that convinced the entire nation of Judah to "go along" with the revival? The answer is obvious. It was the presence of the powerful Scythian army that convinced Judah's "closet pagans" to "feignedly" obey God's laws.

Josiah kept this great Passover in the "eighteenth year of his reign" *(II Kings 21-23)*, which would date it to about 621 B.C. The fact that the Prophet Jeremiah was God's representative during this time argues that Jeremiah organized or presided over Josiah's joint-Passover between Judah and the portions of the ten tribes of Israel "who were present." The fact that the Scythians readily consented to observe the Passover and Days of Unleavened Bread implies that they were already familiar with these observances!

Consider this question: what prompted King Josiah to restore the Temple of God in the first place? Perhaps it was the invading Scythians who prompted his action. The Scythian army in Palestine was so large that Egypt paid tribute money to them to spare Egypt an invasion. Scythians were known to kill their own royalty for indulging in idolatry and pagan practices, and Judah's people were heavily engaged in paganism when the Scythian Israelites returned. Did the familiarity of the Scythians with God's laws and their obvious military superiority inspire King Josiah of Judah to obey God's laws and restore God's Temple?

There is no conflict between I Kings 17:18, stating that God removed all of the ten tribes from Palestine around 721 B.C., and II Chronicles 34 which records that many Ephraimites, Manassehites, Simeonites and Naphthalites were living in their old tribal homelands of Palestine around 620 B.C. The Israelites in Palestine during Josiah's reign were the "Scythians" (or "Sacae") who had reoccupied Palestine. Secular history calls them "Scythians," but the Bible simply refers to the Scythians by their traditional Israelite names.

The role of the prophet Jeremiah in Israelite history has been unappreciated. He did not simply utter pronouncements from God. He was very actively involved with the leaders and political events of Israel and Judah. He surely played a key role in the reforms of King Josiah and the observance of the Passover during the reunion of the Israelite Scythians and the Jews of Judah. The Bible also relates that Jeremiah was present at the destruction of Jerusalem approximately 35 years later. Although King Josiah repented when he heard the law of God read from a long-lost scroll found in the Temple, the last king

VIEW OF JERUSALEM.

of Judah, Zedekiah, contemptuously burned a scroll of the law when it was read to him. *(Jeremiah 36)* When the Babylonians conquered Jerusalem, Zedekiah was forced to watch the execution of his nobles and sons just prior to having his eyes "put out." *(Jeremiah 52:10-11)* Zedekiah paid a terrible price for his flagrant disobedience to God's laws and instructions given through Jeremiah. *(See Jeremiah 38)*

Jeremiah, his assistant, Baruch, and Zedekiah's daughters survived and traveled to Egypt with a remnant of escaped Jews. *(Jeremiah 43:6-7)* As discussed in an earlier chapter, Jeremiah and his party then traveled to Celtic Ireland, which was long a Phoenician-Israelite colony, and participated in a new revival of the laws of God among another group of dispersed Israelites. On his voyage to Ireland from Egypt, Jeremiah's ports-of-call would have included the thriving city of

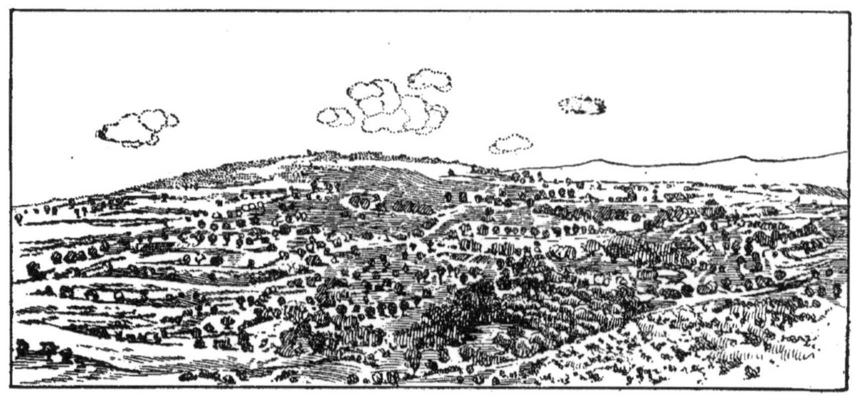

The Hill of Samaria.

Carthage in North Africa and the Celtiberian port of Gades in ancient Spain. Jeremiah had witnessed the last revival of Judah as well as its fall; he had celebrated a Passover with the Israelite Scythians from the Black Sea region, and had visited Carthage on his way to Celtic Ireland. Jeremiah had more experience with the scattered nations of Israelites than anyone else in his time. We are not yet finished with the life of Jeremiah; however, the "rest of the story" will be told in book four of this series. We must now return to the narrative about the Scythians.

Why did the seemingly invincible Scythians, the sons of Isaac (i.e. Sacae), abandon the Mideast so soon after subduing it? There are two possible answers. When the kingdom of Israel and her capital of Samaria fell, Assyria brought in foreigners who had no affinity for the land. *(II Kings 17:24-34)* When the Scythian Israelites returned to Palestine, they were likely disappointed in what they found. The "land of milk and honey" about which their grandparents had reminisced was now a "land of weeds and foreigners."

The Scythians likely decided that Palestine was simply not worth the effort, and withdrew into Scythia where the expansive terrain was far more suitable for their chosen lifestyle. Also, the population of the Scythians was now far too large to seriously consider cramped little Palestine as anything but a remote colony. Besides, the other purpose for their southern invasion (revenge upon Assyria) had been satisfied, so there was no compelling reason to stay in Mesopotamia either. **The voluntary Scythian withdrawal from conquered territory is evidence that the motives for their invasion did not include imperial expansionism.** Indeed, Herodotus observed the following about the Scythians' "isolationist" attitude, stating that the Scythians:

> "...dreadfully avoid the use of foreign customs, and especially those of the Greeks...So careful are the Scythians to guard their own customs, and such are the penalties [Herodotus refers to the death penalty for pagan religious activity] that they impose on those who take to foreign customs over and above their own."[68]

The Scythians' decision to withdraw from conquered territory was consistent with their traditional isolationism. They preferred living in their own "wide open spaces" to the burden of ruling over nations of foreigners with unfamiliar customs and lifestyles.

Herodotus offers examples of the Scythian zeal in forbidding idolatry and the worship of "foreign gods." In one instance, King Saulius of Scythia executed his own brother for participating in the rites of a Greek "mother-goddess" festival and wearing pagan "images."[69] In another instance, a Scythian king (Scyles) participated in a Greek ritual in which devotees allowed "Bacchus" to possess them in frenzied rites. Knowing the strict Scythian laws against such rites, King Scyles tried to prevent any Scythian from learning about his "secret life," but his actions were discovered. The Scythians rejected him as king, and selected his brother, Octamasades, as the new king. Octamasades pursued his paganized brother, and beheaded him in Thrace, modern Balkan Europe, where Scyles had sought refuge.[70]

The fact that the Scythians executed even their own leaders who worshipped pagan gods illustrates the strictness of the Scythian law against idolatry. Combining this fact with the Scythian custom of avoiding swine's flesh, the Scythians were faithfully practicing two key features of the laws of God given to the Israelites under Moses. Who else but displaced Israelites would be doing this?

After the Scythians returned to the steppes, the Babylonians soon became the masters of Mesopotamia, capturing Jerusalem and taking the remainder of Judah into captivity. The Medo-Persian

TOMB OF CYRUS THE GREAT

Empire then replaced the Babylonians, and it was in their rule that King Cyrus allowed a contingent of Jews to return to Palestine under Ezra and Nehemiah. The Jews flourished under Persian rule, and they occupied high positions of governmental authority. Daniel served as the king's Prime Minister under Darius *(Daniel 6:1-3)*, Esther was a queen of Persia *(Esther 2:15-18)*, Nehemiah was cupbearer to a Persian king *(Nehemiah 2:1)*, and Mordechai was promoted by a Persian king. *(Esther 9:3-4)* Interestingly, Esther became Queen of Persia as a result of winning an empire-wide "beauty contest" judged by the king of Persia. *(Esther 2:1-18)*

Two biblical passages about the time of the Persian kings offer insights into the past history and locations of the tribes of Israel during the period of the Persian Empire. When a small contingent from the tribes of Judah, Benjamin and Levi were rebuilding the walls of Jerusalem under Ezra and Nehemiah, their enemies obtained a temporary restraining order from a Persian king. Ezra 4:20 records the edict of the Persian king which noted that:

> "There have been mighty kings also over Jerusalem which have ruled over all countries beyond the river; and toll, tribute and custom was paid unto them." *(KJV)*

Those "mighty kings" who ruled everything west of the Euphrates River and accepted tribute money from their subject nations could only have been David and Solomon. Persian records remembered them.

The second account is in Daniel 9:7. In the midst of a prayer confessing the sins of all Israel and Judah against God, Daniel makes this statement:

> "To thee O Lord, belongs righteousness, but to us confusion of face...to the men of Judah, to the inhabitants of Jerusalem, **and to all Israel, those that are near and those that are far away, in all the lands to which thou hast driven them**..." *(RSV)*

Daniel here refers to "Judah" and "Israel" as separate entities, as do the other biblical writers. Notice he mentions that **some Israelites of the ten tribes were "near" to Daniel and others were "far away" in "all the lands" where they were driven from Palestine**. Daniel provides biblical confirmation that by his lifetime the tribes of Israel had been widely scattered in "many lands." Those Israelites near Daniel would be the descendants of the Israelites carried captive into Asia by the Assyrians. Those Israelites were in "the cities of the Medes" and "eastern Assyria" as noted earlier. Both locations were close to Daniel and within the immediate Persian Empire. Other Israelites were "far away"...in many lands. These would include the Scythian Israelites in the Black Sea region, the Carthaginians, Spanish Iberians, Celts in western Europe and the British Isles, and even Phoenicians and Carthaginians in the ancient Americas. Daniel 9:7 documents that educated Jews knew the ten tribes of Israel had been widely dispersed across the globe by about 540 B.C. Secular evidence, examined in earlier chapters, confirms that Daniel's observation about the widespread scattering of the ten tribes was absolutely true.

The Persian-Scythian Wars

After Assyria fell and the invading Black Sea Scythians withdrew into south Russia, the eastern Scythians (descendants of Israelites taken captive by Assyria) could take advantage of the power vacuum and migrate elsewhere. Apparently, many did so, migrating out of Mesopotamia into the region east of the Caspian Sea, where they were later located. Tamara Rice comments on the dramatic expansion of the Scythians in Asia after they withdrew from Assyria and Palestine:

> "The Scythians had ruled a large portion of western Asia for twenty-eight years. They were now back in Urartu...at this date...some turned eastward again, to occupy the tract of steppe lying **between the Caspian and the Sea of Aral**, blending there with Dahai kinsmen to form an ethnic group from which the Parthians were to spring some three hundred years later. Others may have pushed on **as far as India**...whilst others remained in Armenia.[71] *(Emphasis added)*

This account confirms there was an explosion of Scythians into the region east of the Caspian Sea soon after the Black Sea Scythians returned to their homeland. However, the Scythians east of the Caspian Sea were the ones who had lived "east of Assyria" in Mesopotamia. Freed from Assyrian constraints, they moved northeast to the region east of the Caspian Sea. The Israelites taken captive around 740 B.C. and settled in eastern Assyria were sunworshippers when taken captive, and they had not participated in the religious revival experienced by the Black Sea Scythians. The Black Sea Scythians zealously forbade idolatry and pagan customs; however, the Scythians east of the Caspian Sea were pagan sunworshippers. This indicates the easternmost Scythians were descended from captive Israelites in Mesopotamia who had retained their sunworship practices. The above quote mentions the "Parthians" sprang from this group of Scythians. The Parthians will be the subject of the next book in this series.

In approximately 530 B.C., King Cyrus of Persia invaded the Scythians who were located east of the Caspian Sea.[72] The Scythian tribes attacked by Persia were the **Massagetae** and the **Dahae**, with the *Encyclopedia Britannica* noting that the Dahae were also called the **Dana** or **Dahans**.[73] The names of these Scythian tribes indicate that they were descendants of the Israelite tribes of **Manasseh**, **Dan** and, possibly, the **Ephraimite clan of Tahanites.** *(Numbers 26:35)* A queen named Tomyris then ruled the Massagetae. Although her name has come to us via Greek accounts, the Hebrew name **Tamar** is the root word of "**Tomyr**-is." The name Tamar appears twice in the Bible for females in the royal family of King David. *(II Samuel 13:1 and 14:27)* God had promised that David's descendants would rule over the ten tribes of Israel, so the presence of a Queen bearing a Davidic-Hebrew name supports the conclusion that these Scythians were Israelites.

Like the Scythians in the Black Sea region, the Massagetae were also called "Sacae" or "Saccae,"[74] confirming that they also bore the name of "Isaac." Herodotus records that the Massagetae were called Scythians and that "the Massagetae wear the same kind of clothes as the Scythians and live much the same."[75] The evidence clearly supports the conclusion that the Massagetae and their related tribes were part of the widespread ten tribes of Israel.

Herodotus records that Cyrus "set his heart on subduing the Massagetae."[76] The Massagetae were living in peace, but Cyrus launched a war of aggression against them. With Persia's invasion imminent, Queen Tomyris sent the following message to Cyrus: "King of the Medes, cease to be so eager to do what you are doing...rule over your own people, and endure to look upon us governing ours."[77] It is noteworthy that the Scythians had a "live and let live" attitude, but Persia persisted in its aggression. After initial fighting, Queen Tomyris of the Massagetae offered Cyrus the Great of Persia a second chance to cease hostilities and go back to his own land, but warned him:

> "If you do not so, I swear by the sun, the lord of the Massagetae, that, for all your insatiability of blood, I will give you your fill of it."[78]

The above confirms that the eastern Scythians were sun-worshippers, descended from the three and one-half tribes of Israel who were sunworshippers when they went into captivity about two decades prior to the fall of Samaria. This group included one-half of the tribe of Manasseh, and it would be appropriate for the Manassehites (the "Massagetae") to be their leading tribe.

History tends to look upon the Persians as "civilized" and the Scythians as "fierce barbarians." Yet, it was the Persians who launched a war of unprovoked aggression, and the Scythians who twice offered a peaceful solution even as they fought in self-defense. Who were the real "barbarians?"

Cyrus should have heeded Queen Tomyris' warning. Herodotus described the ensuing battle:

> "Tomyris, since Cyrus would not listen to her, gathered all her host together and fought him. Of all the battles that were fought among the barbarians, I judge this to have been the severest...finally the Massagetae got the upper hand. The most of the Persian army died on the spot and, among them, Cyrus himself...Tomyris sought out his corpse among the Persian dead, and...she filled a skin with human blood and fixed his head in the skin, and, insulting over the dead, she said: 'I am alive and conqueror, but you have...rob[bed] me of my son [Tomyris' son died in the war]...Now...I will give you your fill of blood, even as I threatened.' There are many stories of the death of Cyrus, but this...seems to me the most convincing."[79]

The invading Persian army was "wiped out" by the Scythians defending their homeland. Persia's famous emperor, Cyrus the Great, was killed and his corpse mutilated. We do not know the total casualties in this war, but they must have been immense. Persia ruled a vast area and could assemble armies of over a million men. Herodotus lists the army assembled by Xerxes against the Greeks at 1,700,000 men.[80] Since the expedition against the Massagetae was led personally by Cyrus the Great, his army surely numbered in the many hundreds of thousands. Yet the Massagetae annihilated the Persian army. Scythian isolationism is evidenced in the fact that they did not invade Persia when it was glaringly vulnerable after this battle. Scythia had no imperial designs.

About eighteen years later, in 512 B.C., the Persians launched a second large military expedition against the Scythians, but the Persians now feared and respected the Massagetae. This time, Persia attacked the western Scythians near the Black Sea. Needless to say, these Scythians had no desire to be conquered, and put up an effective defense. Their defense was so successful, in fact, that the Persians came close to losing their whole army a second time. With an army of 700,000 men, King Darius passed through modern Turkey, crossed the Bosporus on a bridge of ships, and attacked the Scythian-Israelite homeland north of the Black Sea by marching through the territory of modern Bulgaria and Romania.[81]

HEAD OF A PERSIAN KING.
From a bas-relief.

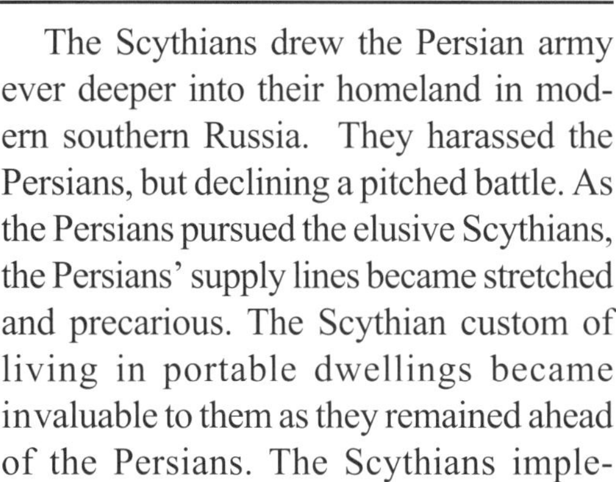

The Scythians drew the Persian army ever deeper into their homeland in modern southern Russia. They harassed the Persians, but declining a pitched battle. As the Persians pursued the elusive Scythians, the Persians' supply lines became stretched and precarious. The Scythian custom of living in portable dwellings became invaluable to them as they remained ahead of the Persians. The Scythians implemented a "scorched earth" policy, burning the vegetation ahead of the Persian army.[82]

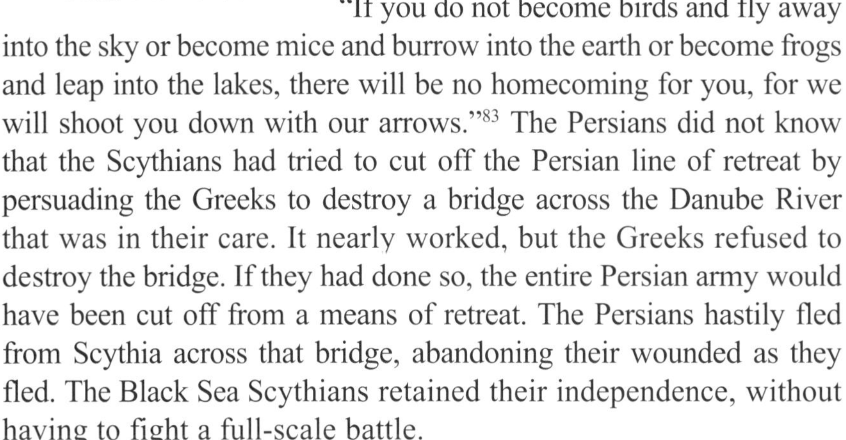

Herodotus records that the Scythians finally sent a herald to Darius with a strange gift of a bird, a mouse, a frog, and five arrows. The Persians were told to ascertain the meaning of the message themselves, which they guessed to mean: "If you do not become birds and fly away into the sky or become mice and burrow into the earth or become frogs and leap into the lakes, there will be no homecoming for you, for we will shoot you down with our arrows."[83] The Persians did not know that the Scythians had tried to cut off the Persian line of retreat by persuading the Greeks to destroy a bridge across the Danube River that was in their care. It nearly worked, but the Greeks refused to destroy the bridge. If they had done so, the entire Persian army would have been cut off from a means of retreat. The Persians hastily fled from Scythia across that bridge, abandoning their wounded as they fled. The Black Sea Scythians retained their independence, without having to fight a full-scale battle.

Is it not strange that modern history stresses the historical accounts of the Assyrian and Persian Empires when in three great wars fought between their empires and the Scythians, the Scythians decisively won all three? History teaches a great deal about the losers of these wars, but rarely mentions the victorious Scythians.

Tamara Rice writes in The Scythians, that:

> "all the mounted nomads of the Scythian age **spoke the same Iranian tongue**, whether they came from the Dniester or the banks of the Oxus...**the majority were linked by some sort of racial tie**. A definite affinity is indeed suggested by the nature of their art, which shows well-nigh identical features over so wide an area."[84] *(Emphasis added)*

The reference to the Scythians of the "Dniester" and the "Oxus" Rivers denotes both the Black Sea Scythians who defeated Darius, and the Scythian Massagetae who slaughtered the army of Cyrus the Great east of the Caspian Sea. Scythian numbers and influence became so widespread across Asia that evidence of their culture has been found from central and Eastern Europe to Manchuria.[85]

The Scythians were racially related tribes with a common language, attire, and lifestyle. Clearly, they shared a common heritage. As we have seen in this chapter, these Scythian tribes called the "Sacae" or "Saka," named after Isaac, were "linked" via their common origin in the old ten-tribed kingdom of Israel.

Some have speculated that the Scythians migrated to the Russian steppes from northern Asia. However, all the evidence strongly refutes that speculation. Their language — they spoke an "Iranian tongue" — confirms that they originated in the Mesopotamian-Fertile Crescent region, and that they had migrated northward into south Russia. If they had originated in northern Asia, they would have spoken a Mongolian language. Also, many examples of the excellent

Scythian artwork have been preserved into modern times. In their own artwork, the Scythians depict themselves as a bearded, Semitic race, further confirming their origin was in the Middle East.[86]

The only Semitic nation which left the Fertile Crescent just before the Scythians settled in the Black Sea region were "the ten tribes of Israel." Soon after the ten tribes of Israel "disappeared" from Palestine, the Scythians — bearing the name of Isaac — "appeared" near the Black Sea and spread throughout the Russian steppes. Based on the overwhelming evidence presented in this chapter, the conclusion is obvious: The ten tribes of Israel became known as "Sacae" or "Scythians" after they migrated into Asia.

Although the Scythian tribes were racially related, they were not a united "empire." Tribal loyalties were paramount, and Scythian tribes even fought each other as they competed for living space. Inter-tribal warfare was typical of Israel's tribes. The Bible records that Judah (the tribes of Judah and Benjamin) and Israel (the ten tribes) frequently fought each other. The tribe of Benjamin was almost wiped out in a civil war it fought with the other tribes in the pre-dynastic period. *(Judges 20-21)* The tribe of Ephraim also fought a losing war against the tribes of Manasseh, Gad and Reuben. *(Judges 12:1-6)* This indicates even the brother tribes of Ephraim and Manasseh could come to blows. The fact that the Scythians put tribal loyalties above their common racial relationship was consistent with their Israelite history.

Jacob fathered his twelve sons via four different mothers. As the twelve sons of Jacob took wives, the tribes became even more diverse. Joseph had an Egyptian wife *(Genesis 41:50-52)* while Judah married a Canaanite woman. *(Genesis 38)* We do not know the ethnic background of all the wives of Jacob's sons, but as they took wives and concubines of different backgrounds, their bloodlines and progeny became even more diverse. As a result, the tribes did not look and act alike. Indeed, some tribes did not get along well with certain other tribes. Their natural state was to subdivide into tribal units; being united was the **exception**, not the **rule** in their history. Their brief times of unity were facilitated by divine action working through strong personalities such as Moses, Joshua and Kings David and Solomon.

The Apostle Paul and the Scythians

This chapter began with a quote from Josephus, the Jewish historian, who recorded that the descendants of the ten tribes of Israel were exceedingly numerous and living in Asia during his lifetime. This fact was known to other educated Jews of his time. One educated Jew whose life overlapped that of Josephus was the Apostle Paul. Paul was a member of the Pharisees, a Jewish sect *(Acts 23:6)*, and a student of Gamaliel, a venerated Jewish teacher. *(Acts 22:3)* Did Paul know the Scythians were the ten tribes of Israel? A careful reading of Colossians 3:11 indicates the answer is "yes." Paul wrote:

> "Where there is neither Greek nor Jew, circumcision nor uncircumcision, **Barbarian [nor] Scythian**, bond nor free: but Christ is all and in all." *(KJV)*

Paul here draws four sets of dichotomies to illustrate that all are free to become Christians, regardless of one's lineage or personal circumstances. "Greek nor Jew" is easy to understand, but consider the dichotomy between "Barbarian" and "Scythian." The Greek word translated "barbarian" means "foreigner" or "alien."[87] Paul grew up in Tarsus in Asia Minor, so he was more familiar with the Black Sea Scythians than were the Jews from Judea. Paul had to battle the xenophobia of the Judean Christian Jews who did not want to have personal dealings with gentiles (i.e. "foreigners" or "aliens"). In Acts 10, it took divine action to induce the Apostle Peter to interact with gentiles, and in Galatians 2:11-13, Paul had to oppose Peter's tendency to "backslide" into avoiding gentiles. In Colossians 3:11, Paul strongly implies that "foreigners" and "Scythians" were opposites of each other. Why did Paul **not** regard the Scythians as "foreigners" (gentiles)? He asserted the Scythians were not racial "foreigners" because he knew they were Israelites from the ten tribes of Israel.

The Greek word used by Paul for "Scythians" is significant. A concordance will confirm that the Greek word translated "Scythian" is **skuthes**. It begins with the Greek character for "S" with the next consonant being a "k."[88] Paul referred to the Scythians with a word beginning with "**S-k**," the consonants of the root word for "**Saka**," which designated the seed of Isaac. Paul was a brilliant Hebrew scholar, and surely knew the promise of Genesis 21:12 that Israel's seed would be known by the name of "**Isaac**." It is doubtful that Paul would have referred to the Scythians by such a name unless he knew they were, indeed, the seed of Isaac.

The various Scythian tribes lived for centuries in the Russian steppes. However, the eastern Scythians were eventually pushed into, and absorbed by, the Parthian Empire. The Parthians were also Sacae Scythians, and their empire will be discussed in the third book in this series. The Black Sea Scythians remained in their area for a longer period of time, but they also eventually "vanished." As we shall see in the fourth book in this series, they did not "vanish." They simply came to be known by new names when they migrated elsewhere.

This concludes our chapter on the Scythians and their Israelite heritage. Given the substantial role and power of the Scythians in the ancient world, modern ignorance about them is a huge oversight. The Scythian invasion and defeat of the Assyrian Empire was a very major event in the ancient world. The Scythians also defeated the Persian Empire in two major wars. Indeed, they wiped out an entire Persian army and killed the famous Persian emperor, Cyrus the Great. At one time, Scythian territory stretched from Eastern Europe to China. With such an expansive and dominant history, it is incredible that history texts contain little or nothing about the Scythians! In contrast, the ancient Greek historian, Herodotus, recorded much about them.

If the Scythians had received historical coverage commensurate with their role in history, Scythia's identity as the descendants of the ten tribes of Israel would become obvious. Perhaps that is why their prominent role in ancient history for too long has been de-emphasized.

Whether by deliberate policy or just a subconscious act of human nature, Scythian history has been ignored because mankind, in general, does not want to be reminded of the reality of the Creator God's preeminent and ongoing role in human history. The Apostle Paul observed that man's natural state of mind is one of "enmity" against God *(Romans 8:7)*, and that people frequently do "not like to retain God in their knowledge." *(Romans 1:28)* Mankind does not mind the concept of "God" as long as he is distant and ephemeral. But human nature becomes uncomfortable when God's reality gets "up close and personal."

If historical texts included all of the knowledge contained in this series of books on Israelite history, God would become "up close and personal" to mankind. People would then realize that God kept His promise to multiply vastly the Israelites' population, implementing biblical prophecies and demonstrating that a living Creator God guides the destiny of nations. That makes people uncomfortable, so mankind's history texts dwell extensively on the nations and empires which were not Israelite and de-emphasize those ancient nations and empires which were composed of people descended from the ten tribes of Israel.

The ten tribes of Israel remained a major power in world events long after their migration out of Palestine. The last two chapters have presented abundant evidence that the Carthaginians and "Sacae" Scythians were both descended from the ten tribes of Israel. We are not yet finished with the Scythians. Their history overlaps events in the Parthian Empire, and we will examine more about Scythian history in the next book on Israelite history.

The next book will reveal the fascinating, but forgotten history of the most powerful ancient empire composed of descendants from the ten tribes of Israel. That empire was Parthia! Parthia and Rome were two of the largest and most powerful empires that ever existed on the earth. They were concurrent empires that became rivals in an ancient "superpower" struggle that lasted for centuries. The fascinating history of the Parthians and their great rivalry with the Roman Empire will be discussed in the next book in this series. Rome and Parthia were equals in the ancient world. You have heard much about Rome and, most likely, nothing about Parthia. The next book, *Parthia: The Forgotten Ancient Superpower And Its Role In Biblical History,* will restore Parthia to its rightful place in history and reveal why modern texts do not want to say much about the vast and powerful Parthian Empire.

ENDNOTES: CHAPTER FOUR

1.Josephus, Antiquities, XI, V, 2

2.Keller, p. 246

3.Gawler, Our Scythian Ancestors Identified with Israel, p. 9

4.Culican, The Medes and the Persians, p. 46

5.Webster's New World Dictionary, see "Cimmerian," p. 135

6.Encyclopedia Britannica, Vol. 20, Heading entitled "Scythia," p. 237

7.Encyclopedia Americana, Vol. 24, Heading entitled "Scythians," p. 471

8.Tamara Talbot Rice, The Scythians, pp. 19-20 and p. 44

9.Ibid., pp. 104-105

10.Polosmak, Natalya, "Siberian Mummy Unearthed," National Geographic, October, 1994, pp. 87-88

11.Ibid., p. 95

12.Encyclopedia Britannica, Vol. 20, Heading entitled "Scythia," p. 238

13.Xenophon, Cyropaedia, V. ii. 23-26

14.Pliny, Natural History, IV, xii, 80

15.Boris Piotrovsky, Liudmila Galanina and Nonna Grach, Scythian Art, plates 49-50, 120-121, 127-129, 134, 158, 166-173, 184-187, 202

16.McClintock, John and Strong, James, Cyclopedia of Biblical, Theological and Ecclesiastical Literature, Vol. IX, see "Scythian," pp. 489-490

17.Rawlinson, The Sixth Oriental Monarchy, p. 20

18.Culican, p. 50

19.Encyclopedia Britannica, Vol. 2, Heading entitled "Babylonia and Assyria," Subhead: "Second Assyrian Empire," p. 857

20.Ibid., p. 857

21.Culican, p. 51

22.Rice, The Scythians, p. 45

23.Encyclopedia Britannica, Vol.20, Heading entitled "Scythia," p. 238

24.Culican, p. 51

25.Gawler, p. 9

26.Ragozin, Media, p. 414

27.Herodotus, The History, 4.17

28.Culican, p. 136

29.Rice, p. 22

30.McClintock, James and Strong, John, Cyclopedia of Biblical, Theological and Ecclesiastical Literature, Vol. VIII, see "Phoenicia," p. 157

31.Piotrovsky, Galanina and Grach, Scythian Art, see extensive series of photographs following p. 21

32.Charriere, Georges, Scythian Art (Crafts of the Eurasian Nomads), Introduction, p. 13

33.Ibid., p. 7

34.Herodotus, The History, 4.17-4.20

35.Herodotus, The History, 4.46

36.Gawler, p. 5

37.Ibid., p. 5

38.Ragozin, Media, p. 418

39. Herodotus, The History, 7, 64

40.Turner, Sharon, The History of the Anglo-Saxons, Vol. 1, p. 101

41.Gawler, p. 6

42.Young's Analytical Concordance to the Bible, Hebrew Lexicon Section, see words "Bayith" and "Beth," pp. 7-8

43.Bristowe, Oldest Letters in the World, pp. 8-9

44.Hall, H. R., The Ancient History of the Near East, pp. 406-407

45.Benjamin, Persia, see illustration on p. 79

46.Encyclopedia Britannica, Vol. 17, Heading entitled "Persia," p. 563

47.Encyclopedia Americana, Vol. 21, Heading entitled "Phoenicians," p. 950

48.Fell, America B.C., p. 168

49.Harper's Bible Dictionary, see "Dress," example no. 9, p. 227

50.Herodotus, The History, 7. 64

51. Ibid., 4. 63

52.Ibid., 4. 76

53.Ibid., 4.5 and 4.7

54.Gawler, p. 5

55.Collier's Encyclopedia, Vol. 17, Heading entitled "Scythian," p. 434

56.Keller, The Bible As History, pp. 272-273; and Ragozin, Assyria, p. 423

57.Keller, P. 272

58.Encyclopedia Britannica, Vol. 2, Heading entitled "Babylonia and Assyria," Subhead: "Scythian Influence," p. 857

59.Encyclopedia Britannica, Vol. 13, Heading entitled "Kalakh (Calah)," p. 241

60.Encyclopedia Britannica, Vol. 2, Heading entitled "Babylonia and Assyria," Subhead: "Scythian Influence," p. 857

61.Ibid., p. 857

62.Herodotus, The History, 1. 106

63.Herodotus, The History, 1. 104

64.Ibid., 1. 105

65.Keller, p. 273

66.Encyclopedia Britannica, Vol. 2, Heading "Babylonia and Assyria, p. 851

67.Herodotus, The History, 1. 106

68.Ibid., 4. 76 and 80

69.Ibid., 4. 76

70.Herodotus, The History, 4, 78-80

71.Rice, The Scythians, p. 45

72.Herodotus, 1. 201-204

73.Ibid., 1. 201; and Encyclopedia Britannica, Vol. 17, Heading entitled "Persia," p. 566

74.Benjamin, Persia, p. 96; and Rawlinson, George, The Sixth Oriental Monarchy, pp. 117-118

75.Herodotus, The History, 1. 201, 215

76.Herodotus, The History, 1, 201

77.Ibid., 1, 206

78.Ibid., 1, 212

79.Ibid., 1, 214

80.Ibid., 7. 60

81. Herodotus, The History, 4.87-97

82.Ibid., 4. 122

83.Ibid., 4. 131-132

84.Rice, The Scythians, p. 42

85.Ibid., maps on pp. 40-41 and 104-105

86.Piotrovsky, Boris; Galanina, Liudmila; Grach, Nonna, Scythian Art, pp.120-121, 126-129, 158-159, 166, 168-173, 184-187, 196-197, 202

87.Young's Analytical Concordance to the Bible, see word "Barbarian," p. 70

88.Ibid., see word "Scythian," p.844

A 19th century view of the Valley Of Jehoshaphat in the Crimea. The Keraim, or Crimean Jews, believe that they are descended from the lost tribes of the house of Israel. (See the evidence presented in *The Story Of Celto-Saxon Israel,* by W.H. Bennett, page 197)

Epilogue

This book has presented abundant archaeological, historical and linguistic evidence regarding the destinations of the tribes of Israel as they scattered in many directions from ancient Israel. While it is true that many Israelites became captives of the Assyrians and were relocated into Asia, both the Bible and Assyrian records indicate most of the Israelites escaped the Assyrians.

You now know that the Phoenician fleets transported many Israelites to new homelands in Phoenicia's colonies in Carthage, Spain, the British Isles and Western Europe. These refugees became the Carthaginians and the Celts. There is indisputable physical evidence that the Carthaginians and Celts continued to explore, mine and trade with the New World. Carthage had considerable contact with ancient Mesoamerican civilizations, influencing them to build Egyptian-like pyramids and copy the degenerate Carthaginian practice of human sacrifice.

The evidence in this book affirmed that a large body of the ten tribes of Israel also migrated to the Black Sea region of Asia. They were called the "Sacae" Scythians, as their tribes bore the name of the Hebrew patriarch, Isaac. Their artwork and much additional evidence confirmed that they originated as Semites from the Mideast. The Scythians carried on the Israelite wars with Assyria, finally destroying Assyria's empire. Scythia twice defeated Persian invasions and it annihilated the Persian army of Cyrus the Great.

Biblical evidence supports the above conclusions. Hosea 1:10 specifically prophesied God would vastly multiply the population of the ten tribes of Israel *after* they left Palestine. A century *after* the ten tribes fled to Asia, God addressed a message to them in Jeremiah 3:11-12. The Bible clearly indicates the ten tribes of Israel would not become "lost." This book ends with the degenerate Carthaginian empire destroyed by Rome, but the Scythian tribes were still independent and strong in the Black Sea region and as living far east as western China.

The next book will continue the forgotten saga of the ten tribes of Israel. Even greater surprises await the reader in the next book on Israelite history. While Carthage and Scythia were powerful empires, another Israelite Empire rose in south Asia that dominated the entire region for half a millennium. They were allies and relatives of the Scythians. The Greeks and Romans preserved much information about this forgotten empire, and it became Rome's most powerful adversary.

When this now-forgotten empire was attacked by Rome's legions, the Roman armies were often militarily outclassed. Famous Romans such as Crassus and Mark Antony led expeditions against this Asian empire, but their Roman armies were totally defeated. This powerful Asian empire even developed rudimentary forms of a very modern technology, but you will need to read the next book, *Parthia: The Forgotten Ancient Superpower And Its Role In Biblical History,* to learn what this modern technology was which began in this mysterious ancient Asian empire.

This powerful but forgotten ancient empire was called Parthia. Even the Romans acknowledged Parthia as Rome's equal. Yet if you look in history texts and encyclopedias, you will find vast numbers of pages about Roman history and little or nothing about the Parthian empire. Because Roman historians preserved so much information about the Parthian Empire, it is bizarre that almost nothing is mentioned by modern historians about it. Why has the extensive history of the Parthian Empire been removed from historical accounts? Very likely, it has been slighted and de-emphasized in historical accounts for the same reason the empires of the Phoenicians,

Carthaginians and Scythians have been mostly removed from historical texts by today's modern revisionists. They don't want to talk about these empires because they are Israelite Empires founded by the descendants of the ten tribes of Israel. Their histories demonstrate that the God of the Bible has literally been guiding the affairs of nations throughout human history.

Modern history texts don't mention these empires because modern evolutionists don't want you, the reader, to know what really happened in the ancient world. They want you to bow down at the altar of the modern god of evolutionary theory. To accomplish that end, they must hide the truth about the Israelite Empires. If the truth were known, more people would realize the Bible is a profoundly accurate historical book that can only be the inspired revelation of a Creator God. The theory of evolution will collapse if it is confronted by the true facts of ancient history; therefore, important accounts about all Israelite empires have been conveniently "left out" of history books.

The following volume about Israelite history will reveal the untold, factual history of Parthia, one of the greatest and most-powerful empires ever seen in the ancient world. Even Rome tried many times to conquer Parthia, but could not do so. What are our greatest sources about Parthia's history? It is the very writings of the Greco-Romans themselves! They understood Parthia's greatness and their records reflect Parthia's substantial role in the ancient world. As the reader will see, evidence that Parthia was an empire of the ten tribes of Israel is very extensive.

Another fascinating historical mystery involves the Parthians. It is the famous visit of the Magi (or Wise Men) who came to visit the Christ-child. Matthew 2:3 records that the Romans and the whole city of Jerusalem were afraid when the Magi came. *Parthia: The Forgotten Ancient Superpower And Its Role In Biblical History* will reveal the reason for their fears. A hint: The Magi were part of Parthia's nobility! The next book in this series will document much biblical and secular evidence that the life of Jesus Christ, the central figure of the Christian religion, was greatly affected by the geopolitical relationships between Rome and Parthia. The visit of the Magi was one such event. The next book also includes a plausible explanation of another historical mystery: Why does the Bible say almost nothing about Jesus Christ's life between ages 12 and 30? Readers of the next book will learn the likely answer.

Finally, the next book will continue to affirm that the Abrahamic Covenant, revealed in the biblical book of Genesis, has guided the affairs of nations and empires and determined the course of human history. God really has favored certain nations over others at times during world history. God's unconditional promise to Abraham requires him to grant major blessings to the descendants of Abraham. The greatest blessings, called the "birthright," were permanently given to the tribes of Ephraim and Manasseh, two of the so-called "lost" ten tribes of Israel. The following book will confirm that the tribes of Israel, who were guaranteed a prominent role throughout history because of the "birthright" promise, also inherited those blessings in the empire of Parthia. You, the reader, have not been told the whole truth about the history of the ancient world. This series of books on the history of the Israelite people, will reveal to you "the rest of the story," and restore a balanced view of world history.

Be prepared for more surprising revelations in *Parthia: The Forgotten Ancient Superpower And Its Role In Biblical History,* the third volume in this series about Israelite history, which reveals the hidden history of the powerful, but forgotten Parthian Empire.

Bibliography

Allen, J.H., Judah's Sceptre and Joseph's Birthright, 19th Edition, Destiny Publishers, Merrimac, MS, 1917

Encyclopedia Americana, Grolier, Inc., Danbury, CT, 1988 Edition

Benjamin, S.G.W., Persia, T. Fisher Unwin, London, 1887 and G.P. Putnam's Sons, New York, 1888

Bloom, Ernest and Polansky, Jan, "Translation of the 'Decalogue Tablet' from Ohio," Epigraphic Society Occasional Publications, Vol. 8, Part 1, 1980

Boland, Charles, They All Discovered America, Pocket Books, New York, 1963

Bristowe, Mrs. Sidney, Oldest Letters in the World, Allen and Unwin, London, 1923

Encyclopaedia Britannica, Encyclopaedia Britannica, Inc., Chicago, 1943 (175th Anniversary) Edition

Camden, William, Brittania, Bishop and Norton, 1610

Capt, E. Raymond, The Traditions of Glastonbury, Artisan Sales, Thousand Oaks, California, 1983

Carpenter, Rhys, Beyond the Pillars of Heracles, Delacorte Press, 1966

Carter, George, "A Note on the Elephant in America," Epigraphic Society Occasional Publications, Vol. 18, 1989

Carter, George, "The Mammoth in American Epigraphy," Epigraphic Society Occasional Publications, Vol. 18, 1989

Ceram, C.W., The March of Archaeology, Alfred A. Knopf, New York, 1958

Charles-Picard, Gilbert and Colette, Daily Life in Carthage, MacMillan, New York, 1961

Charriere, Georges, Scythian Art, Crafts of the Early Eurasian Nomads, Alpine Fine Arts Collection Ltd., New York, 1979

Church, Alfred J., Carthage, T. Fisher Unwin, London, 1890

Church, Alfred J., Early Britain, T. Fisher Unwin, London, 1889

Coleman, Nick, De Danaan blends old and new for great Irish sound, Minneapolis Star & Tribune, March 3, 1986

Collier's Encyclopedia, P. F. Collier & Son, New York, 1957 Edition

Connon, F. Wallace, The Stone of Destiny, Covenant Publishing Co., London, 1951

Culican, William, The Medes and the Persians, Praeger, New York, 1965

Edey, Maitland, The Sea Traders, Time-Life Books, New York, 1975

Davidy, Yair, Lost Israelite Identity, Russell-Davis, Jerusalem, 1996

Davies, Nigel, Voyagers to the New World, Morrow, New York, 1979

Dawkins, W. Boyd, Early Man in Britain, MacMillan and Co., London, 1880

Dictionary of Christ and the Gospels, Charles Scribner's Sons, New York, 1906

Dobson, Rev. Cyril C., The Mystery of the Fate of the Ark of the Covenant, First Edition, Williams and Norgate, London, 1939

Edey, Maitland, The Sea Traders, Time-Life Books, New York, 1974

Epigraphic Society Occasional Publications, Fell, Barry, "Punctuation at Los Lunas," Morehouse, George, "Geological Study at Los Lunas," Vol. 13, 1985

Epigraphic Society Occasional Publications, "An Elephant Petroglyph," Vol. 17, 1988, p. 195

Farley, Gloria, "The Shawnee Creek Stone of Oklahoma," Epigraphic Society Occasional Publications, Vol. 18, 1989

Fell, Barry, America B.C., Wallaby, New York, 1976

Fell, Barry, Saga America, Times Books, New York, 1980

Fell, Barry, "A Christian North African Inscription from Comal-calco," Epigraphic Society Occasional Publications, Vol. 17, 1988

"An Interview with Barry Fell," New England Social Studies Bulletin, Fall, 1978; Printed in Epigraphic Society Occasional Publications, Vol. 7, Pt. 2, 1979

Fell, Barry, "The Micmac Manuscripts," Epigraphic Society Occasional Publications, Vol. 7, Part 2, 1979

Fell, Barry, "A Punic Calendar from Comalcalco," Epigraphic Society Occasional Publications, Vol. 17, 1988

Fell, Barry, "A Punic Inscription on an Atlatl Weight from Georgia," Epigraphic Society Occasional Publications, Vol. 18, 1989

Fell, Barry, "Tanith in North Carolina", Epigraphic Society Occasional Publications, Vol. 18, 1989

Gawler, Colonel J.C., Our Scythian Ancestors Identified With Israel, Guest, London, and MacLaren & MacNiven, Edinburgh, 1875

Goodspeed, Edgar J. (translator), The Apocrypha, Vintage/Random House, New York, 1959

Gordon, Cyrus, Before Columbus, Crown Publishers, New York, 1971

Hall, H.R., The Ancient History of the Near East, Methuen & Co., London, Seventh Edition (Revised)

Halley, Henry, Halley's Bible Handbook, Special Abridged Edition, Grason, Minneapolis, 1964

Hannay, Herbert B., European and other Race Origins, Sampson, Low, Marston & Co., London, 1915

Harper's Bible Dictionary, Harper & Row, San Francisco, CA, 1985

Harrison, Richard J., Spain at the Dawn of History, Thames and Hudson, London and New York, 1988

Herm, Gerhard, The Celts, St. Martin's Press, New York, 1975

Herodotus, The History, Translated by David Grene, University of Chicago Press, Chicago, 1987

Hitti, Philip, Short History of the Near East, Van Nostrand, New York, 1966

The Holy Bible, King James Version, The Open Bible Edition, Thomas Nelson, Nashville, Camden and New York, 1975

Jefferson, President Thomas, Jefferson's Letters, Arranged by Willson Whitman, E. M. Hale and Co., Eau Claire, WI, published circa 1940

Johnston, Thomas C., Did the Phoenicians Discover America?, Lames Nisbet & Co., London, 1913

Josephus, Complete Works of Josephus, Translated by William Whiston, Kregel Publications, Grand Rapids, Michigan, 1969

Encyclopedia Judaica, Keter Publishing House, Jerusalem, 1972 Edition

Keller, Werner, The Bible As History, Second Revised Edition, Morrow, 1981

Lawless, Emily, Ireland, T. Fisher Unwin, London, Circa 1905

Lenhart, Robert, "The Adena Tablets," Epigraphic Society Occasional Publications, Vol. 13, 1985

Leonard, Jonathan, Ancient America, Time-Life Books, New York, 1967

Margoliouth, Moses, The Jews in Great Britain, James Nisbet & Co., London, 1846

Marx, Robert, In Quest of the Great White Gods, Crown Publishers, New York, 1964

McClintock, John and Strong, James, Cyclopedia of Biblical, Theological nd Ecclesiastical Literature, Harper and Brothers, 1887

Mitchel, John, The History of Ireland, D & J Sadlier & Co., New York, 1869

Moore, E.R., "Inscribed Stones from Kent County, Michigan," Epigraphic Society Occasional Publications, Vol. 7, Pt. 2, 1979

Moore, Thomas, History of Ireland, Lea & Blanchard, Philadelphia, 1843

Piotrovsky, Boris (with Liudmila Galanina and Nonna Grach), Scythian Art, English version translated by Viacheslav Sobolev, Phaidon, London, 1987

Pliny, Natural History, Translated by H. Rackham, Harvard University Press, Cambridge and London, 1989 printing

Pohl, Frederick J., Atlantic Crossings Before Columbus, W.W. Norton, New York, 1961

Polosmak, Natalya, "Siberian Mummy Unearthed," National Geographic Magazine, October, 1994, pp. 87-88

Ragozin, Zenaide, Assyria, 2nd Edition, T. Fisher Unwin, London, 1887

Ragozin, Zenaide, Media, 3rd Edition, T. Fisher Unwin, London, 1897

Rawlinson, George, Phoenicia, T. Fisher Unwin, London, Circa 1895

Rawlinson, George, The Sixth Great Oriental Monarchy, Dodd, Mead & Co., New York, 1872

Rhys, Sir John, Celtic Britain, E. & J.B. Young and Co., New York, 1882

Rice, Tamara Talbot, The Scythians, Thames and Hudson, London, 1958

Sammes, Aylett, Britannia (Antiquities of Ancient Britain), Roycroft, London, 1676

Smith, R. Bosworth, Carthage and the Carthaginians, Longmans, Green & Co., London, 1878

Smith, R. Bosworth, Rome and Carthage: The Punic Wars, Charles Scribner's Sons, New York, 1923

Smith, Roberta C., "Ancient Celtiberian and Mediterranean Peoples in the New World," Epigraphic Society Occasional Publications, Vol. 7, Pt. 2, 1979

Sodders, Betty, Michigan Prehistory Mysteries, Avery Color Studios, Au Train, MI, 1990

Steede, Neil, "Inscribed Bricks from Comalcalco," Epigraphic Society Occasional Publications, Vol. 17, 1988

Stubbs, Brian Darrel, "A Curious Element in Uto-Aztecan," Epigraphic Society Occasional Publications, Vol. 23, 1998

Sullivan, A. M., The Story of Ireland, M. H. Gill and Son, Dublin, 1898

Thebaud, Rev. Aug. J., The Irish Race, Peter F. Collier, New York, 1878

Totten, Norman, "South to Eldorado," Epigraphic Society Occasional Publications, Vol. 7, Part 2, 1979

Turner, Sharon, The History of the Anglo-Saxons, Longman, Hurst, Rees & Orme, London, 1807

Tytler, Alexander, Universal History, Fetridge and Co., Boston, 1854

Universal Jewish Encyclopedia, Patron's Edition, The Universal Jewish Encyclopedia, Inc., New York, 1942

U. S. News and World Report Magazine, March 30, 1987, and October 5, 1987 Issues

Waddell, L. A., The Phoenician Origin of Britons, Scots, and Anglo-Saxons, Williams & Norgate, London, 1924

Webster's New World Dictionary, Second Concise Edition, Avenel Books, New York, 1975

Warmington, B. H., Carthage, Robert Hale, London, 1969

Williams, Larry, The Mountain of Moses, Wynwood Press, New York, 1990

Wise, Terrence and Healy, Mark, Hannibal's War With Rome, Osprey Publishing, Oxford, Great Britain, 1999

Xenophon, Cyropedia (English Translation by Walter Miller), Harvard University Press, Cambridge and London, 1989 printing

Young, Robert, Young's Analytical Concordance to the Bible, Wm. B. Eerdmans Publishing Co., Grand Rapids, 1978

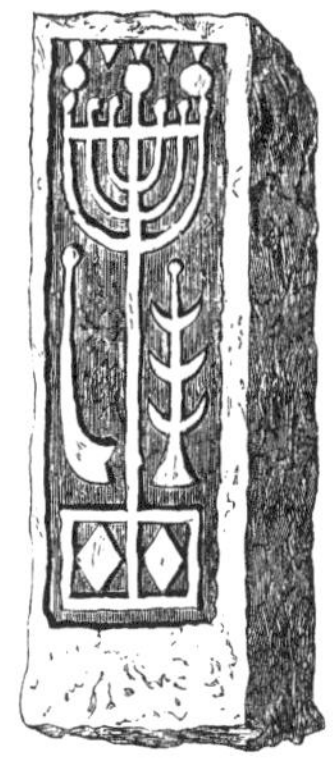
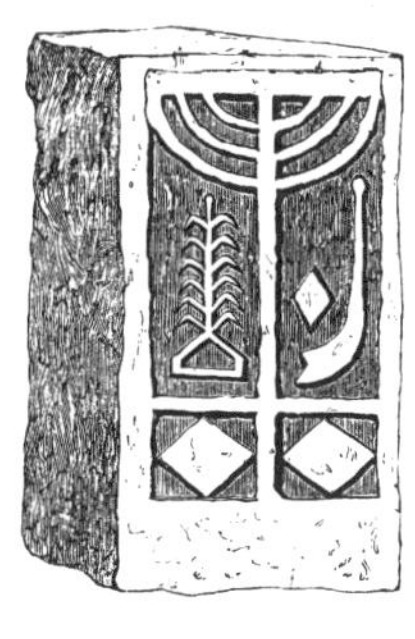

Early Hebrew tombstones from the Caucasus region

THE STONE LIBRARY
ON THE WALLS OF WHICH
ASSYRIAN RECORDS
WERE KEPT
ASSYRIAN PALACE

Index

Scripture References

OLD TESTAMENT

GENESIS:

NUMBERS:

DEUTERONOMY:

JOSHUA:

JUDGES:

I SAMUEL:

II SAMUEL:

I KINGS:

II KINGS:

I CHRONICLES:

II CHRONICLES:

JOB:

PSALMS:

ISAIAH:

JEREMIAH:

EZEKIEL:

DANIEL:

HOSEH:

AMOS:

JONAH:

ZECHARIAH:

MALACHI:

NEW TESTAMENT

The Valley of Baksan in the Caucasus, part of the route taken by the lost tribes of Israel on their trek into Europe.

Index

Persons, Places, Subjects

A

B

C

D

F

G

H

J

L

M

O

P

Q

R

S

T

U

V

W

X

Y

Z

[End]

A STEVEN COLLINS PHOTOBOOK TOUR OF THE HOLY LAND

Steven M. Collins and Yair Davidy at the ancient site of Meggido. This was an important Biblical site in the Carmel Mountain range. The Greek form of the word appears in the prophetic symbolism of Revelation 16:16 as "Armageddon," or the "hill of Meggido."

Israelite Altar Model in Shiloh. The city of Shiloh was an early center of Hebrew worship and figured in the Messianic prophecy of Gen. 49:10. It was a symbol of God's judgment in Jer. 7:12-14; 26:6-9.

The Mountains of Ephraim as seen from Shiloh. Ephraim was the second son of Joseph (Gen. 41:50-52) and gave his name to his tribal descendants as well as to the entire northern ten-tribe kingdom.

A Roman Acqueduct located at Caesarea, a town built by Herod the Great on the Mediterranean shore. The Apostle Paul landed here after his second and third missionary journeys. (Acts 18:22; 21:8)

"The Lost Tribes Of Israel" Series by Steven M. Collins

Over 275 pages each! See our website or write for current list of books and prices

BOOK ONE: THE ORIGINS & EMPIRE OF ANCIENT ISRAEL

This book begins with the call of Abraham and the elements of the unconditional Covenant which God made with the Patriarchs and their descendants. Strong evidence is presented that the real Mt. Horeb, on which Moses and the Israelites received the Torah and made a covenant with God, is not in Egypt's Sinai desert, but rather in another location identified both in the Bible and by physical evidence existing to this day.

The role of the Israelite tribes in the ancient Sea Peoples is shown to parallel accounts about them in the book of Judges. This book then reveals new information about King David, the warrior king who united the tribes of Israel, made lasting alliances with Tyre and Sidon, and built an Israelite Empire. Both the Bible and secular history contain evidence that David's forces crushed the Assyrian Empire (which fueled Assyria's desire for revenge upon Israel in later centuries). Greek historians discussed much about the power of the Phoenician Empire from about 1100-700 B.C., and they identified the land of Israel as being part of the homeland of Phoenicia's Empire. Much evidence is offered that the Phoenician Empire was, in fact, the Empire of Israel and its allies from Tyre and Sidon.

This book documents that the Israelites were not only major players in ancient history, but actually became the leading power on earth under Kings David and Solomon. When it is realized that the Israelite tribes had major roles in that ancient time, it becomes easier for the reader to understand that the ten tribes have also had major roles in the world's geopolitics from that time forward.

BOOK TWO: ISRAEL'S LOST EMPIRES

The worldwide scope of the Israelite/Phoenician Empire! This book offers readers the truth about the extensive navigational and maritime skills of the ancient Israelites and Phoenicians, and reveals their worldwide reach. They established a network of colonies throughout the Mediterranean Sea, in Western Europe, the British Isles and North America. Considerable new evidence is offered to document the extent to which they explored North America in a search for metals and raw materials to meet the need for Solomon's Temple and other building projects.

Israel and Judah became two separate and often-hostile kingdoms after the United Kingdom of Israel fell apart during a very bloody civil war. The Kingdom of Israel gradually degenerated as a nation as they disobeyed God, but remained a dominant naval power. The drought in Elijah's time stimulated waves of Israelite migrations from their homeland and they founded new colonies for their people, including Kirjath-Hadeshath (identified in modern texts by its Roman name: "Carthage").

Simultaneous with the rise of Carthage to power in the Mediterranean world, another new power rose to prominence in Asia. This new power was Scythia, and its tribes were named the Sacae. The term "Sacae" preserves the name of the Hebrew Patriarch, Isaac, fulfilling God's promise in Genesis 21:12 that Isaac's name would be placed on Abraham's "birthright" descendants. Scythia's Israelite origin is extensively documented. The names of many Israelite tribes and clans are present and identifiable among the Sacae tribes. The Scythians also renamed all of the rivers emptying into the Black Sea, giving each one a name based on the name of the Israelite tribe of Dan.

BOOK THREE: PARTHIA, THE FORGOTTEN ANCIENT SUPERPOWER AND ITS ROLE IN BIBLICAL HISTORY

This book details the history of the greatest Israelite empire in the post-exilic period: Parthia. Even Roman writers acknowledged it was the equal of the Roman Empire. In fact, its forces frequently defeated Roman armies in many wars, and Parthia was the only empire that Rome actually feared. Just decades before the birth of Christ, its armies drove the Romans completely out of Palestine, Syria and Asia Minor, forcing the reigning King Herod to flee for his life. This ancient superpower rival of Rome that lasted for half a millennium was the Parthian Empire. Its Semitic/Israelite origins are well documented as well as the fact that its single dynasty was descended from King David. The Parthian Empire rose to power as Carthage fell, and the names of Israelite tribes and clans are in evidence within the Parthian Empire. Parthia's first capital city was named after "Isaac." Josephus, the famous Jewish historian, records that the ten tribes were a very numerous people in Asia and he identifies them as living in Parthia's empire. Secular histories have long acknowledged the Parthians were related to the Scythian tribes, and Scythian "Sacae" tribes often assisted the Parthians in their wars against Greece and Rome. Parthia and Rome fought battles that were among the largest and most pivotal ever fought in the ancient world. The Roman Triumvir, Crassus, met an ignominious death fighting the Parthians and Mark Antony led a large army into Parthia, but was driven out and barely escaped with his life.

Some of the events of Jesus Christ's life become more understandable when they are examined in light of the politics that prevailed between Rome and Parthia at that time. One group of the Parthian elites that chose Parthia's emperors was called the "Magi" or "Wise Men." A delegation of these high Parthian officials worshipped the young Jesus.

BOOK FOUR: ISRAEL'S TRIBES TODAY!

When Parthia fell, it triggered one of the greatest migrations of people in human history. Many Semitic nations and tribes that had lived in the Parthian Empire for centuries fled out of Asia into Europe in search of new homelands. This migration took centuries to fully accomplish. This mass Semitic migration is known to historians as the Caucasian migration into Europe. It was given that name because of the many millions of Parthian and Scythian refugees who fled Asia by squeezing through the Caucasus Mountain region; hence the name "Caucasian." Parthian nations and tribes which bore such names as the Sacae, the Kermans (Germanii), the Getae and the Jats became known as the Saxons, Germans, Goths and Jutes when they invaded Europe. They also transplanted Parthia's feudal system of government into Europe. The mass invasions of these "barbarians," as the Romans called them, eventually led to the complete fall of the Roman Empire. Secular histories long ago documented the above facts, but they have usually been deleted from historical accounts because modern evolutionary historians are uncomfortable with the facts.

The invading Semitic Caucasians eventually formed the population base of modern Europe, Canada, Australia, New Zealand, the United States, and other nations. These nations rose to world prominence, amassing the dominant share of the world's power, resources, and wealth. Was this all an historical accident...or was a divine purpose being worked out? A mass of interesting Bible prophecies are here shown to be fulfilled in the world today.

Also available and highly recommended!

The Story Of Celto-Saxon Israel

Nearly 250 pages! (236 + xii) Available in either soft or hard cover.

This is the story of a missing branch of God's chosen people, the Israelites. Ten tribes of the northern Hebrew kingdom of "Ephraim" were conquered, taken into captivity by the Assyrians in the eighth century, B.C., and never heard from again. Jewish and Christian scholars have long speculated on their disappearance, and Christ in the New Testament alluded to their continuing existence. Where did they go?

Historian and scholar, W.H. Bennett, a long-time Fellow of the Royal Geographic Society, spent over fifty years following their trail. He examined leads such as language, heraldry, culture, and prophecy fulfillment, solving at last the mystery of their disappearance from the Middle-East scene, and their identification in the world today.

Over 175 maps, charts, and illustrations help tell the story of these lost Israelites. Twelve valuable appendices include little-known historical evidence of dispersed Israel, including Assyrian and Persian monuments, the Hebrew connection with Gaul, the Chief Rabbi's and the lost tribes, and much more. The information in this book is an important key to understanding the fulfillment of the Biblical promises and covenants in our modern world.